Freya Stark (1893–1993), 'the poet of travel', was the doyenne of Middle East travel writers and one of the most courageous and adventurous women travellers in history. She travelled extensively through Syria, Palestine, Lebanon, Iran, Iraq and Southern Arabia, where she became the first western woman to travel through the Hadhramaut. Usually solo, she ventured to places few Europeans had ever been. Her travels earned her the Founder's Gold Medal of the Royal Geographical Society and she was  created a Dame in 1975. She received huge public acclaim and her many, now classic, books include *Traveller's Prelude*, *The Valleys of the Assassins*, *Ionia*, *The Southern Gates of Arabia*, *Alexander's Path*, *Dust in the Lion's Paw* and *East in West*.

D1639021

Tauris Parke Paperbacks is an imprint of I.B.Tauris. It is dedicated to publishing books in accessible paperback editions for the serious general reader within a wide range of categories, including biography, history, travel and the ancient world. The list includes select, critically acclaimed works of top quality writing by distinguished authors that continue to challenge, to inform and to inspire. These are books that possess those subtle but intrinsic elements that mark them out as something exceptional.

The Colophon of Tauris Parke Paperbacks is a representation of the ancient Egyptian ibis, sacred to the god Thoth, who was himself often depicted in the form of this most elegant of birds. Thoth was credited in antiquity as the scribe of the ancient Egyptian gods and as the inventor of writing and was associated with many aspects of wisdom and learning.

IONIA

A Quest

Freya Stark

TPP

TAURIS PARKE
PAPERBACKS

Published in 2010 by Tauris Parke Paperbacks
An imprint of I.B.Tauris and Co Ltd
6 Salem Road, London W2 4BU
175 Fifth Avenue, New York NY 10010
www.ibtauris.com

Distributed in the United States and Canada Exclusively by Palgrave Macmillan
175 Fifth Avenue, New York NY 10010

First published in 1954 by John Murray (Publishers) Limited

Cover image: © Izzet Keribar / Lonely Planet Images

ISBN: 978 1 84885 191 7

A full CIP record for this book is available from the British Library
A full CIP record is available from the Library of Congress

Library of Congress Catalog Card Number: available

Printed and bound in India by Thomson Press India Ltd

To
Harold Nicolson
and Vita Sackville-West

The author's thanks are first due to Herodotus, born in the early years of the 5th century B.C. in the Dorian city of Halicarnassus in Caria, traveller in the Levant and maker of History, and the constant companion of this journey. Of his life little but its work is known: except that he was the son of Lyxes, and ended his days in the South Italian colony of Thurii: and Sophocles at the age of fifty-five wrote for him a song.

Thanks are due also, for great kindness and helpful advice, to Mr. and Mrs. David Balfour and Mr. and Mrs. Seton Lloyd in Smyrna and Ankara; to Mr. R. E. Wilkinson; to professor A. Andrewes; to the Hon. Steven Runciman; to Carlo della Posta di Civitella: and to Miss Barclay Sanders.

NOTE

The Latin variant has been used for all classical names with the exception of some few outside Turkey. For Turkish place names English phonetic spelling has been used with the addition of Ö Ü ö ü. As on many maps produced in Europe, the distinction between the dotted and dotless i has not been made, although in modern Turkish they are pronounced somewhat differently.

Contents

Illustrations

Preface

A thousand, aye, ten thousand years are but a point one
cannot see, nay the smallest part of a point.

SIMONIDES, 6th cent. B.C.[1]

In the autumn of 1952 I travelled about the western coasts
of Asia Minor, and counted, at the end, fifty five ruined
sites that I had visited: in only one of them—and that was
Pergamum—had I met another tourist, sightseeing like myself. Some of these vanished cities were buried in earth, or
had sunk away in swamp, so that only a few places of wall, a
cornice or shaft of column, remained, neglected or forgotten:
in many, the steps of their theatres were split by the roots
of trees or hidden, hardly accessible, in thorns. Here, like a
manuscript of which most of the words are rubbed away, lay
the record of our story, of what—trickling down slopes of
time towards us by devious runnels—has made us what we
are today. A great longing came to me to know more, and
to bring a living image out of these dots and dashes of the
past. More particularly, to discover what elements in that
breeding ground of civilization can still be planted to grow
among us now. This then is the double search of this book—a
guide-book in time as it were, among the ruins, and it may
require patience in the reader to read as in the writer to write

it, for the questions it asks lead far and I have been anxious
to base my results on as solid a groundwork of historical fact
as my means allow.

I ventured on this enquiry with a very inadequate equip-
ment of learning. I read the ancient words in translations
only; and kept a mind open because it is blank towards the
controversies that thicken as one presses to the outer edges
of time. I started therefore from a level of ignorance shared
with the majority of those readers who may not have made
a particular study of the ancient world: sharing their difficulties, I have been careful in the notes at the end of my book to
give them references to works and even to pages from which
my facts and many of my opinions were taken, so that those
who are interested to do so may be able to reconstruct the
journey and come perhaps to different conclusions. They will
see that the authorities are not chosen by an expert: many
of them I rather fear are such as the historian might reject.
Yet they build a picture that an average tourist in the days of
Ionia might have felt at home with. However unhistorical,
it gave me pleasure to think of the things Pausanias saw, the
monuments of a doubtful past, as he went to and fro; and
the notes at the end of my book are meant not only to help
my reader to reconstruct the argument, but also to warn him
against taking the authorities more solemnly than is intended.
I am also adding to this foreword a synopsis of the history
of my period, which all who do not happen to have the first
3,000 years of human history at their finger-tips will be well
advised to look through.

Every reader, as he reaches the end of my book, may decide
for himself what part of this world might still be reconstructed
in our time. It would be too summary, I think, to assume that
none of it can be recovered. The ingredients that made it, as I
see them, and as I try to describe them under the names of the

various towns of Aeolis and Ionia that follow, were: climate and the healthiest of foods—olives, and fish and corn and wine; leisure, and a simplicity of pleasures; precariousness, to make good moments sharper; and commerce like a river where ideas as well as wealth move up and down. Add to these enough solitude to divide one city or one human being from the next one; curiosity and toleration, which produce truth together; beauty, under whose wing great words are written; a life where personal decisions are demanded; and freedom for women and men. Above all, a tradition that, to be a 'lively oracle', must be surrounded by the Unexpected, friendly to it, and instrinsically honourable in itself: so that in periods of emptiness the symbol may be preserved with piety, ready for a new breath of the spirit when it comes.

All these ingredients, and doubtless many others, are found in the fragments that are left us of Ionia: and the reader himself, if he has the patience to follow my rebuilding of cities, will decide which of them are valid and practicable today. To my mind, only two—climate and solitude—are unattainable to great numbers of human beings at this time: as for the rest, the flexibility of our natures and the wealth of our tools could procure them, if we followed them as that supreme good which, during one indelible blossoming in time, they showed themselves to be.

'We sit, wicked men, among pleasant things, upon a seat rock o'er-hung, thinking we see and seeing not';[2] and the imagining of Ionia is academic in our day. But a moment may come when we recognize the face of our world, as we mould it, to be death; and we will then think no change too drastic, no renunciation too high, for the recapturing of what once demonstrated, by its actual existence, the infinite possibility in men.

Synopsis of History
(May be omitted by the well-informed.)

However effortless one wishes to travel, it is impossible to touch the coast of Asia Minor without hitting about 5,000 years of the life of mankind at once; and an outline is necessary for the understanding of this book. Its origins begin long before history—in a dim time when round-headed travellers from Anatolia, drifting westward, filtered among the long-headed dark Mediterraneans, earlier settlers, perhaps from Africa.[1]

To these, living their neolithic life on the islands of the Cyclades, in Cyprus and in Crete, the gift of metal travelled—first copper and then bronze—chiefly from the north-east. And fragments of Sumerian culture came across from Mesopotamia by unrecorded ways.

About 2400 B.C. or thereabout, the ancient Minoan bronze age in Crete began. A vast Hittite empire was digging its roots into Cappadocia. Mesopotamia was already flourishingly civilized, and tablets of her traders on the Anatolian plateau have been discovered and dated to about 1900 B.C. Crete is, as it were, in the middle of our stage, with the three great powers, Hittite, Sumerian, and Egyptian in the south, shedding their influence from the wings.[2]

About 2000 B.C., the earliest Indo-European Ionians begin to trickle quietly down as peaceful settlers, adopters of Minoan ways, in the Aegean lands. Others follow them, more aggressive, pouring from the north, their routes still controversial. Tribes akin to the Greek descend on Asia Minor— Lycians, Carians, Lydians, Phrygians, Mysians. The people who dug shaft graves in Mycenae on the mainland of Greece overshadow the Ionians, and their settlements spread round Corinth and Mycenae, and elsewhere.

A period of great disorder follows. In 1400 B.C. the palace of Knossos and the Minoan supremacy of Crete are violently destroyed. 'Sea Raiders' are mentioned in the hieroglyphs of Egypt. The Homeric age flashes along with piracy, rapine, echoes of splendour, dominated at sea by Mycenae. In the 12th century, among many events—unsung—of the same kind, the siege of Troy occurred, inspired by the riches of the Asiatic mines; and the Hittite and Egyptian empires try to settle the Levant with a treaty of peace in 1269 B.C.

Through this turmoil, a shadowy wraith of history appears hovering about the coasts of Asia Minor. Cretan and Mycenaean settlers leave legends in places which later and more authenticated adventurers were soon to inhabit.[3] About 1200 B.C., the Dorians descend into Greece by the northern path, with iron already familiar in their hand. At the same time, the Hittite empire crumbles in its northern parts, and Assyria, emerging from the east in 1100 B.C., crosses the Euphrates. For the next four centuries, the Hittites are kept busy on their southern frontier till they vanish altogether, and Phrygians and Lydians become powerful, historic and important neighbours of the Greeks in Ionia, organizing commercially the great military highroad of the Hittite empire from east to west. The Asian highroads, whether in their nebulous, unverified, prehistoric stages, or in their Hittite accidentally

civilizing form, or in their ascertainably commercial character under Lydia and Persia, are of such capital importance
that they vie with Crete in the history of Ionia.

The descent of the Dorians disturbed Achaeans and earlier
visitors on the mainland of Greece, and the best recorded
colonizing of the coast of Asia Minor took place soon after. But
some cities, like Miletus, carried their life on unbroken from
the earlier Cretan and Mycenaean age, and the whole of our
philosophy, and most of the civilization of the Graeco-Roman
world and therefore of ours, poured out to us through that
narrow channel. Most of the cities, however, began afresh
or began altogether, deriving their foundation from some
Aeolian or Ionian leader, and preserving only a faint legend,
the marriage of a bronze age hero with some nymph or river
(mixture of foreign and aboriginal), to mark their forgotten
life. The Aeolian cities were founded north of Smyrna; and the
Ionian, twelve of them, between Phocaea and the Maeander
to the south: their Panionium, their temple to the Heliconian
Poseidon, was built on the headland of Mycale, about 700
B.C.—when Assyria was defeating the last of the Hittites near
Aleppo.

For the next hundred and fifty years, the history of the
Greeks in Asia Minor is closely linked with that of the Lydians and Phrygians and the commercial road—with a less
immediate influence from the west, and a certain coming and
going with Egypt through the Carians south of Maeander,
who 'although the other peoples were not yet having very
much intercourse with the Greeks nor even trying to live
in Greek fashion nor learn our language . . . yet . . . roamed
through the whole of Greece [Asiatic] serving . . . for pay'.[4]
The establishment of a Grecian port at Naucratis in the
Nile delta, in the 7th century, was important since it re-
opened Egypt;[5] and the coast of Ionia now basked in the most

encouraging climate for civilization—that of a maritime community at cross-roads of traffic, with vast reservoirs of wealth at either end.

A need for expansion accompanied the commercial initiatives of Lydia, and the opening of new markets followed; and particularly a strengthening of the ties with the mainland of Greece.[6] A shuttle weaves to and fro between the tyrants of Miletus and Corinth; and the Oracles play their political part. Herodotus records that Midas king of Phrygia was the first barbarian to send offerings to Delphi, and Gyges king of Lydia the second. The Lydian dynasty continued through Ardys, Sadyattes, Alyattes to Croesus and the overthrow of Lydia in 546 B.C. These kings show a constant preoccupation with the Ionian and Aeolian cities, whether in a warfare which always (except in the case of Smyrna) spared them so as not to ruin the trade, or in peaceful transactions that soon spread westward to Athens and Corinth and Sparta, and brought the name of Croesus familiarly down to our day.

The two centuries before the birth of Herodotus, the 7th and 6th, were a splendid age, though most of the works that belonged to them are lost, and few are more than fragments. But the names tell their story: Archilochus, Callinus, Tyrtaeus, Arion, in poetry and music, with Lydian Alcman and the Lesbians—Terpander, Sappho, Alcaeus; and Mimnermus, Simonides, Stesichorus, Ibycus; and Anacreon who overlapped with Aeschylus' first play; Lasus who perhaps taught Pindar, and invented the saying that 'the cleverest thing in the world is taking pains'; Theognis and Phocylides.[7] To these two centuries the Seven Wise Men belong with Thales of Miletus, and the philosophers Anaximander, Anaximenes, Xenophanes, Pythagoras; and Anaxagoras and Empedocles who spill over into the century of Athens.[8] In painting and architecture, little is left but the reputations

of their day—of painters like Bularchus, Apelles and Parrha-
sius, and Bypalus worker in gold; welding of iron by Glaucus
in Chios, and Rhoecus and Theodorus of Samos, casters in
bronze. The builders of the temples are obliterated by those
of later ages. But here and there some terra-cotta like that
of the goddess in Smyrna, some early sculpture like the lion
by the wayside near Miletus, with gay, secret, and haunting
aloofness bear witness to a world that was valid and has gone.
Not all of the names are from Asia; but the impulse came
from that coastal strip where the west and east, meeting to
co-operate, produced the civilization that we know.

At this time, beginning in the 8th century and continuing
into the 6th, Ionians and Dorians, and the Aeolians and Lydians too in lesser measure, established colonies from Spain
to the Black Sea—a geographic event more momentous than
anything that followed until the Cape of Good Hope was
rounded two millenniums later.[9]

The only serious interruption of this prosperity in Ionia
were the two Cimmerian invasions of 678 and 652 B.C. Little is known of these invaders but that they came like a
mist from the north and overran the inland regions, till they
spent themselves on the Taurus against the Assyrians and
turned. They were most deadly to Phrygia and Lydia; King
Gyges spent years of his life fighting them and died during
their second invasion and the young king of Phrygia committed suicide. When they reached Ionia, they sacked Magnesia
and burned the temple in Ephesus, but left no enduring
trace.

In 611 B.C. the Assyrian empire fell to the Medes. Dis-
turbance gradually crept along the eastern highway. In 546,
after a rapid and brilliant campaign, Cyrus the Persian took
Sardis; Croesus, out-generalled and besieged, was captured;
and the Persian empire succeeded to the Lydian in Ionia.

Miletus alone, always the least tied of the cities to the fortunes of Lydia, had kept herself uninvolved in Croesus' downfall: the other coastal places were taken by conquest—and the Persian showed the same regard for their commercial usefulness as the Lydians had done before him. But the local 'tyrants' he ruled through were disliked in the maritime cities and it was the feeling against them, together with affection for their defeated neighbours, rather than any violent hatred of the Persians, that inspired the Ionian revolt of 499 B.C. The battle of Lade and the destruction of Miletus followed—the extinction of the visible ancient Aegean world.

Athens sent twenty ships to help in the revolt: and this was the beginning of Marathon and all the Persian war. After the battle of Salamis, the fleet of Xerxes wintered in Aeolis, and the defeat of the Persians in Asia took place a year later, in 479, at the headland of Mycale, on the same day as the battle of Plataea. The Persian king kept the mainland of Asia, but another defeat, soon after 470 on the Eurymedon, prevented him from recovering the coast. In 449 came that 'famous peace which limited him to a distance of a day's journey on horseback from the Grecian sea; and by which he engaged that none of his galleys or other ships of war should ever come within the Cyanaean and the Chelidonian isles.' When the Peloponnesian war divided the Greeks, and brought rival generals seeking friendships in Asia, the Persian governors again appeared on the coast, and 'their tax gatherers were then left amidst the cities in alliance and friendship with the Greeks'.[10] Then Various treaties, most notoriously that of Antalcidas in 386 B.C., handed back the Ionians to their subjection.[11] But free or subject, with the break in their Asiatic intimacy, the great and ancient line of the Ionian commerce with Asia was impaired.

In 334 B.C. Alexander the Great liberated the coastland, and an economic unity might have been re-established but for his early death. Even as it was, it survived in great measure. His generals divided the Levant between them: Antigonus, Lysimachus, Seleucus, Antiochus, fill Ionia with rivalries and battles for over a century: until Ilium, and then Smyrna in 196 B.C. appeal for help from Rome.[12] This brings the Hellenistic period to an end.

Rome is outside my history; so are the journeys of St. Paul, the Christian and Byzantine, Seljuk and Ottoman stories: I hope to find them, if I am spared, on later visits to Asia Minor, on the plateau of Anatolia and along the southern coasts. But the lands around Smyrna belong to the past of Greece, and to our present and to the present of Turkey; for now once more the highway of Asia touches the sea as far as Anatolia is concerned. At the end of the first world war, on May 15th, 1919, the Greeks of the mainland landed again in Ionia. On August 5th, 1922, Mustafa Kemal was made Commander-in-Chief against them and re-took Smyrna on September 9th.[13] The ruins of this war are still everywhere visible in coastal places. But the Greeks have now gone, and the great country is turning over to a new history: and if one lesson is clearer than another, and yet seems impossible to remember, it is this—that a sea-power can scarcely ever hold the edge of an alien mainland from the sea. Let this be taken for granted: so that the friendly link in Europe may be re-established, and commerce can go up and down from Asia by the slow valleys, as from the beginning of time; and where the sea receives it, in the loveliest harbours of the world, intended for peaceful traffic, the cities of civilization may flourish again, in their new ways.

Dates

(The earlier are approximate.)

B.C.

Hittites establish their power in Cappadocia	2500
Cretan bronze age civilization: Ancient Minoan period begins	2400
First Greeks descend into the Aegean world	2000
Tablets of Assyrian traders on the Anatolian plateau	1900
Cretan-Mycenaean civilization on the mainland (period of the shaft graves of Mycenae) begins	1700
Destruction of Knossos: dominance of Mycenae. Beginning of the Homeric age	1400
Conquest of north Syria by the Hittite empire	1376
Treaty between Hittite and Egyptian empires: steadies the Levant	1269
Attack on Egypt repulsed, of Achaeans, Tyrsenes, Lydians, Cilicians, etc.	1229
The iron age begins in Greece	1200
Fall of the Hittite and rise of the Phrygian power	1200
Reported date of the siege of Troy	1184
Assyrians under Tiglath Pileser I first reach the Euphrates after the Hittite decline	1110

B.C

Descent of Dorians into Greece	1100
Later legendary colonization of Greek Asia Minor	1000
Assyria crosses Euphrates, finally conquers Hittites of N. Syria	879–709
Ionian federation of 12 cities centred round the Panionium	700
Midas son of Gordias, king of Phrygia	693
Gyges, king of Lydia	687–652
Cimmerian invasions	678–652
Psammetichus I, and founding of Naucratis in Egypt	663–609
Assyrian empire and Nineveh fall to the Medes	612
Alyattes, king of Lydia	585
Croesus, king of Lydia	561–546
Expansion and colonization by the Greek cities of Asia Minor	8th-6th centuries

Poets and musicians of the 7th century:

Archilochus of Paros, Callinus of Ephesus, Tyrtaeus of Sparta, Mimnermus of Colophon, Alcman, Terpander and Sappho and Alcaeus of Lesbos, Arion of Methymna. Bularchus, painter.

Poets and musicians of the 6th century:

Stesichorus of Sicily, Simonides of Ceos, Lasus, Solon of Athens, Phocylides of Miletus, Theognis of Megara, Ibycus of Rhegium, Anacreon of Teos, Bypalus of Chios (worker in gold).

Philosophers of the 6th century:

Thales of Miletus, Anaximander and Anaximenes of Miletus, Xenophanes of Colophon, Pythagoras of Samos, Parmenides of Elaea, Heraclitus of Ephesus, Anaxagoras of Clazomenae, Empedocles of Acragas.

B.C

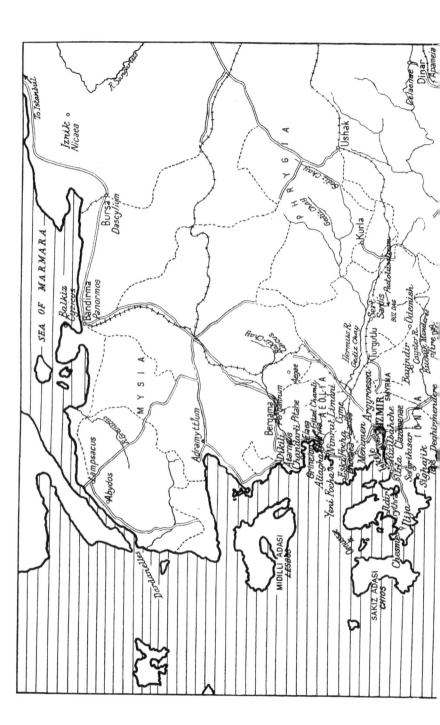

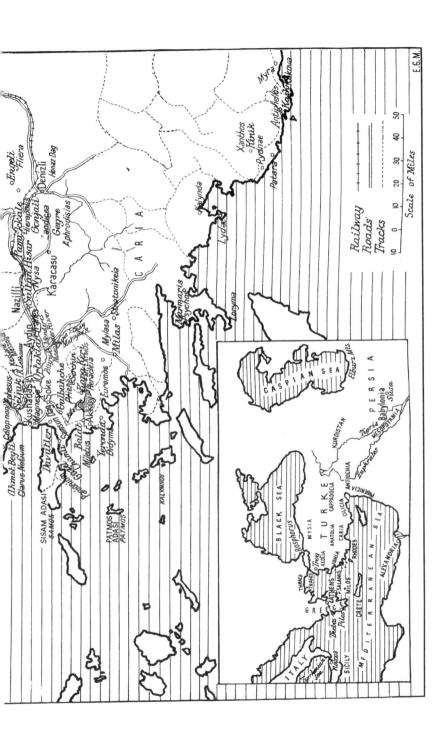

Railway
Roads
Tracks

10   0   10   20   30   40   50
Scale of Miles

E.G.M.

Ahmet Beyli Colophon Ephesus Keçikalesi
Clarus-Notium   Nazilli
                    Kuşadası   Seljuk Lithrae
                  Davutler   Aydin
                        Magnesia   Ortaklar Nysa
                  Samson Bay Söke Menderes Pişirkent
              SISAM ADASI   Bulbahçe
                  SAMOS   Balat Berbrun Geyre
                        Güllübahçe   Heracleia
                  Miletus Akköy
                  Yeronda Bryma Euromos Mylasa
                  Didyma   Milas Stratonikeia

                                  C A R I A

PATMOS   Marmaris
PATMOS ADASI   Sychço

              KALYMNOS   Loryma

Denizli
Fiera Erşeli

Pamukkale Gonjali Honaz Dag
              Aphrodisias

Karacasu

Kalynda

Lydae

Xanthos
Günik
Pydnae
Patara
Antiphelos
Kaş Kalkova Myra

CASPIAN SEA

P E R S I A

Elburz Mts.

KURDISTAN

Tigris MESOPOTAMIA Babylonia
Euphrates   Susa

BLACK SEA

Bosphorus
Troy MYSIA
AEOLIA ANATOLIA
IONIA CARIA CAPPADOCIA
RHODES CILICIA ANTIOCHIA
                  PHOENICIA

T U R K E Y

AEGEAN SEA

ALEXANDRIA

THRACE
THASOS ATHENS
      SALAMIS
Thebes Pilos MILOS
G R E E C E CRETE

ITALY
SICILY
Tyrrhenian Sea
Naxos
M E D I T E R R A N E A N   S E A

1

Dawn in Ionia

How can you hide from that which never sets?

HERACLITUS, 6th cent. B.C.[1]

It was the 4th of September, and I watched Cape Sunium
fade, lit by a dull western afterglow on one side and by the
moon dripping plates of light on the other. The boat was a
Turkish boat, the most comfortable I have travelled in across
the Mediterranean. She slipped along evenly, and split the
smooth surface of the sea as if it were silk. From the horizon,
darkening not in a sharp line but indefinitely, like blotting paper, a colour of violets deepened and encompassed our world.
There were few passengers; they talked in quiet groups, easy
together, each group more separate from the other than in
Europe—the millennial intercourse and separateness of the
Levant. The Turkish stewards and sailors walked about, with
longer arms than most people, and a landsman's walk, and
that absence of vanity in clothes which the change to Western
costume seems to have produced. They stood aside, bowed

the head, and murmured a salutation when an officer passed, with a graceful respect, free of servility, which I was to come to recognize as the charm of Turkish manners.

Two middle-aged women moved about like battleships, so square and broad below; they were built in the Doric order, and made everything look fragile around them. The darkness of violets deepened into night; one listened to the whisper of the sea. What an accurate word, for the sea—to whisper— used by Coleridge who had never known this inhabited, conversational Aegean. Soon, among the surrounding shadows, were shadows of islands; they handed us on from one to another; we were among the Cyclades; their lights, their music floated out like hands to clutch and let go In the trough of small waves that had risen with the night breeze a fishing boat passed, a glow-worm with dim lanthorn that lit the lower edge of a yellow sail. I turned into my cabin, and lay with my porthole wide open still listening to the voices of the islands, and wondered what I was travelling to find. Curiosity led me, pure, disinterested curiosity, the human thrust in time.

If we are to criticize the British for anything, as we cannot get out of the habit of doing even now that we are poor—it would be for our lack of this virtue. When we thought to govern Italy through what we called the A.M.G., I used to watch Brigadiers in motor-launches militarily conducted up the Grand Canal in Venice; their eyes were fixed straight forward, absorbed in strategy, or possibly tactics; I longed to make them turn to the centuries drooping dilapidated on either side of them like afternoon flowers in stone, lit by a water-light, silver-rooted, that had come from so far. Never did I see them turn, this way or that; a leisurely mind seemed unable to rise in anything above a major.

Curiosity ought to increase as one gets older. The earth grows bigger, it ceases to contain itself, it laps beyond its sphere; and Time comes less and less to be confined in this tangible air. Education tells us always all the things that are known. Perhaps, I thought, with the night about me and the mysterious music of the islands—it would be safer to ponder only about what is *not* known? What a stimulus! This, if you come to think of it, is what education was all through the Middle Ages and the Dark, owing partly to ignorance, but also to religion. And that is what it was in the early days of Greece when the sun, rising every morning out of mystery and 'tumbling into a hole'[2] at evening, was a matter for speculation and delight. Was that due to the newness of the world? Impossible, for the bronze and the stone ages had already gone by. Was it a climate that simplifies small repetitive preoccupations such as those which fret us over underwear and draughts? Or were the people not too many? Or did slavery solve the domestic problem, both upstairs and down? Whatever it was, the Ionian curiosity gave a twist for ever to the rudder of time. It was the attribute of happiness and virtue. To look for the causes of it is a hopeless quest in Greece itself; the miracle appears there, perfect, finished and inexplicable. But in Asia Minor there may be a chance, where Thales of Miletus, 'having learnt geometry from the Egyptians, was the first to inscribe a right-angled triangle in a circle, whereupon he sacrificed an ox'.[3]

Thales probably did go to Egypt, but it appears that his geometry was so simple as not to deserve the name. I know this, and I could go into the matter, but I will not. I have little expert learning, and the books I have read, such as they are, are easy, pleasant, all translated, or written in English: the ins and outs, the dates, the documents, the delicacies of attribution, are there attainable for anyone who wishes to study them. But I am looking not for history but for happiness, a secret to be pursued with accuracy of a different mood; and surely to be found; for—out of most hard and barbarous times, out of strangely modern vicissitudes, sacking of cities, emigration, slavery, exile—it still hangs unmistakable, elusive, like a sea-spray in the sun, over the coastline of Ionia.

'. . . then the Persian captains . . . summoned the Ionian tyrants, who fled to the Medes after their rule was put down by Aristagoras of Miletus, and at that time chanced to be making war against Miletus with them; and they spake thus unto them: Ionians, now let each one of you . . . send messages unto them and promise this, that they shall suffer no harsh thing because of their rebellion, neither shall their temples or their houses be burned, nor shall they have any harder lot than they had before; but if they will not obey but must in any case do battle, then threaten them and tell them all that shall befall them, saying that when they are put to the worse in the battle they shall be brought into bondage and we shall make their sons eunuchs and carry their maidens away to Bactria and give their land unto others.'

So Herodotus speaks of what happened only a few years before his birth: and after a siege, Miletus *was* taken and

'the greater part of the men were slain by the long-haired Persians, and their women and children accounted of as bond-servants, and the temple at Didyma spoiled and burned both the shrine and the oracle. . . . The Milesians that were taken alive were led to Susa; and King Darius did them no harm, but made them dwell by the Red Sea [i.e. the Persian Gulf] where the stream of the river Tigris entereth the sea.'[4]

Such was life in the age of happiness.

Not security, but some other thing is the secret; and if I have not found it in my voyage, I have perhaps come nearer to it than I was before. But even if I find it, how shall I give it a name? These things have an unreal reality, like mermaids, difficult to hold. They exist, but the uses of language fail, because their substance is thinner and finer than words. Yet words may reconstruct the landscapes and the thoughts they gave; and the right words have a magic to call up what is not there—the foot as light as thistledown and *gone,* the robe that is only a silken rustle disappearing, the gleam flashing quicker than sight—these things may appear, evoked from their reality as fragments of words or pottery or bronze or marble evoke them, through twenty-five centuries of time.

It is an immense ambition, but I propose to act about it in a modest way, by putting together a straight chronicle, merely, of what I thought and saw; trusting to that intrinsic necromancy which allows language to say a little more than the author himself can imagine.

To catch even the echo a thousand times weakened and repeated of the authentic voice of happiness, is worth a journey. To have heard it and not to hand it on, however faintly, would be grudging indeed. I shall try—asking only this of my readers: that they believe in the forgotten rapture. If they doubt, let them read the fragments left us, let them see the smiling faces of the young men and women (when the Acropolis museum opens itself again at last); let them look into the busy lives of those philosophers, running their politics, their poetry, their engineering, their hypotheses between one exile and another. The felicity, the zest and buoyancy of life were there, and they flourished in danger.

'Great Peace bringeth forth for men wealth and the flower of honey-tongued songs and for the Gods the yellow flame of the burning of the thighs of oxen and fleecy sheep upon fine-wrought altars, and for the young a desire for disport of body and for flute and festal dance. Meanwhile in the iron-bound shield-thong hang the warps of the brown spider, headed spear and two-edged sword are whelmed in an ever-spreading rust, and the noise of the brazen trumpet is not; nor is reft from our eyelids that honey-hearted sleep which soothes the spirit towards dawn. The streets are abloom with delightful feasting and the hymns of children go up like a flame.'[5]

That song was not written in an age of peace. The knowledge is too sharp, the cry too much from the heart. It is nearer to:

Our bugles sang truce for the night-cloud had lowered
And the sentinel stars set their watch in the sky;
And thousands had sunk to the ground overpowered,
The weary to sleep and the wounded to die.[6]

Yet when the 19th century is placed beside it, that Greek passion for life shows clean as a sword and as strong; fearless too of danger as a sword.

'So long as man possesses the flowery bloom of youth there is much that his light heart deems to have no end, counting neither on age nor death. . . . Wherefore be thou wise in time and fail not when the end is near to give thy soul freely of the best.'[7]

Perhaps that is part of the answer, but it is a long way yet to go. In the 'honey-hearted sleep' before dawn I passed the southern tip of Mytilene and came on deck as we rounded the corner of the gulf of Smyrna. The sea had a satin sleekness of early morning. It lay reflecting, in pale green sheets of brilliance, the splintered red bars of the sky. Behind low hills, still black and closed as buds of flowers, the hidden sun threw up his quills of light. It was the moment when the play begins, when the curtains of the full day are drawn. Out of the smooth sea, in front of the sun, a dolphin leaped full into the air, one fin vertical above his head, and his tail in a curve beneath him. He hung there, as he may have appeared in the shield of Odysseus,[8] as many a Minoan atrist saw him, black against the light; and he gave me a shock of ecstasy, as if he were a messenger from the world I was seeking.

The Amphorae of Clazomenae

The Agora in Smyrna

2

Smyrna

The Family in the Levant

And what countrified wench in countrified clothes fires your breast, though she knows not how to draw the gown over her ankles.

SAPPHO, 6th cent. B.C.[1]

Clad in a fair muslin gown.

ALCMAN, 7th cent. B.C.[2]

The modern Smyrna has much more affinity with ancient commercial Ephesus than with the tiny island, the 'first civilized state ever planted on the west coast of Asia Minor',[3] from which Pelops was said to be driven by the Phrygians, and Tantalus was famed to derive his wealth, and which now lies silted up with land in the far north-eastern corner of the bay. Professor Akurgal and Mr. John Cook from the British School in Athens have been excavating it, and the little city, two or three acres altogether on a low mound now grown with

cypresses and vines, was an island in the sea when Alyattes
the king of Lydia besieged and took it, about 575 B.C.[4]
Before that it loses itself in legends, and its name, like that of
Myrina and other cities about here, is said to derive from the
Amazons—nymphs who tossed their spears and clashed their
cymbals round the altars of the Mother Goddess. When the
Olympians came, they transformed and incorporated them,
with many other traditions, in the newer era of the gods. But
the historic city, as we see it excavated today, was inhabited
by Ionian refugees from Colophon, who snatched it from the
Aeolians, their hosts and benefactors, on a day when these
were celebrating a festival of their own outside the gates:
with the Greek matter-of-factness, the accomplished deed
was recognized; the dispossessed Aeolians were distributed
among the remaining communities of their race; and Smyrna
herself was allowed to belong to the Pan-Ionian league.[5]

The city-feeling of a community gathered within walls for
defence, round a temple for worship, beside buildings for
traffic, counsel and shade—the most deeply-rooted feeling
of the Mediterranean so different from the forest-hidden
villages of the North—is strong already in this most ancient
Smyrna. The excavated steps of her water-gate are sharp and
new; the walls of the temple, twice enlarged, still stand; in it
the goddess was found, a haunting, archaic terra-cotta, with
necklace and long hair. The earliest houses, ovals of mud and
stone, go back to the 9th century B.C. In the days of the siege,
in the 6th century, they had become rectangular and larger,
with doors and windows, like the two-roomed boxes the
Turks still build on the modern slopes of the citadel, which
is more or less where Alexander the Great fell asleep under
a tree on his march through Asia, and was visited by Nemesis
and advised to build a city round the steeps of Pagus, where
the walls of his general Lysimachus still appear today.

I have been up there sometimes to walk in the morning, with Ionia on the one side and Aeolis on the other, spread below; and nearby, in a shapeless depression, the stadium where St. Polycarp was burned; and have thought of that old bishop, 'how he would describe his intercourse with John and with the rest of those who had seen the Lord, and how he would relate their words. And whatsoever things he had heard from them about the Lord, and about His miracles, and about His teaching, Polycarp, as having received them from eye-witnesses of the life of the Word, would relate. . . .'[6] And when they found him, in a cottage in the country nearby, he offered his captors food while he prayed for two hours, for the Church and the world: and was brought up late to the height of the citadel, when the games were over, and no lions were available, and was therefore burned in a hastily collected fire.

I have never been on this height without seeing men with pickaxes delving for stones for their houses in the remnants of the ancient wall. The city spreads below, from the hill to the harbour, shining at night like a jeweller's cluster, with sprays of brilliance out at sea—for the harbour is too small and goods come pouring from Asia Minor, and the ships have to wait their turn and anchor for days in the stream that flows through that part of the bay which the earth of the Hermus river has not silted; and they glow at night as if each craft were carried on a cushion of light of its own.

But in the daytime, the city sinks away in the vastness of its landscape. Its suburbs around it, villages charming when you know them, show here and there white houses half hidden in trees; the olive-bearing lowlands hold out their rich and quiet beauty: but the eye travels by gradual slopes, by lines subtly divergent, to empty mountains; the landscape is all repetitive variations, outline beyond outline, like the tones of a voice beyond the words. This, I came to feel, was the beauty of the Ionian scenery, keyed to a perfection so delicate and unobtrusive that, like the more elusive woman, it needs both devotion and time. In this kind of country, where the crowd and the loneliness are so near together, the tender-eyed nymph, Persuasion, 'sister of Orderliness and Fortune and daughter of Foresight' was thought of and personified by Ibycus the poet, who lived at the court of Samos and invented the three-cornered lyre, and discovered the identity of the evening and morning star. In the solitude of the hills, he was murdered by bandits, and called to some passing cranes to avenge him; and in the crowded theatre of Ephesus, when some cranes passed over the audience across the open sky, one bandit said to the other: "See the birds that Ibycus asked to avenge him"—and was overheard and so gave himself away.[7]

I liked to climb through the steep streets of the poorer houses in Smyrna, untouched by the great fire. One can still see a piece of column here and there by a threshold, and find the agora tucked away out of sight, with dew on its grass in the shadow, above Roman vaults where they kept their stores of grain. An old woman once appeared here, climbing up out of the earth by steps made from the scattered blocks of marble; she rested a copper water-pot upon them with her shaking old hands, saying that it came from a spring—once no doubt the agora fountain—and was cold and good for a disease which my Turkish was too poor to understand. From this place one walks down by a street of low shops to the flat and ugly part of the town, where a landlocked harbour was once blocked up by Tamerlane to trouble the knights of Rhodes, and was seen, full of water and with small boats, in the late 18th century, by Pococke and by Chandler.[8]

The harbour disappeared; and the town that covered it was burnt thirty years ago; and is now built again. There are boulevards, and a kultur-park for the international fair, a parachute tower, and wise Turkish planting of trees—yet the city of Smyrna has still not re-crystallized into a harmonious whole. Wealth and peace and time must make it do so. The beauty of its placing will help, and opulence is in the Ionian climate—blossoming under Lydian and Greek, casting an incongruous pleasing glamour over the Victorian English who settled here and traded, and softening the contours of even the dour old Turkish régime. *Eothen*'s Smyrna, gay with a variety of costume when every race clung to its own, still showed 'classic heads, crowned with scarlet and loaded with jewels or coins of gold' from the overhanging windows: and when Sir Charles Fellows went to the Casino ball in 1838, many women wore 'the gold-embroidered skull-cap, the turban of hair with flowers and jewels, the velvet jacket richly embroidered with the gay mameluke sleeves', while the band of the *Sapphire* frigate and the officers in uniform added to the brilliance of the room, and the Pasha himself joined the festivity, dressed rather quietly in red and blue but with very large diamonds.[9]

   In the residential street near the British Consulate where I first lodged, the overhanging windows are still used for the same purpose—to provide variety and amusement for any free and casual moment in the female domestic life. They stand out, supported on intricate cast-iron brackets of the Victorian age, painted pale grey—and there must have been a large consignment, for this specimen of Western export can be followed through street after street in Smyrna, and even in the small towns around. The bow window gives an English feeling to a Turkish street, in contrast to the little box houses on the poorer hills beyond. But the modern plate-glass, the chromium, the hybrid of expensive luxury, remind us—more radically than by mere form—of more distant and wealthy centuries when the town below its acropolis lay with crescent-shaped harbour and many two storied colonnades, with a temple to the Mother Goddess and a gymnasium seen by Strabo, and a sanctuary of Asclepius copied from Pergamum, and a shrine to Homer beside the sea. It also had, outside the city walls, as it were in Langham Place, a Sanctuary of Voices, seen by Pausanias. It was, by common consent, the most beautiful of all the cities of Ionia, sacred to Aphrodite,[10] and the sea 'floated beneath it like a pedestal'.[11] And it was the first city in Asia Minor, after Ilium, to place itself at the beginning of the 2nd century, B.C. under the protection of Rome.

In my lodging, this inner thread of history continued also, different and yet the same. My hostess had the swift Aegean beauty that belonged to Crete. She was slight, and fine, and always busy. Habits of seclusion were probably never recognized by her, even in thought; but they are the natural condition of the Levantine life. The grocer round the corner, the church on Sundays, a walk now and then along the sea-front when the husband is at home, and visits to the most intimate relations—little else takes a woman out of doors. Even shoes are re-soled on the doorstep, by a little stooping man who walks along with a portable table, stool, and tool box, and settles on the pavement to work wherever he is required, as the builders of temples once did in their time. The fruit, or vegetable seller, the carder of mattresses, the seller of socks and ties, all walk along the street and call their wares.

Anything more distant or more difficult is seen to by the husband as he comes and goes in and out of the public world. It is he who fixes the frigidaire, or brings the news, or buys the carpet; and by doing so, turns the house and its tiny court into a small realm—like the harim in Asia. However many men there might be, a feminine atmosphere pervaded it, made pleasant by the mistress's quick neatness: and the seclusion explained what the travellers of last century notice so often—'at every window and doorway . . . at all hours, a fully-dressed head, ornamented with flowers or jewels'.[12] Women can dress once for all in the morning if they have the whole day at home before them. Both in my first lodging and in the second, which was Greco-Italian, I came down to breakfast charmed by the sight of my hostess up so early, with ringlets braided and white fingers manicured and soft, and that look of relaxed luxuriance recognizable in the marbles of Aphrodisias, produced by the cultivation of beauty within doors.

The mistress of the house was French and her husband British; and King George and the Union Jack held the middle wall in the parlour, while St. Joan knelt over the table by my bed. So it must have been, under one symbol or another, ever since the first colonists went out in the long-oared vermilion[13] ships and built new cities for their gods, remembering the communities they came from. There are few things more touching than this loyalty to a state that has never been seen. The placid old mothers who came and went talked Greek, and it was Greek in the kitchen; but the two western countries were entertained with less intimacy but more honour in the parlour, like uncles who have made a fortune abroad.

The centre of the household was the son, whose getting off to school, after the master's departure, made a second climax in the day. Our host went, overflowing with cheerfulness, kindness, and the many odds and ends he was asked to attend to before lunch-time. He was the king of his domain, the fountain of all it does and thinks, and a trifle harassed; and when his wife had seen him out of the breakfast-room, her own less obtrusive royalty became apparent: the house showed itself for what it was, a temenos or temple area, the centre of the most ancient religion the Mediterranean knows.

"So much trouble and expense; we can't afford another," she would remark—attending to the boisterous affair of her son's schoolday, while her look entered, as it were, a long avenue of love. The boy was spoilt as his father must have been spoilt before him. Drawn by the power of affection, in an atmosphere without a bite in it, he will grow up to the same kindly servitudes in the traditions of his home.

Through the ups and downs of history this private sovereignty of the family has brought the Greco-Roman civilization more or less safely through. It is the closed door and open window described by Kinglake, which makes a small but defensible sanctuary of every home. It is Aphrodite who rules.

'Her do thou contemplate with thy mind, nor sit with dazed eyes. It is she that is known as being implanted in the frame of mortals. It is she that makes them have thoughts of love and work the works of peace. . . .'

Empedocles in his subtle observation makes a distinction. Love, says he, produces a universal harmony, a love of like for *unlike*: but *Strife,* the divider, drawing the elements apart, uniting each to its own, produces in all things the love of like for *like*.

'At one time all grew together to be one only out of many, at another it parted asunder so as to be many instead of one. Fire and Water and Earth and the mighty height of Air; dread Strife too . . . and Love in their midst . . . For even as they (Strife and Love) were aforetime, so too they shall be; nor ever will boundless time be emptied of that pair.'[14]

In the family history of the Levant it is strife which has bound the tie so close, holding the family together in a devotion made rigid through centuries of fears. Love is an affair of kindred, a meeting at the same church, a drawing of like to like; it stops at a barrier which Christianity sought in vain to overcome. And its fundamental origin in strife, creating from ancient time the separateness of Greek and barbarian, goes far to explain both the transitoriness and the perfection of that civilization of the dawn.

Most loves in our time also are guarded by strife. The fence of race; the notice at the frontier; the war of class; the team spirit; the party system; not one of these loyalties but Strife around it holds the ring. Shut in from outer clamours, the Mediterranean world established in the family an enclosure of safety. Now the family itself shifts away from Aphrodite, shrinking to an ever smaller nucleus the area of peace. Nor will anything public make good the deficit, since every frontier is doomed to produce an opposition beyond it. Nothing short of the universal—the kingdom of heaven or the heart of man—can build the unfenced peace.

3

Clazomenae

The Philosophic Weather

. . . touching upon all the cities of men, small and great alike.
For those which of old were great, the more part of them are
become small, and those that in my day are great, the same
were small formerly. Therefore . . . I will make mention of
both alike.

HERODOTUS.[1]

I had not been many days in Smyrna before I came to the
conclusion that it was impossible to travel without a guide.
The difficulty was not space, but time: even by limiting myself
to Ionia as I had intended to do, the number of things that
have happened there is overwhelming. I was then reading
Herodotus, and it seemed to me that here was the perfect
travelling companion, to take one to the cities that he speaks
of, whether they still exist or no. By this choice I could at
one stroke disregard two thousand and more years of history
(for I was going to leave a little margin in the matter of

date): I would be led to the world I desired: and as for not finding things standing—I am one of those who *prefer* neglected ruins, places untouched even by the archaeologist, where one's thoughts can build their own palaces, and the past, draped and veiled in its garment of earth, lies like the sleeping beauty undiscovered and undisturbed.

So I went first to Clazomenae, which was one of the twelve cities of Ionia,[2] and easy to reach from Smyrna westward, some thirty kilometres along an asphalt road.

Herodotus has not much to say about it, beyond the fact that it was in Lydia, and spoke the same dialect as Ephesus, Lebedus, Colophon, Teos and Phocaea; and had a part with the other eleven and with Smyrna in the sanctuary of the Panionium at the foot of the mountain opposite Samos,[3] which I visited also, later on. He says further that the people of Clazomenae—with others of their neighbours, both Ionian and Dorian and the Aeolians of Mytilene—built the chief of the Greek sanctuaries in Egypt in the port of Naucratis, given by Amasis in the delta of the Nile.[4] This was in the 7th century B.C., and shows that they were mercenaries as well as traders, and took their turns in furnishing port officers to their Egyptian harbour.

When they first came into the neighbourhood of Smyrna, they were a roving band driven to the shores of Asia by the inroads of Dorians in Greece; and being leaderless, asked for a captain from the colony of Colophon,[5] already settled nearby: so provided, they tried their luck in the north, under Mount Ida, and failed; and failed again, when the Colophonians gave them a piece of their land west of the track from Smyrna to Ephesus, which they left of their own free will. Then at last they settled on a promontory which stands out from the southern shore of the gulf of Smyrna, and stayed there till fear of the Persians drove them to an island, in sight close by. It is now reached by a causeway first built by Alexander the Great, but is still unattainable, for the island is the modern quarantine station, and forbidden to the public. The old name, turned to Kilizman, moved up the hill on the mainland, and, having so Turkified itself into a village, has now changed both sound and meaning, and calls itself the Red Garden, Kizilbahche: while the little harbour, simply known as Urla Iskelesi, or landing-stage of Urla, still sits peacefully by the main road in the sun. Fields of tobacco, and olive trees, are round it, on the strip of land that ends in the smooth landlocked mirror of the sea: and square mounds of bricks, baking slowly and smoking from a fire inside them, carry on in a poor way an industry that once spread lovely earthenware all over the Aegean. Amphorae are still made, and the quayside was stacked with them, red graceful curving shapes aslant in rows, like the pots in Omar Khayyám's poem, with rough white arabesques for decoration.

The fishermen were mending their nets, taking life easily in the shade; and two caïques, there probably for the loading of the amphorae, lapped empty and deserted, tied to the broken shafts of pillars, whose shadows, lengthening like their history, slanted across the tiny harbour in the afternoon. There was no melancholy: the colour of the caïques alone would have prevented it, bright red and green with a splash of turquoise that went half-way up the mast and stopped: but there was a feeling as it were of absent-mindedness, of a past definitely done with and forgotten, never to be remembered again.

This too was an illusion, for nothing is more alive than the past of Clazomenae. From here in the early 5th century B.C. the young philosopher Anaxagoras,[6] a man of good family, set out—perhaps as a soldier—to join the army of Xerxes as it marched to the Hellespont: he would make by sail or oar across the gulf of Smyrna, and then walk or drive for three days, under the walls of an Aeolian city (Argyroessa possibly), along the Hermus valley, to Sardis. Hence the great host set out from winter quarters through Aeolis and Mysia and the Troad, to Abydos where Xerxes—watching the international troops go over into Europe across the pontoon bridge—wept because not one of them would be alive in a hundred years.[7] Anaxagoras may have been among them, and at all events reached Attica, and remained there when war departed and philosophy came back into her own. He was, they say, the first of the philosophers to settle in Athens, and lived there some thirty years: and his teaching, fostered in the learning of Ionia under the great men of Miletus, was handed on to Pericles and to Euripides. This was the chain. Plato speaks of him as a 'scientific man', and adds that Pericles 'having attained a knowledge of the true nature of mind and intellect, which was just what the discourses of Anaxagoras were mainly about, drew from that source whatever was of a nature to further him in the art of speech.'[8]

The fragments Anaxagoras has left tell enough to explain his theory of the world substance, of which every part, however small, contains a due proportion of everything that is. Into this mass, still resting like a nest flat on the cushion of air, an outer force, an independence, a *nous* inserted motion. It is not the atomic theory, but already it is coming very near it, and we hear in its echoes the voice of Dante, 'the love that moves the sun and the other Stars'. As the mass moves, 'these things revolve and are separated off by the force and swiftness. And the swiftness makes the force. Their swiftness is not like the swiftness of any of the things that are now among men, but in every way many times as swift . . . ' and 'the dense and the moist and the cold and the dark came together where the earth is now, while the rare and the warm and the dry (and the bright) went out towards the further part of the aether'. I remember much the same sort of description from my father, explaining the solar system to me as a child.

And what did Anaxagoras look upon with eye or memory from the gentle slope of Clazomenae when he wrote that 'What appears is a vision of the unseen'? How fortunate, to leave a sentence like that out of so few bare pages, for a heritage through the accidents of twenty-four hundred years?

He went about noticing, and discovered among other things that the fish which the Clazomenians caught in their nets woven of broom, breathed through their gills. He saw how the sea rose from the waters in the earth, for when these evaporated the remainder turned salt; and he knew the moon to have no light of her own, but to get it from the sun. He knew that winds sprang up when the sun rarefied the air; and that thunder and lightning were heat striking on clouds. He thought that earthquakes were the air above that struck the air below and made the nest of the world to rock between them: and he recognized sensation as pain.

What one finds in the early Ionian philosophers is a passionate interest in weather—how easy to understand when one looks on the landscape they saw.

Clazomenae, we happen to know, was uninhabited even by the aboriginal 'Lelegians' when the band led from Colophon walked across to explore and settled on the low slope with the island before it.[9] They were within a day's march from Erythrae, Teos, Lebedus, all Ionian colonies, but all hidden by promontories or hills; only the little island of Smyrna lay barely in sight. For the rest, the limestone reared its ridges from the sea or settled into it with soft and undulating lines, and the islands stood 'like the backbone of an ass crowned with savage wood'[10]; and probably the stretches cushioned with spiky camel-thorn were fewer, and the pines more frequent on what are now the bare or cultivated headlands of the sea. But the weather was then as now always in sight, not dull for long with heaviness or sunshine, but varied across the arch of an immense horizon, where the storms and sunlight and their rainbows and their changes are visible at play. Islands and thin gulfs, sea and land interwoven, may produce this animation. England too has it, with fringed coasts and a surrounding sea; and perhaps there too the naturalist and the poet learned to observe with a countryman's eye when the towns they lived in were still small enough to look out of.

The ancient writers are supposed to have no feeling for scenery; and this may be so if we think of a static background, passive to be looked at and admired; this is the landscape of the towns, where the 'picturesque' is invented. But the Ionians were accustomed to look straight out on a country horizon; and they saw what the sailor or the countryman sees, that something is always *happening* there. 'There's a squall coming,' or 'You'll find it's getting a bit thick over the moor': this outlook is radically that of the Ionian poets; it is possibly weather rather than landscape; but in any case it is the outlook of someone who *sees*.

From

> The south west shifts 'tween cloud and clear
> The north west nought but cloud doth bear,[11]

we soon come to the morning star, 'the white-winged fore-runner of the sun' by Ion of Chios, who wrote a hymn to Opportunity, the 'youngest of the children of Zeus'[12]:

'Fearless of heart with the halcyons over the bloom of the wave, the spring's own bird that is purple as the sea',[13] Alcman, of Lydian origin, sings in the 7th century. He was so weather-minded that he saw the Muses as daughters of Heaven and Earth, and not of Memory and Zeus; and wrote:

'The wood-beflowered mount of Rhipé that is the breast of dusky night'[14]

watching how the headlands that dip to the west are the first to meet the darkness.

And what of Ibycus, who speaks of:

'Love like the North wind from Thrace, aflame with the lightning'?[15]

It may not be scenery, but it is vision—the eyes of men who live with an open country round them and look at what they see.

In this sort of visibility the philosophers of the early centuries are at home, noticing like sailors and poets, with an added scientific ardour to look farther round the corner. No one interfered with them in a world where curiosity reigned supreme. Anyway, 'No man would enjoy very many delights who heeded the censure of the people' as Archilochus said in the early 7th century, from the island of Paros.[16] Athens, different and old-fashioned, was outraged by Anaxagoras who announced the sun to be a red-hot stone and the moon made of earth with hills and valleys, and who spoke in a friendly way, perhaps, of the easy-going Persian rule, under which his youth had grown: so that he was brought up for trial, and rescued by Pericles, who seems to have smuggled him out of prison and away. He came back to the liberal atmosphere of Ionia, not to Clazomenae but to Lampsacus, a colony from Miletus, where he taught and died, and asked that the school-children be given an annual holiday to remember him by when he was dead. This was still done many years later, and the citizens also put up in their market-place, in his memory, an altar to Mind and Truth.

How pleasant it is when the fragile things, the defenceless, come through!

The thoughts of Anaxagoras echo down the ages in their transformations, while Clazomenae sits forgetting in the sun. Her amphorae have forgotten the fine texture they once were worked in, when the clay was built in to sarcophagi still called by the name of Clazomenae in museums, decorated with figures, Asiatic rosettes and sphinxes, and warriors no longer Asiatic but touched with the joy of Ionia, dancing with shields and immense horse-tailed helmets, and so very little in the way of clothes on underneath. And the poets remember. Keats who saw the Portsmouth vase: and that young Frenchman who recognized the old Aegean shape in the raised arms of death:

O mort des anciens jours, j'ai compris ta douceur . . .
Quand j'ai vu ses deux bras relevés sur sa tête.
Comme au sommet vermeil d'une amphore de Crête
Les deux anses du bord qui s'élèvent en choeur.[17]

4

Teos

Anacreon and the Poetry of Living

This is the sort of thing we should say by the fireside in the winter time, as we lie on soft couches after a good meal, drinking sweet wine and crunching chick-peas: 'Of what country are you, good sir? And how old were you when the Mede appeared?'

XENOPHANES of Colophon, 6th cent. B.C.[1]

Before reaching Clazomenae, a side road branches off to the left and makes by a shallow dip for Seferihisar, at twenty-four kilometres' distance; and there turns westward, another five kilometres, to Sighajik, a tiny medieval town on what was once the northern sea-front of Teos.

The way must always have been much the same, for it is made by the shapes of hills dipping towards an open space; it climbs in a gentle embrace of light varied with small descents and strips of glades, where the Vallonia oak, *Quercus aegilops,* throws shadows hard as metal from branches that seem to hold darkness even in the sun. On the right, in a middle distance, villages slant among poplars and olives; higher rolling lands lead to Urla, a village where new houses are built for Balkan refugees. We too climb gradually to bare and thorny downs, like moors now that the meagre gathered harvests leave them scorched and brown. Except for the oak glades, the sun reaches everything; hill and valley are equally open, bathed in a variety of light, an extravert landscape that welcomes whatever comes. That, I thought, is what it feels like; there is a *welcome* about the approach to Teos. We left on one side Seferihisar's quiet rural lacework of minarets and trees and followed an older paved road deep in dust, between walls or banked olive roots and gardens and gardens of vines, wells with smooth well-heads of rubbed stone, cypress trees here and there and a growing remoteness and peace. We had met a few carts, covered with patterns painted like those of Sicily, and one car and a lorry had passed along the road: now there were peasants walking here and there: and then the cultivation trickled out in thin grass, bents and rushes, to a low isthmus—we were on the northern harbour of Teos, with the patchwork wall of Sighajik loosely fitted of older and finer pieces, with a poor gate, under a notched Byzantine keystone, leading to blind houses on a village street of earth. The wall has rooms built here and there upon it like teeth with gaps between them, and surrounds the dwindled little place. Two towers, one hexagonal and one square, overlook a landing-stage of ancient stones, where the smallest steamboat ever seen was loading Vallonia acorns in a leisure that seemed to lap across centuries in one endless afternoon.

Teos is little visited, for it is only just free from being a military area. It is hard to imagine a fate more unsuitable for the city of Anacreon.

Sighajik: Walls and Harbour
The Quays of Teos Harbour

The Gate of Sighajik

When he lived, for two centuries already the royal Homeric hexameter had been giving way to lighter songs, whether to the Phrygian flute or Lydian lyre. Exactly what came to the Ionians from Lydia it is difficult to know, but I am inclined to think it was a very great deal—not so much from definite statements as from the way in which writers who belonged to the country, Herodotus and Pausanias and others, take the Lydian influence for granted, like a constant background for whatever they have to say. It is a fact for instance that none of the Greek coastlands, except Minoan Miletus, wished to be detached from Lydia when the Persian invasion came.[2] And in how easy a manner Herodotus writes of the Lydians in Smyrna, telling that, in a time of famine, one-half of them were brought down there from the inland plain of Sardis, and the king's son Tyrrhenus 'obtained boats wherein they set all their furniture, and sailed away in search of livelihood and land', and settled among the Ombrici [Umbrians], where they dwell unto this day:[3] and if one accepts this account of the Etruscan origin (which is I believe unhistorical but I am far too devoted to Herodotus to doubt it), then there are many remarkable similarities between Lydian Etruscan and Greek archaic. A whole atmosphere of intercourse and intimacy is built up by these and many other details.

In music at any rate the tradition of the Lydian influence is dominant, even to the point of military bands. Herodotus describes armies that came every year in summer to ravage the crops of Miletus, marching 'to the sound of pipes and of psalters and of the flute both tenor and bass'.[4] This was in the early days of the 6th century, when King Alyattes took Smyrna and failed before Clazomenae, and drove the Cimmerians from Asia. The origins of these musical instruments went far back—the double flute and the lyre are depicted in

Cretan paintings many centuries before, and the harp exists in the eastern background, lapis and gold, in the third millennium at Ur. Orpheus and the tall men of the north who brought Apollo and the younger gods may have adopted and distributed them: but later Ionians took these things from their neighbours, Lydian for the most part, and brought the new music from Lesbos where the races met.[5]

From here came Arion, in the 7th century, the wandering singer, inventor of the tragic style, the first recorded composer of dithyrambs, the assembler of the chorus, the first to introduce satyrs speaking in metre, the pupil of Alcman and friend of the dolphins. Here or at Cyme in Aeolis, Terpander,[6] also in the 7th century, established the barbitos or lyre to accompany, an octave higher, the Lydian lute; and also thought of the drinking song 'to vibrate in answer to the low-pitched lute at the feasts of the Lydians'.[7] Before the games were instituted or flutes admitted, the singers to the lyre contended at Olympia for a prize; and Alcman and Sappho started in Lesbos the love-song which Anacreon was to confirm. Sappho first thought to strike her lyre with a quill. The artists continually invented technical improvements. Stesichorus in Sicily added a lyre to the chorus, and later poets, Ibycus, Prophrastus the Pierite, Histiaeus of Colophon, and Timotheus, altered the ancient form and increased its strings.[8] Music travelled—through Sicily, to Corinth, to Sparta carried by minstrels, or sung in the nurseries and at the victors' tables by prisoners of war.

There was evident friendliness between the Greeks and Lydians. Long after the fall of Sardis, Pindar writes that 'the loving kindness of Croesus fadeth not away'.[9] Any number of the smaller pleasures of life are attributed to them— games, dice, and knucklebones, ' the ball and every other plaything, saving draughts, whereof the Lydians claim not the invention'.[10] Herodotus speaks of them with constant sympathy, holding them to be like the Greeks 'save in that they cause their female offspring to be harlots'. Even this he observes with more interest than disapproval, adding, as a corollary, that 'they choose their own husbands'.[11] Xenophanes writes of his fellow countrymen of Colophon that 'they learnt dainty and unprofitable ways from the Lydians ... they went to the market place with cloaks of purple dye, not less than a thousand of them all told, vainglorious and proud of their comely tresses, reeking with fragrance from cunning salves'.[12] They stand for the luxuries and pleasures of life.

'Golden-haired love hits me with his purple ball and calls me forth to play with a motley-slippered maid.'

'I thrum and thrum in Lydian fashion the harp of twenty strings,' Anacreon sings.[13]

It is high time to return to him in Teos.

Here he was born, and lived till Teos was taken by the Persians by siege, and its people, and Anacreon among them— 'all entered into their vessels and sailed away to Thrace, where they founded Abdera, which Timesius of Clazomenae founded before them, yet had no profit of it but was driven out by the Thracians.' The Clazomenians were very unlucky in their colonizing—'howbeit he now hath honours as an hero from the people of Teos in Abdera.'[14]

When the trouble was over, the people of Teos came back to their city; there the fame of Anacreon spread, and Hipparchus the tyrant of Athens sent a fifty-oared galley to fetch him, and kept him at his court: and a statue of him, in his cups, was put up on the Acropolis after his death, near the statue of Pericles. He lived till he was eighty-five, surviving, by a few years, the first prize of Aeschylus in 499 B.C., and he died in a time of peace, appropriately, a grape-stone sticking in his throat, having returned to his native Teos long before.[15]

Who would not do so? It is where I should live, if I had the choice of all the cities of Ionia. We drove towards it across the isthmus, by a paved Turkish road that lies straight between the two harbours and therefore probably follows some ancient thoroughfare. The land is flat—flooded, a traveller reports,[16] by winter storms, though I find it hard to believe of such sheltered seas. The road with its rough stones, narrowed between hedges of *Agnus castus* and brambles, that scratched our car and brushed its sides with purple panicles of flowers, soon grew too difficult; we climbed its banks to stubble fields, where the isthmus rises to a shallow watershed, less than a mile in width altogether. Perhaps a canal was once cut across it, since Pliny was able to think of Teos as an island.[17] Now, over all this sloping land, so relaxed and gentle in the sun, the potsherds of the Teians he thick as the leaves of Vallombrosa and the stone foundations of their buildings divide one cornfield from the next. The whole slope is planted with very old olive trees. No house was in sight; the hand of man's labour was everywhere, in space and time, in the evidence of harvest, in trees formerly planted, and in squared stones lying about worked for an earlier day: but his habitation was nowhere: and this emptiness in a landscape so tended was as intimate as that of a house, where someone dearly known is settled with all his things about him, but happens to be temporarily away.

Far out across the beautiful gulf, which silts up like all these western bays, the enchanting outline of Ionia lies, tired gold between the colours of sea and sky. There too no town, no village, no habitation was in sight; little hills that might have been tumuli, at the head of the bay, and long ridges, slender as fingers neither round nor steep, but nervous and so delicate that every contour speaks, lay as if they belonged to careless hands at rest. The headland of Myonessus reached out to southern cliffs unseen, where, in two anchorages, the Syrian fleet hid and the Romans sailed from Teos to defeat them, in their war with Antiochus the Great.[18] The harbour from which they set out at night in haste and confusion, was spread silted and shallow before me; a small current shouldered its stones, butted at and half corroded by these waves. The tongue of land must have held customs offices or warehouses and things belonging to a port—a temple perhaps? Now all is covered with pale turf that shows the sand beneath it, and nourishes flowers on threadlike stems, in thicker clusters where some old cornice emerging spreads its sloping edge of marble to give a triangle of shade.

Half-way on the hillside the ruined shape of the theatre faces south-west. A boy we had found in Sighajik to guide us stooped as he climbed over the seats in what is now an earthen hollow, and picked a Hellenistic coin off the ground. We had walked a long time and had rested, seated on slices of Corinthian column, by a field of water-melons in the shade; had eaten the melons and talked of buried treasure and of people who came to read inscriptions thirty years ago; then we had walked on, stepping across the stone walls and through the scented bay or laurel that divided every field. As he helped me over, Ahmet the taxi-man gave me a sprig, calling it daphne though he spoke in Turkish; the spicy scent has remained in my nostrils like the seal of Teos in the sun. As I stepped over I noticed that the stone on which I stood was roughened by Greek letters carved in even lines.

Teos was known in its day for the grey marble, and used to export it, as well as cups of earthenware ('the heeltaps fly from Teian cups')—and fine cloaks of Miletus wool.[19] The

grey marble shows in a great heap the temple platform of
Dionysus; drums of fluted columns, Ionic volutes, a half-lost
metope of centaurs, they lie tangled in olive roots and oak-
scrub, overgrown with long grass and catmint and fennel;
they were put up by Hermogenes of Caria, long after the
Persians had destroyed the older temple near the theatre,
across the hill.

It is remarkable, in spite of its vicissitudes, how pleasant
are the things remembered in the history of Teos—as if the
amenity of Anacreon had survived. We know that the city
dwindled into poverty so that there was talk of adding to
it the population of Lebedus and making one City out of
two: we know that it quarrelled with its Society of Artists,
so that they removed to Lebedus (after 153 B.C.) and were
enticed eventually by Mark Antony to entertain Cleopatra
in Priene:[20] We know of course that Harpagus took the city
'by approaches', heaping up earth against its walls, and that
the people, alone of all the Greeks except the Phocaeans,
chose rather to abandon their wrecked town than to live in
bondage.[21] But this is all the sadness that we hear. Between
the return of Anacreon and the quarrel with the artists there
were four centuries of summer evenings in their seasons
by quiet shores, delightful songs, processions to the temple
under the hill. The memory of the art of living breathes even
now in a landscape full of kindness, a memory of pleasure
pouring as from a natural cornucopia out of the gentlest
climate in the world. Perhaps the simplicity of the pleasures
wove the charm.

'A wattle basket full of the stalks of fine white celery,'[22]
or: 'little garlands of celery' [which was discovered in Ionia],
'to hold high festival to Dionysus';[23] or 'galingale', for lying
on at meals.[24] In 1852, in Mitylene, they still laid the roast
lamb on aromatic herbs.[25]

'Twas a Lydian hand, Asian born, that invented pitchers, and the offerings of toasts in turn round the board with the naming beforehand of the toast to be drunk'[26] and 'twas an old custom for the guest who began the singing to hold a spray of bay or myrtle, and hand it as he chose, without regard to the order of the seating, to another who continued the song.'[27]

'The star is coming round again, the season is hard to bear with the world athirst because of the heat; the cricket sounds sweetly from the leaves of the treetop, and lo! the artichoke is blowing.'[28]

'And the serving maid, holding the jar aloft, poured out the honey-sweet, mixed one in three' [of wine to water].

This is Anacreon. It seems remarkable that he got so strong a result out of watered wine. Even when he took his drink a little stronger—'and into a pure clean jar let them pour *five* and *three,*'—Anacreon's orgies seem singularly mild.[29]

'Made wanton by marrow-feeding marjoram,' a later poet sings.[30] The athletes themselves, in early days, were trained on wheat-meal, soft and pure, and figs. One can envy people who got so much stimulus out of so little. The easy flow slips effortless into the stuff that poetry is made of—life rather than literature seems to solve the poet's problems.

Apellicon must still be remembered, who was a Teian, and with failing eyesight copied out and saved the works of Aristotle, found in a trench in the ground.[31] And I will end with an inscription put up in Crete to record the visit of two Teian diplomats, who 'have not only shewn the good behaviour expected from visitors, but ... Menalcas, as became a man of culture, has given sundry tasteful performances to the lyre. ... It is resolved by the Directors and City of Knossos that . . . thanks be tendered to the City of Teos for sending the same and likewise to the Ambassadors . . . for their excellent behaviour'.[32]

It was late afternoon and we drove to find some food in Seferihisar. The houses in that neat little village-town are built with marble, with a piece of cornice upside down here and there for a doorstep. In the *lokanta* we ate pilaf and curds off a clean linoleum tablecloth, and drank water from which even the one in three was banished, and felt life quiet after the business and tenderness of memory in what is now a city of the imagination.

> 'And he who once wove poems for women's song, Anacreon whom Teos gave to Greece, the stimulator of banquets, the deceiver of women, the antagonist of flutes, lover of the lyre, sweet, free from pain. Never shall love of thee grow old or die, so long as the boy serves the water mixed with wine, from left to right, and female choirs ply the dance all night long, and the bowl, the daughter of bronze, sits on the cottabus [a Sicilian game] struck by the drops of Bacchus.'[33]

Guide in Teos

Teos: Temple of Dionysus

Teos: Metope of the Temple

Turkish Bridge on the Old Coast Road, Clazomenae to Ilija

5

Erythrae

Exile and Slavery

W. from Erythrae
26.9.52

... to woes incurable, my friend, the gods have ordained the
remedy of staunch endurance ...

ARCHILOCHUS, 7th cent. B.C.[1]

There has always been a surprisingly tough side to the
delightfulness of the Greeks. For one thing, they were
apt to kill their prisoners. My teacher, when we studied
history, explained that this is the only economic way to
deal with them; but economics recommend a number of
things that in the long run do not pay; they belong to an
order where the good of one is the harm of another, and
one hopes that the kingdom of heaven may dispense with
them. The Greek prisoner, at all events, as often as not
was doomed, though the worst horrors of the Peloponnesian
war may have shocked the inhabitants of Asia, still basking
in the Aegean sun. Exile and the wholesale transplanting
of populations was, however, a matter that both Asia and
the Eastern Mediterranean have always taken in their stride,
and it would lead us far afield to disentangle how much of
civilization is rooted in this unhappiness of the past. How
often did the ancient world in its nursery listen to some
foreign lullaby, sung by a captive stranger? It will not bear
thinking of in detail; of the two sorrows, that of scattered and
private slavery is worse than that of a whole population bodily
transplanted. One can gauge the latter in most of the little
coast towns of Ionia today, charred and scarred as they are
by the Greek departure and the Turkish arrival in 1922, and
still looking, in their half-ruined state, like someone else's
garment, too big for its present wearer.

Yet if one could, would one go back beyond 1922? I think
not. The wound is healing, and Turkey has her country to
herself; there is optimism abroad there, a rising sap of life.
And now that the magic region is her own—no longer to be

looked upon as an alien threat, an enchantment that at any moment might be or be imagined to be a poison—now that she can relax and admit herself into the climate that built a past so beautiful and can take up her sovereign inheritance without danger, she too, like all the great empires of the past that touched the beguiling shore, will be illuminated by the land and sea around them.

Greece need not repine. Perhaps, belonging to an empire that for ten years and more has been liquidating itself, I may feel about territorial losses with more detachment than before. In the years immediately following the war a wave of panic went about north Italy and everyone in good society was buying estates in the Argentine; my friends wondered that I should then set about the repairing of my house, which is on the direct route of invasions in one of the least defensible areas in the world. But I looked into myself and considered, and—because the place is so much loved—felt that I would be happier to think of it beautiful even in the hands of strangers, and so continued to work upon it, hoping that, whatever might come, its pleasantness would save it for even a commissar to enjoy. This poor instance is an absurdity—for what house on earth can compare with that of Hellas, which all the world inhabit in their day? And yet the principle is the same.

We drove from Clazomenae to Cheshme, past hot springs—Ilija'—where rich men of Smyrna have built up a semicircular quayside round a bay. The air here is cool from the north, and the houses have bathrooms where natural warm water pours through four-inch taps of earthenware. The ancient Clazomenians too had baths ('incidentally they worship Agamemnon', is added by Pausanias in a rather heartless way)[2]—and so had Teos, 'some in clefts of the rock filled by the tide, others made to display wealth', but the best, then and now were at Lebedus, a little to the south,

unapproachable both to modern bathers and to myself because still a military area.[*]

The poor people of Smyrna and the peasants bathe in
fields where warm sulphur water a stone's throw from the
road wells out at the foot of a rise; and here their huts of
tea-houses with awnings, makeshift and crooked, are spread
by the wayside. The port of Cheshme itself is at the west
end of the peninsula, caught as if by the prong of a fork
between two headlands, and looks straight at Chios across
the water, and has a rectangular Genoese castle, with an
Ottoman minaret and gateway added, protecting the small
harbour below. It was here that I walked through what looked
like double desolation, both Greek and Turkish, in opposite
corners of the town, on a late afternoon, and thought about
the exiles and the slaves. And, coming out to white, hard
country slopes, with olive trees sailing like clouds upon them,
felt the healing quality of Time with the sudden softness of
a bird's wing. It was present but invisible, as the spring
is there when plants recognize it and push into the raw
February world: for there was little but ruin to see. Wrecked
obliterated terraces of vines ran like ribbed sand across the
unhappy headlands; the small, once trim Greek houses lay
in the heaps of their walls: across sunset-spears of light and
shadow peasants rode home between panniers, on donkeys,
or walked two and two in the silent Turkish companionship:
the children already had the gentle gay look of the coast; and
three girls with dark curled hair free of the kerchief, with
faces and figures of the generous Mediterranean, yielding
and sure—no tense barbarian hardness—came walking and
laughing towards their village home. Life was returning.
Here and there a few neater houses under cypress and fig

[*] No longer so now in 1954.

tree showed painted windows or garden walls repaired: the water splashed its half-rainbow into the wayside trough, and the laden animal stopped to drink with an habitual air. The ingredients of peace and happiness were all about. But the Voices that made them articulate have gone: and this snapping of the traditional intimacy, the cutting of a cord that vibrates in all surrounding hearts, makes the misery of exile.

The depth of all we say lies hidden deep under the surface of the words. The fallacy of so-called realism is that it concentrates on illusion; it uses description superficially and not, as the great ages use it, to show from common porches time and eternity implicit in the commonplace. The 'realist' sets description on a pedestal as if it had a reality of its own. This is the art of decadence. The great ages find a more withdrawn reality. 'Amid the flagons, frankincense gives forth its sacred odour, and water stands cool, and sweet and clear.'[3] Subtly, in every day, they find the immortal pulse making a sacrament of life, whatever the god may be; and this image of the eternal in his existence is what the exile loses, because the familiar unconscious ways to find it have been broken, unless he can build something more safely permanent in his own heart. The break is not irreparable, but generations are needed to build a new tradition in a different shape.

Sadness closed about me as I walked back into Cheshme. It must once have been a delightful town; the paved streets were narrow, and charming Turkish houses, whitewashed or blue, hung over towards each other in uninhabited decay: a mosque, disused and open, was surrounded by derelict cemeteries, their marble turbans askew with an inhuman gaiety. There was trouble in Cheshme, and when it was over, and the Greeks had gone, the Turkish citizens probably moved down to the better houses on the flat ground near the quay, where a new life may take root and spread. A Turkish khan or warehouse is there, with two-storied arcade of rounded brick and badly built double gate of entry, ruined: the new mosque is nearby, cheerful and white with a plane tree beside it: the Genoese castle (probably made to protect the commerce that went on in the warehouse), is beyond; and beyond that the square on the quayside, with café, a taxi or two, buses, and an electric power station newly built. It is a very long journey to come down through a little town in Asia Minor!

I had in fact no business to be loitering in Cheshme at all, since Herodotus my guide never even mentions its existence. We stopped there only because we were on the way to Erythrae, now Ildir—which was one of the twelve Ionian cities, and spoke the same language as Chios, different from that of the other ten towns.[4] Of all of them it is the most naturally inaccessible, and even in the days of its strength must have been much easier to reach by sea than by land; for it lies well out on the range that Tmolus pushes westward, and close up to the last dark headland of Kara Burun, the southern clasp of the gulf of Smyrna. Into the sea of this peninsula, which was once all called Erythrae, we rounded a shallow cape north of Cheshme, and pushed out from the land and its dilapidation, uprooted vines and a ruined church where prayers used to be said for the souls of Russian sailors—into a blue width of promontories and islands, solitary and gay. One scarcely visible smudge of houses on the high flank of the enormous headland; Ilijà, with trees and smoke, in the low south in the mist of the sun; farther on, a slope with windmills and the fields of Reisderé, where the track ends; and Erythrae lay beyond them, marooned and apparently pathless in the distance eastward, in a loop of its island-guarded bay.

Somewhere on the cape we had rounded, which goes out in shallows, an image of Hercules, very ancient already in the days of Pausanias, drifted on a raft from Tyre. The people of Erythrae and Chios both tried to secure it, unsuccessfully; until a blind Erythraean fisherman dreamed that only a rope plaited of women's hair could tow it. The women of Erythrae would have nothing to do with this suggestion, but the Thracians, 'both slave and free', cut off their locks, and the men of Erythrae towed the raft ashore. After this, only Thracian women were allowed in the sanctuary, and the rope of hair was seen by Pausanias. As for the fisherman, his sight was restored.[5] How the Thracian women came here, is not said. The Erythraean origins are mixed with Cretan, and Lydian kinsmen and Carian friends, and Pamphylians who took a part when Cleopus the son of Codrus brought his Ionian settlers:[6] the probability is that they found a local community of some sort with a touch of the seafaring Minoans, already settled there when they came.

What they would find now is just as unexpected.

We anchored behind one of the empty islets, once called Hippi'[7], that are like a shoal of swimming hedgehogs with their backs alone above water; we made a fire and cooked our lunch, and swam in the warm sea watching—as pirates must often have done—the little city unconscious on its hill. A feeling of distress came from it. The houses showed white and pleasant as they climbed their slope with trees among them; the shape of a church stood vaguely upon the acropolis above; yet something was so wrong that it conquered the distance; the little place looked dead. It was, I believe, the absence of window-panes: only one house in Erythrae gave back the light. When we came to its landing-stage, we found but a few yards of stones put anyhow together, with half a pink marble column to tie up to, and not a boat or skiff of any kind in sight. A police officer was there to watch for smugglers, and came forward, courteous and pleased

with an unexpected visit; and waved us up between shells
of houses and heaps of rubble when we said we had come
to see the town. With olives and fig trees going back to
wildness and wattled gardens neglected, it lay all ruin and
death in the sun; but half-way up the hill a few stones were
pulled about to build a makeshift square, and the headman's
house or perhaps the schoolmaster's showed the windows
that had caught our eyes at sea. Here like owls in their ruins
a few inhabitants live, not more than a hundred or two, and
came out ragged and friendly from crumbling basements.
They were the Thracians, or as near as may be—Macedonian
Muslims brought here on exchange—sick with malaria and
desperately poor to look at, with fine and nervous features
and delicate hands.

Two young girls, one knitting and one spinning as they
walked, came with us a little way as we climbed to the
acropolis and found a church in ruins, slabs of white marble,
patches of ancient wall. The fine new wall built about 300
B.C. on a three-mile circuit, which presumably enabled Erythrae to resist the general of Lysimachus,[8] is there in sight
below winding its rubble, with facing stones left only here
and there. It still strides across the landscape, north of the city
and round the acropolis into what should be a fertile prosperous valley, with a stream of water rushing through a mill. The
river winds south of the town where once, I imagine, there
was an estuary harbour. The view from the height stretches
far over the screen of uninhabited islands by many headlands
to the closed horizon of Chios in the west; and eastward, over
lands where the garrison watched Lysimachus' general burning their crops; where the Galatian Gauls arrived, ravaging
and extorting ransom;[9] where Attalus came, taking refuge
in the city after his defeat by Philip Vth of Macedon in 201
B.C. From here a road, so poor that it does not even show

in the landscape, goes to Balikovasi on the gulf of Smyrna, as it probably did from the beginning—a long and trouble-some journey always; and visitors, like the Emperor Hadrian, preferred to come by sea.[10]

The best days of Erythrae were probably the earlier days, when the difficulty of the thirty-five miles of the gulf of Smyrna made ships prefer a more westerly harbour. There were wars—'the people of Miletus aided the men of Chios against the people of Erythrae"[11] and the poet Alcaeus dreamed that to the fighters against the Erythraeans Apollo came in sleep with a tamarisk branch in his hand.[12] But the city's life was prosperous and dignified, exporting wine and milestones, and wool; acting, with Sardis, as umpire in the dispute of Miletus and Priene; sending eight ships to the battle of Lade. There were religious monuments, not the temple of Hercules only, but a huge wooden image of Athena with a distaff[13] (like that of our little Thracian com-panion) in each hand: and a temple too to the Idaean dactyls, priests of Cybele and workers in iron, more primitive than the upstarts from Olympus. There was a Sybil too called Herophile, born of a nymph and a shepherd in a cave,[14] still recognizable on the ceiling of the Sistine Chapel, painted by Michelangelo.

All this floats among the débris of history as if it were in the mill-race, carried through the Erythraeans' shrunken fields.

As we came down the northern hillside, we found un-even hidden buildings, jutting out unnaturally, as bones of the dead. Below the theatre hollow, near the town, one side of a temple platform shows ten yards or so of fine smooth moulded stone: it supports a shed now, and the whole sty-lobate might probably be cleared. A little nearer the sea, the main temple ruins lie in heaps of grey pillars, fluted and plain.

The Turkish Gate to the Castle of Cheshme

Macedonian Refugee in Erythrae

Macedonian Refugees in Erythrae

Desolate Erythrae (Ildir)

The town recovered its comfortable look as we sailed away. By a kind accident, the one house with glass in its windows caught the sun. The clear deepening rose of evening festooned the bay with ghosts of all the garlands ever worn there:

> 'and each man had three garlands, of roses two, and the other a wreath of marjoram,'[15]

The colour of dying roses and the dark undercolour ebbed and melted, and, withdrawn in its solitude, the window flashed and died. Out of the past, among its bigger ventures, an unimportant voice is heard—an elementary schoolteacher from Erythrae, talking with Sophocles the poet, as he sits next him at table.

"What a pretty phrase," says Sophocles. ". . . The light of love shines upon crimson cheeks."

"You may be very clever, Sophocles, at poetry," cries the Erythraean, "but all the same Phrynichus was wrong in calling the cheeks . . . crimson. If the painter were to put crimson on this lad's cheeks, he would cease to be pretty. . . ."[16]

The pedantic outraged little voice dies away; he may probably have come from Eretria in Euboea and not from here at all: it does not matter, but with such a stickler for accuracy one would like to be as careful as one can. His idle echo makes a splash like a tiny fish in the evening silence: it is the pedant's voice, so familiar, so ready to teach: and yet the Thracian exiles are still torn from their homes and brought to Erythrae, as if nothing useful were ever learned at all.

6

Chios

Ingredients of Empire

Thou shalt enquire into everything; both the motionless heart of well-rounded Truth, and also the opinions of mortals.

EMPEDOCLES of Akragas, 5th cent. B.C.[1]

In trying to live back into Ionia, one should not underestimate islands. Their presence must always have added to the happiness not so much of their inhabitants—since islanders are apt to be morose—as of those who from a mainland see their interesting shapes, never for any hour the same.

One acquires an eye for them. "Do you see Samos over there?" D.B.* would ask, pointing to the white, empty horizon; and gradually I too came to distinguish a line, faint and indefinite as a sigh in Eternity, so unsubstantial that all we can think of—forgotten hopes, unanswered loves, the vibrating

---

* David Balfour, the Consul-General in Smyrna.

of a wire into silence—are solid and substantial by comparison. Yet it is a rock—a high hard-bitten ridge, washed clean of softened earth by rains and winds. It grows firm as one approaches, light or dark blue according to the slant of the sun, but smoothly vertical; until, with the distance still decreasing, the varieties of surface begin to show—back-bones of slopes and darkness of chasms, and lastly the trees and fields and houses, with only a streak perhaps, a trail of whiteness like a scarf of tulle, where the island rears its head from the sea.

 There is a game one can play with two crescent shapes of white paper exactly alike: by placing them side by side, the one whose points face towards the convex side of the other will appear quite small: and this magic, the denial of the actual testimony of our eyes, is the constant effect of islands. There can be no boredom with anything that varies in such a way as always to tip one's thoughts just *over* the horizon: and the absence of boredom must be one of the main attributes of happiness. So that I think one is justified in counting the islands high among the ingredients of ancient cheerfulness in Ionia.

Even an island as near the mainland as Chios has its mystery as you watch it from the shore—more human in quality and therefore not quite as enchanted as those wrapped by distance in their cocoon of air. With a glass and the sunrays upon it, one could look at Chios from Cheshme as one looks at an anthill, going about its business through the morning hours; at its nearest point to the mainland it is a bare five miles across.

I had no visa for Greece, but we had a Sunday to play with and an easy sea: D. B. offered to give me a view of Chios without landing.

As we sailed across, Hüseyin the Skipper, who has a house in Cheshme, told us about the war, and hunger in the islands. And how a number of the boatmen saw to it that fugitives, who had paid large sums and were trying to escape with all they had left upon them, should never reach the land. Even when they found an honest boatman and managed to cross, they were by no means sure of a welcome: and usually it was the story of Arion, with the dolphins left out. One can understand why the ancient tellers of tales looked, for relief from human squalor, to the more decent animal world and to stories such as that of Coeranus, a 7th-century poet from Miletus, a comrade of Archilochus in the colonizing of Thasos, who once saved a dolphin from the hands of some fishermen: the debt was repaid when, shipwrecked off Naxos, the fish carried him safely to a cave; and, when he died long afterwards, a shoal of dolphins followed his funeral procession as it walked round the harbour.[2]

Even historically, there are pleasanter and older things in Chios to think of than the behaviour of the boatmen in the war. The Paeones, for instance, who, brought from the Strymon (Struma) river and settled by the Persians in a village of Phrygia, 'taking up their children and women, ran away to the sea . . . and crossed over . . . to Chios. And when they were already in Chios, straightway there came a multitude of Persian horsemen at their heels, that had pursued the Paeones; and when they overtook them not, they sent a message to them commanding them to return again. But the Paeones received not their words; and the men of Chios took them to Lesbos, and the men of Lesbos brought them to Doriscus, whence they journeyed afoot and came to Paeonia'.[3]

It must always be a delicate matter in islands to decide what to do about a trouble from the mainland when it comes. There is a temptation to be isolationist while one can. When Histiaeus, plotting against the Persians and seeing himself discovered, crossed over the narrow water, the men of Chios put him in bonds, fearing him as a Persian party man, until he was able—by his wiles—to draw them all into rebellion.[4]

Of all the nations of Asia, the Persian one would think most suited to work happily with the Greek. The impression left of their intercourse is friendly, and I am not sure that the Greeks of Asia Minor did so well for themselves by escaping the Persian rule. Under the Persians as under the Lydians before them, the geographic situation of the coastal cities made easy dealings with the interior a matter of large profits on both sides. Just as the Flanders wool trade has been the main thread of English history, so the great trade routes from Mesopotamia to the Aegean (with the north and south cross of the Bosphorus and Cilician Gates) are the threads which ever string the history of Asia Minor. Hittite sculptures already trace the routes of Anatolia: a king, armed with a bow, stands against a rock above the pass that leads to Ephesus from Sardis; and a vast Hittite figure, miscalled Niobe, is on a cliff of the Hermus valley in sight of the road which American bull-dozers are widening below. We can follow the route inland across Phrygia and Cappadocia to the Euphrates and beyond. Herodotus describes it as the Royal Road, and tells of the system of posts which the Persians instituted, and carried on (in their own country) into the age of railways. After the Hittites, and before the Persians, the Lydians whom Herodotus calls the first pedlars or hotel-keepers (the word is ambiguous), organized its mighty traffic. They were business men and probably ran khans or halting-places at every stage; and they were the first people to think of coined money with a government stamp upon it to facilitate their tolls—so that one of the chief human inventions came by reason of the trans-Anatolian highway. By it the Lydians at Sardis gathered their share of the wealth of northern Asia, and transferred it for western export to the cities by the sea.[5]

The Persians, inheriting the Lydian position on the highway, also inherited the necessity of a friendly maritime people to deal with their traffic when it reached the coast. The Greek cities had the trump cards in their hands; they were repeatedly conquered, and then—because of geography—treated with care by every nation in turn that ran the Asiatic road. When Histiaeus wished to poison their minds against the Persians, he did so by telling them that King Darius planned to transfer them to Phoenicia, and to bring the Phoenicians to Ionia in their stead: it was untrue, but successful propaganda, for it was the measure that might have made them vulnerable by taking their key position away from them; and I imagine that is why Histiaeus chose this particular threat. However this may be, he succeeded; but even in the war that followed there is no sign of any very bitter feeling on either side.

The Ionian bonds with mainland Greece were not then as intimate as they later became. Even after the battle of Salamis, refugees from Chios, trying to persuade the Peloponnesians to venture to Ionia, 'could scarce draw them forth as far as Delos; for all beyond was dreadful unto the Greeks, because they had no knowledge of those parts . . . and in their imagination they thought Samos to be as far away as the pillars of Hercules. And so it fell out that the barbarians for fear and trembling durst not sail farther west than Samos, nor the Greeks farther east than Delos, albeit the men of Chios besought them; and so dread kept watch over the space betwixt'.[6] When the war was over at last, the

Lacedaemonians thought it advisable to remove the Ionians to Greece altogether, where they could be protected; but the more maritime Athenians opposed it strongly, and 'brought into the confederacy the men of Samos and of Chios, of Lesbos and of the other isles . . .'[7] and one could spend years imagining what might have happened if things had gone the other way, if the iron curtain of that day had not descended, and the fates of Ionia had remained attached to the interior of Anatolia.

The problem of an enterprising maritime fringe and a producing but more primitive mainland is so common in history that I think it could now be reduced almost to a formula, with an answer attainable. Rome and Italy in Africa, Britain in Egypt and India, Palestine, the Adriatic, and coasts uncountable—the regions are various, the circumstances differ, but the substance is, I believe, the same. Taking a general view, one may say that intercourse runs smoothly while the inland power remains strong; then, a revolution, a change of dynasty, any internal hitch that dislocates the traffic, ruins a number of influential people in the seaports; they are not altruistic or long-sighted enough to wait, perhaps a generation or two, while the inland perturbation settles back into order; and they try to force it with whatever sea-power they can command. 'Imperialism' is simply the use of inland productiveness for the benefit of the power at the sea-end or other commercial outlet of a trade route: it dislocates the balance of mutual benefit—of the profits which ought to go to the mainland power as far as the coast, and to the trafficking sea-power beyond. The history of Asia Minor is full of examples: the relations of Saracens and Crusaders; of Byzantines with the piratical business men of Genoa and Venice: it is always a question of the mainland traffic and the sea. Given time, and a strong inland power, the trade will make its way through all the changes of the hands that hold it: but it will never remain for very long in the hands of a foreign sea-power, if once that sea-power tries to move inland.

With the great route of Asia Minor this delicate adjustment goes back to the beginnings of recorded history: the fall of the Lydian empire was one of the periodic inland dislocations; it was resettling, remarkably swiftly, into economic harmony under the Persians. But a series of accidents, of sentimental attachments, of individual resentments and impatience, rather than any economic compulsion, turned Ionia towards the mainland of Greece. How doubtful the balance was can be seen by the behaviour of people like Themistocles and Alcibiades. Whatever one may make of their political morality, one must, I think, give them credit for a *vision* above the average—and this vision—helped no doubt by their private and embittered circumstances—brought them to see no great catastrophe in the Persian suzerainty over the routes of Asia. I am inclined to agree with this view. The cities of Ionia had no more to fear from Persian than from Lydian: the greater the volume of trade along the highway, the stronger their own situation on the coast. Nor is this a matter merely of academic interest today. The coming of the Seljuks brought the nomads into Asia Minor, and the machinery of a commerce that had survived through Hittite, Lydian, Persian, Macedonian, Roman and Byzantine was destroyed for centuries. But geography is there, and the condition of a strong mainland power is being supplied by Turkey reviving. It is a pleasure to read Ionian names on ships against the quays of Smyrna, not as trespassers on the land route of Asia, but as the carriers where the land route ends. In 1922 this was interrupted; the sea-power attempted to possess the mainland; the mistake was made which we all seem to make, and the reaction was swifter than most but not different in essence: the sea-power was thrown back to the sea. Turkey, strong enough to hold her land routes safe, can now afford to welcome visitors to her harbours; and the Greek islands may yet become a part, once more, of that long serpent of commerce which glides indestructible, across the highlands of Asia to the western seas.

It is sad to watch this narrow sea-boulevard, as it were, between Turkey and the islands—crowded as it ought to be with shipping—now empty as if gangsters with guns had just been up and down along it. It takes us back with Herodotus to those days before the Lydian adjustment was made when 'Croesus purposed to build ships and lay hands on the people of the isles. But when he had all things ready . . . there came to Sardis, as some say, Bias of Priene, but as others say, Pittacus of Mytilene, and prevented the building of ships, for when Croesus asked him if there was any new thing in Greece, he said: "O king, the people of the isles are buying ten thousand horses, having in mind to make war against thee in Sardis." And Croesus, believing that he spoke true, said: "O that the Gods might put this thing into the hearts of the people of the isles, to come against the children of Lydia on horseback." And he answered and said: "O king . . . thou dost earnestly pray to catch the people of the isles on land riding horses . . . But what else deemest thou that the people of the isles pray for . . . than to catch the Lydians at sea?" . . . Then Croesus . . . ceased from the building of ships and covenanted friendship with the Ionians that dwell in the isles,'[8] and the sea- and the land-power came to their agreement.

Chios was a great power, and sent 100 ships to the battle of Lade (as against 17 from Teos and 8 from Erythrae). Later, in Athenian days, the ships of Chios are constantly mentioned by Thucydides; and it was a naval station for 80 ships under Rome.[9] In the Middle Ages, it was a strong point of the Genoese, and has a castle; and later was mentioned, in

English capitulations with the Porte, as the chief centre with Smyrna for English trade: Henry VIII had J. B. Giustiniani as his Consul in Scio.[10]

We were now making for it with a northerly light summer breeze that bundled us and the waves together towards its eastern shore. Both D. B. and Hüseyin knew it well, and leaving the city with inland-rising gardens and bicycle-dotted roads and a Sunday leisure look about it, we made along the emptier coast towards the south. Yellow slopes lie tumbled here like lion cubs at play round the flank of their mother, for a lean backbone ridge runs parallel with the sea. It is bare enough and poor with little water, but has a thrifty look, as if every slender thread of prosperity were carefully attended to, and in this as in everything else done by man, there is a contrast between the two neighbouring shores.

Somewhere in the island is mandragora, said only to be found in Chios, Palestine and Tibet (though I know it in Cyprus): and here squat dark bushes of mastic grow like clumps of shadow up the hills. There is nothing sweeter-scented than the resin of the mastic if you burn it—the sun and air and light of its home are in the scent; and the drink they make from it too is more aromatic than any others of the kind that I know. Chios was famous for it in ancient times—and for delicate earthenware and variegated marble, woven tapestries and rather sticky wine; and, in the 8th century B.C., for the welding of iron, invented by Glaucus, who made a bronze bowl for the king of Lydia.[11]

We were close inshore: people called to us, bathing from little beaches in the sun; and when we came to an empty cove, with only vineyards and shallow cliffs and clear water, we too threw the anchor down on the ribbed sand and swam, careful not to step out on the forbidden beach. Three young girls, making their way to church perhaps, with coloured

veils on their heads, came suddenly over the cliff, and cried
out and made to turn back when they saw us, explaining in
Greek that they were frightened, but yet coming on again,
as it might have been Io on the shore of Argos or Europa
in Tyre: and one could hear Herodotus, that sensible man,
saying: "to be eager for revenge, they hold foolishness . . . for
it is plain that unless they had so desired themselves, they
would not have been ravished". D. B., however, whether
withheld by Consular scruples about visas or other reasons,
kept strictly to the sea, and the maidens tripped by with a
little trail of gaiety and pleasure. As for us, we turned to sail
northwards, past the Genoese fort and back into the harbour
itself where, without landing, we drank our tea on deck on
the quiet water, and watched the neat buildings and animated
cafés of the town. And in the evening, with the sun behind the
ridges we had been so close to, we made east for Cheshme
with a rising sea.

a greek island 6.8.52

7

Myrina

'New Harvests Cover the Land'

The greatest touchstone of any work is Time, who showeth
even the heart of a man beneath his breast.

SIMONIDES, 6th cent. B.C.[1]

North of Smyrna lay the eleven cities of Aeolis, in a
country so easy, comfortable and fertile that agriculture, taking the place of commerce, seems to have deprived
them of history. Their names and their coins are known,
and a few events thinly scattered are attached to them here
and there: but on the whole one feels them lost in a deep and
rural peace, not lifeless but so embedded in the repetition of
harvests that the ancient bustle has died away; one hears only
the thick fall of the earth when the plough turns it, the stir
of the sickle or the homing feet of flocks through centuries
upon centuries of time.

The good road carries north to Pergamum and passes, without noticing them, by Larisa and Cyme, Myrina, Gryneium

and Elaea. Larisa is in sight, north of the bridge of Hermus
(Ghediz Chay), pushing its landlocked headland out to make
Time visible, by marking what was once the edge of the sea.
Fertile and Pelasgian, she was mentioned by Homer, and
already deserted in Strabo's day. From the road, looking up,
the acropolis shows a fragment of polygonal wall: but why
should one climb, when so little worth hearing seems ever to
have been said or thought about Larisa? She belonged at one
period to the temple of Ephesus; and Cyme was settled with
her conquered inhabitants; and a Pelasgic princess, whose
father had violated her, tripped him up and drowned him in a
cask of wine.[2] That is all I can find out about her. 'For he that
would live completely happy, must before all things belong
to a country that is of good report.'[3]

Ah, noble Simonides!—'*before all things*'—before a
frigidaire or a motor-car, or even a daily paper? And this
abstract contentment is glowing enough to be called *happiness*? Anyway, Larisa seems to have had little report, and I
left her acropolis unclimbed.

But I turned aside on the way back from Pergamum to try
and find Myrina.

Myrina too is dismissed by Herodotus my guide in the
shortest way: what led me off the highroad was its own
intrinsic charm and the sight of two hills stretched out to sea,
that looked like the summits of a double acropolis, which
indeed they were.

The lands of ancient Myrina, and suburbs probably with
gardens, lay spread for a great distance on the easy slopes
east of the modern road to Pergamum; but the centre of the
town was built in the west round its double harbour, which
I now made for with Ahmet the taxi-man, leaving his small
nephew to guard the car by the roadside.

It soon turned out that we had branched off from the road on the wrong side of a river which flowed out of sight, beyond fields of cotton. Peasants standing about, picking the white wool bundles out of their dark pods, told us that we had far to go and could anyway not cross, the river being deep and without a bridge. In the face of all experience, including my own, I assured Ahmet that one can often paddle across estuaries; and indeed what looked like a shallow sheet of water lay reflecting the afternoon sun two miles or more away.

So we walked, between one field and the next, calling to the peasants for direction. It was all cotton or tobacco, separated by ditches smothered in rushes and scented with catmint, with vineyards trailing ragged hedges here and there; and in the corners of the fields, resting on a mattock or a garment, lay the porous amphora, double-handled, with the labourer's water for the day.

A young lad came riding on a lean pony, a loose yellow kerchief on his head, and two milk-cans in his saddle-bag. He dismounted, and turned to lead us, and let me ride through the afternoon light, now rich and beautiful, long past its meridian. It shone on the pale grass of the two little acropoleis, on scraps of ancient wall half-way up their slope, on the folded edge which—now a mere boundary of cultivation— must once have marked a poorly fortified line.

The defencelessness of these Ionian and Aeolian cities filled me with surprise. They had no chance to hold out against anything at all serious from the land; and when the Persians came, Harpagus took them one after the other 'by approaches', piling up mounds of earth against their walls.[4] Very many of them, if one reads Thucydides, appear to have had no walls at all. The fact is that the first seafarers must have found

these coasts very lonely. The inland power, Hittite or Lydian, was tied to Asia, its intercourse and traffic absorbed by
the long stages that led to Mesopotamia, its kings in friendly
intimacy with the Assyrian court; when King Meles of Lydia
went into a three years' exile to obey an oracle, he turned
naturally eastward and chose Babylon as his refuge.[5] And
when the Lydians began to be interested in overseas trading, with a need for more markets as their inland territory
expanded, their relations with the coast were not fundamen-
tally warlike, the object being to keep the cities subservient
but prosperous—so that diplomacy was usually sufficient and
the fortifications of the headlands were made to serve chiefly
against skirmishers or pirates from the sea.

I began to recognize the sort of promontory that the Greek
adventurer, skirting the coast in his fifty-oared longboat,
would make for: an isthmus narrow enough to cut a canal or
drag ships across, and protection for a harbour on both sides.
The height above, the defence at the back, were secondary;
the sites are all chosen with a sailor's eye. A river estuary,
with a habitable promontory giving shelter both north and
south, and rich flat lands around, was an ideal situation—and
such is the site of Myrina.

For quite a long time, from my height on the pony's back,
I had been watching the estuary; it ran out in a sheet of
smooth water, with a curving line of dark blue sea-waves at
its edge: and no sign of a ford. But an old fisherman and a
boy sat crouched in a skiff, brooding on their own reflection,
surrounded by a halo of the evening.

The real river now opened before us, about thirty feet
wide, deep and cool, with sea lavender and rushes on its
banks. Its name was once Pythicus and is now Koja Chay, or
Güzel Hisar which means Fair Castle. It was blue as moonlight
and moved by à deep invisible current, and came from an

open valley in pastoral hills that led to the pass of Magnesia, by Aegae, whence Themistocles in exile made secretly, in a lady's Utter, for the Persian court at Susa.[6]

The need of our crossing was explained to the fishermen, and they pushed their boat in among the rushes. The pony was left to wait in the Eastern way, without being tied—for there is never anything to tie up to—and the lad came with us, calling joyfully to the peasants of the northern shore. A group of us soon walked among ruins, raising the scent of fennel from rubble of old walls in the sun.

There is nothing above ground to speak of, except shapeless lines tumbled and fallen and potsherds so crowded that they still seem to hold the gossip of streets and markets and particularly of fountains, when all else has disappeared. On the north side of the isthmus, hardly three fields across, the sea laps over dark red conglomerate stone—what is left of a mole and quay now under water; for the whole of this coast has subsided two feet or so in the last two thousand years. A few untidy bits of later masonry stand on the isthmus; and a temple, probably, shows four broken column shafts, one of them fluted, still upright in the ground.

Carts drawn by oxen were there from a distant village, collecting stones for building; one of the columns was already split in half all down its length, showing the fine white marble it was made of, 'even the heart of a man beneath his breast'. Fig and pistachio and maple grew as they liked here, and cotton in the hollow between the ports, and corn on the once-walled heights. Little box-like houses such as one still sees in Smyrna probably once clustered down these slopes, with flagged streets between them; and many-oared boats in the two harbours. The bright blue river wound against the walls, and peasants with their animals came to market on

the flat ground beside the temple from the wide flat lands
outside.

As far as I could, in Turkish practically non-existent which
only Ahmet the taxi-man understands, I tried to ask mercy
for the remaining columns; but the peasants laughed and said
they needed houses; and saw us back in a body to where the
fishermen sat waiting with their coiled nets in the bottom of
their boat.

The river now had a silver evening sheath over its darker
blue, like the light side of a mirror, and out of its depth fish
were leaping, half-fish and whole fish, quivering with pleasure
in the last red freedom of the day. Islands in the west, and
the coastline that hides Phocaea lay black and voluptuous
under the rayless disc of the sun. On the southern bank the
peasants in the fields were picking up their tools. There was
nothing but cotton to think of in the landscape, and a plot here
and there of melons, and some vines. Myrina, who was an
Amazon like Smyrna, and buried under a tomb in the Trojan
plain,[7] was sinking again into her obscurity and twilight.

The fishermen ferried us back and left us, and began to
throw their circular nets in the dusk. The darkness of the
under-water made widening ripples where they hit. The
leaping fish were below now, asleep or being caught by their
doom. A flash or two in the sun, in the shelter of 'a city
of good report'; and then the net of Fate and the darkness,
while new harvests cover the land. In the days of the Persians,
fishermen must have thought of this as they threw their catch
to the bottom of the boat while Harpagus was 'netting Lesbos
and Chios, one man taking hold of the hand of the next so
that they stretch from the sea on the north to the sea on the
south . . . hunting out the people'.[8]

While I jogged along, the vanished city and the Fair Castle
river melted away into wonder like a tale. The young peasant

with flat face from the central steppes of Asia gave a whack to the pony now and then: I was far more remarkable to him than all the history he turns over every day with his spade. We got back to the main road and to Ahmet's nephew waiting anxiously in the car in the dusk: and drove easily, some forty miles, to the lights of Smyrna.

8

Gryneium

Solitude and Patriotism

Not houses finely roofed or the stones of walls well builded,
nay nor canals nor dockyards make the city, but men able to
use their opportunity.

ALCAEUS, 6th cent., B.C.[1]

The Landscape, as one penetrates into Aeolis, changes
with a scarcely perceptible gradation; it loses the Mona
Lisa subtlety of Ionia, that delicate art which implies by with-
holding. The Chinese or Persian draughtsman, simplifying
his tools, makes the line of a brush or pen sensitive enough
to carry the whole weight of his meaning: and I feel this to
be the secret also of the Ionian landscape—held in flawless
contours and lit by a pure light, and almost independent of
detail or of colour. So Herodotus must have felt, for he says
that 'these Ionians chance to have their cities established in
the fairest place for climate of all men that we know. For
neither the parts to the north nor the parts to the south are

like Ionia; for those are oppressed by the cold and the wet, and these by the heat and the drought'.[2]

That is the accent of affection. From what I remember, there is no particular difference of climate, and the worst rain I have met outside Dartmoor was in Ionia. The 'climate' that Herodotus felt so clearly was, I believe, this strange and detached perfection, this feeling in the landscape that the *essential,* with the very minimum of trimming, is always there. Perhaps this is also as near as can be to a definition of classic art?

However this may be, Herodotus goes on to say that the Aeolians 'chanced to have built their cities in a more fruitful land than the Ionians, but one not so blest by the seasons': and as one drives northward towards Pergamum, the fruitfulness appears in an exuberance of slopes and fanning valleys where the olive-grown hillsides under their naked summits shimmer and toss, like 'azure-eyed Argive ships'[3] round a headland.

And nowhere in the world can the olive be so beautiful— not even in Zante, not even below Amphissa, nor on the terraces of Sicily or the hills of Provence. Nowhere else, except perhaps in the clefts around Cyrene, and there in a meagre way, have I seen it look *indigenous.* It grew wild a hundred years ago in Mytilene,[4] and as it stands now about its landscape in careless profusion, no longer so carefully clipped as before the Greeks departed, one knows it to be at home. When the tree is ripening and hangs over-jewelled, with every pendant berry graceful on a stem of its own, swaying in the winds' arms, with that backward toss that shows the small white edges of its leaves like teeth—it relaxes languidly, because so heavily laden, like the beauty—a little over full— of the later marbles, or those Lydian women transparent in

rose-coloured gauze, who flitted about the pleasure park of
Sardis.[5]

Gryneium was another of the Aeolian towns that crossed
the northern road, after the 'Harbour of the Achaeans, where
are the altars of the twelve gods',[6] three miles or so beyond
Myrina; and, as at Myrina, the tourist cuts through without
noticing that it is there. It ran mostly along what are now
rather empty slopes to the east of the main road; but it was
celebrated for a temple of Apollo, which stood west of the
road on a low, almost flat, very small headland of its own,
washed on either side by quiet waters enclosed in a bay where
Pitane, the most northerly of the Aeolian coast-towns, shows
in the distance. There on the water's edge the temple stood:
and its squared temenos and the blocks of its foundation
remain with trees growing out of their stones, and cornfields
in between. Pausanias travelled along the road of his day
and saw it, a temple of white marble, in 'a most beautiful
grove of Apollo, with cultivated trees and all those which,
although they bear no fruit, are pleasing to smell or look
upon'.[7] It must have shone reflected in the water as its poor
descendance is reflected now.

Where the shallow ploughing turns bits of black or red
earthenware over and over on the ground, I found a piece
of the white marble with two Greek letters carved upon it.
The drums of columns lie about, fluted and plain; on one of
them, under a thorny dwarf-oak unworthy of the adjectives
of Pausanias, a shepherd boy was sitting watching his sheep
browse in the sacred courts. One of the temple treasures
seen by Pausanias was a linen breastplate, not very useful in
war, he thinks, but helpful to hunters because the teeth of
lions and leopards break off in it. He himself cannot have
been much of a hunter, I believe, or he would not speak so

casually of what, however sporting one may wish to appear, must anyway be an uncomfortable moment. The breastplate was a beautiful work, like that, perhaps, which the king of Egypt sent to the Lacedaemonians, of linen woven with cotton and gold, so fine that every thread was twisted with 'three hundred and sixty threads, all visible'.[8] Another such was in the temple of the Athena of Lindos in Rhodes, also dedicated by Amasis, during whose reign in the 6th century B.C. a constant stream of communication passed between Greek and Carian mercenaries in Egypt and the shores of their homes; and temple walls no doubt were hung about with souvenirs of travel and votive offerings after a safe return.

The distance of these towns one from another, and the loneliness then as now of the hills between them, explain the love of the Greek for his city. The only similar condition I can think of in modern life—rapidly disappearing—is the pioneering West of America and Canada. Great monasteries in the Middle Ages must have spoken with a voice of the same kind. But the monastery's life was always a little beyond the level of every day, and even the most earth-bound monk could not enclose all his affection within the walls; while as for the New World—the church soon ceased to be the pioneering centre and the cities of the Middle and the West have been built round the general store. The friendly quality of the store, its anxiety to look after the people of its district, the way that—even in New York—the great festivals of religion centre round shop windows, all is I believe reminiscent of lonely little centres where the enterprising merchant (or the Company up North) provided all the novelty there was.

In the Greek city, the centre was a Hero or a God. The oars dipped at the headland, the olive-grey slopes, fields

of chick-peas and wheat and barley, and villages with roofs
of reeds appeared. The city shone from far away. Above
her landing-stage, the fluted columns showed double in a
waveless bay. One could see porticos beyond, and the agora
with its market shops, citizens' houses round little courts, and
the straight street for chariots, with other streets branching
off from it, less well attended to, if one can judge from the
general ways of the Levant today. And after the very early
years, one saw the fine walls of cut stone, block upon block
laid with the delicacy of sculpture, so that, even now, the
remaining stretches, that climb hillsides far beyond the visible
ruins of Greek cities, have an exquisite vitality as if the pride
and enthusiasm of their building shone in every join.

'The people should fight for their law as for a wall,'[9] says
Heraclitus. Men have lived in the stones they put together,
from Avebury to Chartres and beyond; but no one, I believe,
after the Greek, has put so much of himself into surfaces of
walls, straightforward and entirely unadorned.

Here in the city even the gods were your own, bound
with a give and take which only the Roman faith shows today
in places quite remote. I am asked now and then by friends
to light candles for them in churches where a Madonna is
more efficacious than elsewhere; in fact, Protestant as I am,
I prefer to pay my candle to St. Anthony, when I owe one,
in his own church at Padua which happens also to be near
my home. This I do unreflecting. But how else could you
act in Asia Minor twenty-five centuries ago, where the sky
and the temple-roof (under which the god lived familiar in
his half-twilight) were framed by hill summits whose barren
pebbly ridges enclosed all the safety one could know? And
there was not merely safety, but also pride. For these cities
were the seaports of a great Asiatic road; and no labour was
thought too heavy, either in the quarrying of the marble from

its hill, or the fluting and working and chiselling of it to its final form.

'The city is the teacher of the man.'[10]

The sound of it comes personified through the ages. The friendships between cities have a personal depth about them. When a play represented Miletus after her fall, the Athenians wept in their theatre, and fined the author a thousand drachmas 'because he had put them in mind of their troubles'; and Miletus itself, when Sybaris was taken, shaved the heads of its men and went into deep mourning, 'because these two cities were the closest friends of all the cities that we know'.[11]

Heartfelt devotion, strangely enough, explains, I believe, not only the power of the city, that could inflict the punishment of exile, but also the almost inhuman lengths of treason to which an exile would go in order to get back.

'Sotades, proclaimed a Cretan as he was, was victorious [in the Olympic games of 384 B.C.]. But at the next festival he made himself an Ephesian, being bribed to do so by the Ephesian people. For this he was banished by the Cretans.'[12] As if we should banish Charlie Chaplin if he were to become American.

Alcibiades and half the remembered names and parties, of his century and the one before and after, have made the perfidy of exiles too notorious to be gone into. But the point about them is that they are mentioned in a matter-of-fact manner by the ancient historians, as if there were a *mitigating circumstance* in the public opinion of their day: and this I believe was so, and was the recognition that love of city, like love of woman in a French *crime passionel,* allowed a man to get away with almost anything.

The high passion has come down in the world, but I have still found it, centred on small places in poor and lonely

lands—as in South Arabia where there is danger between
one settled township and the next, or the high villages of the
Elburz and Kurdistan. If you meet someone from there in
a foreign country, they will talk of their homes in soft and
rounded voices, as one talks of one's love: it is moving to
hear a tough rugged man speak so of a little plot of barren
hills and sparing water which scarce three or four hundred
people in the whole world know.

Lucian describes cities as hives where 'each man has his
sting and stings his neighbour';[13] but this was in an easier and
later day. And though history makes it certain that there was
truth in the simile, and though I have little learning to imagine
how a Greek city worked in detail, yet I am convinced that
I know what the Aeolian mercenary felt as he rounded the
promontory which gave the temple of Gryneium and the hill
above it to his sight. It was a feeling which had the meaning
of geography behind it; not only the city, but all the spaces
separating it from all other cities, and all the difficulties of
news and of travel were in the sentiment of home: even now,
as one sails in a small craft along the loneliness of the more
southerly peninsulas of Asia Minor, this feeling catches one in
sight of some ragged nestling township in a bay, the evening's
goal, although no ties bind one and there is nothing intrinsic
to admire—it is an emotion built up out of its contrary
emotions, humanity after loneliness, the beauty of a star.

And here as far as I can see it, is the one thing we cannot
recapture out of the ancient day.

'Had we but world enough and time': we can compass
time, if we set about it and cut half the modern speed gadgets
out of our lives; but space is not to be invented. It can still
be found, with increasing difficulty; it is already the luxury
of our age; but a day is threatening when every house in
the world will have another house in view: and then the

feeling of the Greek for his city, or of the Hebrew for that matter—for the city that is set upon a hill—will become as incomprehensible as the dead languages of these coasts—whose words can be deciphered when the meaning has gone. Already in the Roman age, when there was almost a ribbon development along the southern seaboard of Cilicia, and when the population of Asia Minor had grown to be far denser than it is now,[14] the feeling had changed.

'The poet says dear city of Cecrops; and wilt thou not say, dear city of Zeus?'[15]

The crash of the whole ancient world was required to make us turn from the city of our fathers to the city of God as Augustine saw it under the darkness of the Vandals. If the world now is to be deprived of both these safeties, we may be poor indeed.

9

Pitane

Toleration and Truth

from Gandooli looking N.
30.11.52

Particularly at the present time, when all places can be reached
by water or by land, it would not be right to use as evidence
for the unknown the works of poets and mythologists.

HERACLITUS, 6th cent. B.C.[1]

Heraclitus, who came from Ephesus where all the races of
Asia and the Aegean met and mingled, was something
of a misanthropist; no doubt, seeing so many people about,
he exaggerated the travelling facilities of his time. Today it
would be difficult to say that all places in Turkey can be
reached by land or water, and two months went by before
I was able to get to Chandarli, the ancient Pitane. This was
because the bridge over the Caicus, or Bakir Chay, was being
renovated, and it was impossible to get a car across.

I wanted to see Pitane for various reasons. Partly because
it has a castle; and also because Arcesilaus,[2] who was head
of the Platonists of the Academy about 250 B.C. and came
from this little town, was 'the first to argue both sides of a
question'. This is 'poets and mythologists giving evidence for
the unknown' with a vengeance, since no one can tell who
first considered both sides; it was probably Adam over the
apple. But Arcesilaus existed—a pupil and fellow countryman of Autolycus the mathematician,[3] who travelled with
him to Sardis and wrote a book about the rising and setting of
stars and the moving sphere. Arcesilaus then studied under
Xanthus the musician and Theophrastus in Athens, and became head of the Academy there, loved for his generous and
charming nature and living on the revenues which his brother
sent him from Pitane. However good at seeing both sides, his
tolerance—like that of many philosophers—stopped short of
a rival school, and when asked why the Epicureans made con-
verts but never lost them, he is reported to have explained that

Gryneium: Temple of Apollo

Village Woman of Ionia

The Castle of Pitane (Chandarli)

The Castle of Pitane (Chandarli)
The Village of Pitane (Chandarli)

'a man may become a eunuch, but a eunuch never becomes a man'.

An easy road branches west off the main coast road, some way before the bend to Pergamum, whose high cloud-like citadel can be seen or guessed in the distance. The open country of the Caicus plain, bright violent green after the autumn rain, lay between. The road, passing north of the unobtrusive mounds of Elaea, the port of Pergamum, curved gently with the curve of the bay, and reached the Caicus where the bridge was mending. Between banks of moist rank grasses overhanging, the river oozed with slow rhinoceros wrinkles in the mid-current; and into it, with obvious enjoyment and no feelings of hurry, a gang of workmen were lowering a pine trunk, to take the place of one of the wornout piles. They greeted us in a friendly way. The mukhtar and the doctor from Pitane, who had arrived to stroll about in the enjoyment of other people's work, came to give the city's welcome: the friends who were taking me were the Consul-General of Smyrna and his wife, so that we were almost an official occasion; they would have invited us if they could. But alas, the bridge was in a skeleton condition: its traffic—the motor-bus service that connects Pitane with the world—had to work in two sections, one on either side of the stream, and the passengers threaded their way across on foot: we were asked to return in a few weeks' time.

We did so, and the bridge was still not complete; but as it had reached the stage of having planks laid loose across the supporting beams, the workmen cheerfully devoted an hour of the government's time to making us happy. While they removed some heavy wooden structures, and prepared to lift the off-wheel over the narrow places to the delight of D. B. and the disquiet of his wife, I wandered along the farther bank, from where one can see the estuary pouring, by streaks of pale blue sea and yellow sandbanks, into a bay so wide and shallow that clouds alone can sail about it, reflected as if in another sky.

If one were suddenly turned upside down (and perhaps we often are without knowing it?) it would be impossible to tell which sky was the right one. Led on by this fascinating deception, my thoughts now turned to the little town we were going to visit, where—according to Strabo,[4] bricks floated in water, and—according to the mythologist—the equally tricky mirage of philosophic tolerance began.

So much is supposed to have happened there, that 'I am Pitane' was made into a proverb to describe people who suffered the ups and downs of fortune.[5] The present deadness is mere illusion: the road after the bridge, winding gently to a ridge where columns in the ditches and a few white stones on the hillside lie forgotten, is loud with history for all its dusty silence. The Pelasgians captured Pitane, and the Erythraeans set it free. Oriental influences have been discovered in its cemetery. Its wine 'unfired and of the finest scent', was famous; and the lord of Pergamum lent thirty talents so that the town might buy a piece of land from Antiochus the First. Mithridates in a later day took refuge here, was invested by Gaius Flavius Fimbria and escaped by sea; and returned in 85 B.C. to negotiate a peace with Sulla.[6] And then in the Middle Ages, the Venetians or Genoese built the castle where, side by side on the ground, an array of old-fashioned guns lie stamped with the name and arms of George III of England.

These ups and downs we know: and how many more must lie about, just beyond that surface which memory reaches? Lydian and Persian invasions wrecked Pitane; it must have been visited by Seljuk and Ottoman wars; even now it has an entire quarter built for refugees: whole generations have been submerged without a ripple in history as we know it. Strangely, the hurly-burly produced the climate of tolerance.

Here, in Grecian Asia Minor, the spirit of abstract enquiry began—theories of the universe with the background of Asia and Crete, and news of Babylonia along the trading road. Archelaus, the teacher of Socrates, was possibly Milesian:[7] his training certainly came through Anaxagoras and the Milesian school: they took their curiosities and an open mind—a combination unknown to the world before—to revolutionize the West in the limpid light of Ionia.

On the mainland of Greece this apparition has always seemed as Renan called it—'the only miracle in history.' The excitement about Ionia is that here it is no miracle, but the result of causes natural enough if one is patient to hunt for them among the shallows and shiftings of a past that can never be clearly known. The Greek poets of that time were fond of personifications: 'Lovely Infallibility and dark-haired Uncertainty,'[8] writes Empedocles. Leaving the former for a more arrogant and ignorant day, we may take the nymph of Uncertainty for our guide.

By herself she is unable to produce tolerance—or indeed anything much at all: she is apt to become bigoted in danger. But she produces Curiosity. Perhaps the 6th century of Ionia would never have blossomed if a daily press had then been in existence to deceive with the illusion that Uncertainty is dead. We are drugged to forget how little our strides carry, however stretched they may be; the real position remains almost unchanged since the yardstick is infinity. The modern world has made its foreground definite, with discoveries of science and of fact; but this in itself distorts the picture, since we forget that the foreground is not reality. When less was known the sight travelled farther because the proportion was more accurately kept. Adventure and mystery, perhaps the greatest mortal ingredients of happiness—love being immortal—were not polished away from the surfaces of things by exact but unimportant information. Events came looming full of possibilities as well as fears, 'dark-haired uncertainties'—down the road from Sardis where the beaten Cimmerians had vanished—from the west where the islands lie like stepping-stones—from Egypt where Herodotus was taught to ponder the ages of the gods.[9]

Uncertainty alone is apt to be paralysed by fear; but Commerce and Uncertainty together make an adventurous pair, and the coastal cities experimented them to the full. Commerce gave well-being and leisure: there is no poverty about the philosophers of Ionia. The revenues sent from Pitane; the social standing of Anaxagoras in Clazomenae; Heraclitus who belonged to the Ephesian kings; the story of Thales, renting olive presses in a year when the harvest promised well, to prove that a philosopher could be clever at making money—all is financial easiness at the end of the trading road.

The trading road was a constant stimulus, a teacher of geography, a reminder that this world is not all the same. The tradition is that the Ionians, Hecataeus and then Anaximander, invented maps—and the first map known to be described was engraved on a table of brass and shown by Aristagoras of Samos at the end of the 6th century B.C. to the Spartan king.[10] It seems to have been a sort of route report of the Asiatic highway since the nations are listed in the order in which they dwelt along it.

From this background, first made as it were articulate by commerce, a variety of strange and distant objects reached the marble wharves and markets by the sea: and in the temples, the eastern raptures of Cybele and Dionysus mixed with the privacies of Minoan religion and new gods of Olympus exploring from Thrace. In the light of Commerce and great political insecurity, 'lovely Infallibility' vanishes, and the critical mind is created. Enquirers begin to look with doubt, and to wonder whether Orpheus 'ought to be called a philosopher considering the sort of things he said about the gods'.[11] Herodotus, on the borderland, comes to one of his sensible conclusions, and, accepting the evidence, hopes that 'Gods and heroes may not be displeased with me, that I have said so much. . . .'[12] In comfort, but with an awareness of the mystery and precariousness of life, among beliefs so diverse that the absurdities of all are apparent, the love of abstract truth is awakened, disinterested and passionate: the rectitude of tolerance is born. It is scattered among the poets of these centuries:

'Gold is disclosed by the Lydian touchstone, and the worth and skill of a man is proved by almighty Truth,'[13] says Bacchylides in the 5th, echoing Mimnermus of the 7th century: 'Betwixt thee and me let there be truth, the most righteous of all things.'[14]

And tolerance comes because the attaining of truth is only possible in the sight of things as they are; and things as they are have many facets. She is born out of Uncertainty and Commerce, by Curiosity and Truth. And the mildness of her voice is recognizable at once. In the 6th century Xenophanes of Colophon noticed that 'the Ethiopians make their gods black and snub-nosed; the Thracians say theirs have blue eyes and red hair'; and comes to the conclusion that: 'There never was nor will be a man who has certain knowledge about the gods and about all the things I speak of. Even if he should chance to say the complete truth, yet he himself knows not that it is so. But all may have their fancy.' And adds that 'if oxen or horses or lions had hands, and could paint with their hands, and produce works of art as men do, horses would paint the forms of the gods like horses, and oxen like oxen, and make their bodies in the image of their several kinds'.[15]

When this is said, the decks are clear; the ship of the human mind is free to find whatever fixed stars there are to set its course by. As far as we have travelled to the present day, no one has yet superseded the modest sincerity of the Ionian words.

D. B. meanwhile, steering with a fixed look over the loose boards of the bridge of the Bakir Chay, had crossed to the western bank. We were eating our lunch in a hollow of lime-stone, with the square towers of Pitane rising opposite rather like Windsor Castle, on a long low spit of land. An ancient harbour, now a lagoon with a causeway, showed oxen dragging a cart over uneven stones. A boy came cantering along the dusty road riding a bareback pony: there was no other traffic, or even movement, about the town in sight: with its bridge cut, it lay unattached like a gathering of driftwood, temporarily stranded by a bank in the river of Time.

The same atmosphere, of life almost imperceptible, continued when we reached it. A pedlar had spread his wares— lamps of blue glass, plastic combs, cups and saucepans—on the ground below the castle where windowless house-walls looked down on them. The castle itself stood mild and neglected as a superannuated soldier in the sun. Salt-eaten gates too tired to use their hinges let us into an oblong court; there was a stairway at each end, grown with weeds, and a *chemin de ronde* where we looked down on the tiled roofs and little courtyards of the town. From its dusty ways, the castle, with four big and two smaller towers, rises out of a sloped glacis of more ancient stones; and the Turks in a later age renovated the southern wall and pierced it with arched openings for their guns. These, side by side, showing the stamp of George III and the English arms, look as if they themselves had forgotten how they come to be resting in such a depth of foreign oblivion.

On the headland beyond, the new village built for Balkan refugees spreads good box-houses with grass growing green around them and a foreign clatter of geese. The recurrent theme of exile, like a leit-motif through the ages, alone recalls the vanished features of the first Pitane, the oldest of the Aeolian cities. The bay itself has silted with the earth of the Bakir Chay, and only its bony architecture—the southern headlands between Cyme and Phocaea—show faint sun-steeped outlines beyond younger sandbeds indefinite in the water, not yet solidified to stone. In the evening light we returned, with Pergamum gleaming high and wooded among purple hills. Smooth grassy nearer shoulders hung dark and fed with rain. Under a sunset sky like watered silk, we passed the trees of the headland of Apollo at Gryneium, shivering with gold and yellow haloes reflected in the sea.

10

Pergamum

The Raiders of the Border

Wasped headdress of a Cimmerian, with wooden rings in his
ears, and about his ribs a hairy oxhide that had been the
unwashen cover of a wretched shield . . . but now he goes in a
coach, wearing earrings of gold like a mix-with-all, and carries
an ivory sunshade as though he were a woman. . . .

ANACREON, 6th cent. B.C.[1]

Auge, the daughter of Aleus of Tegea, was descended
from the nymph Callisto whom Zeus had turned into
the Great Bear and lifted up to Heaven. Having borne a child
to Hercules she was put to sea in a chest with her infant son and
'came to Teuthras, lord of the Caicus plain, who fell in love
with her and married her. Her tomb still exists at Pergamum
above the Caicus; it is a mound of earth surrounded by a
basement of stone and surmounted by a figure of a naked
woman in bronze. One of her nephews joined the Argonauts
and was later killed by the boar of Meleager'.[2]

If it had not been for this social snippet by Pausanias, I should have felt obliged, reluctantly, to omit Pergamum from my tour of Aeolis, for the city itself scarcely appears in history until Xenophon lodged there.[3] It seems, however, to have existed for a long time, obscurely, on the borderland of civilization. A borderland atmosphere, largely of bloodshed and raids, hangs over its earlier days. After the accomplishment of their march, the Ten Thousand came down to it through Antandros and Adramyttium, behaving in the Homeric way habitual to the visitors of the Caicus plain. For when Xenophon arrived in Pergamum in the destitute condition which anyone who has travelled about in Asia will probably sympathize with, he was instigated by his hostess and encouraged by omens to attempt the capture of a Persian who lived with his family and property in the plain below. Hellas was the wife of Gongylus of Eretria, to whose ancestors King Darius had given these lands as well as Myrina and Gryneium on the coast.[4] She was an energetic woman, not inclined to waste the providential arrival of a small army, and suggested that an attack by night with three hundred men might be successful: and having encouraged Xenophon, 'she sent with him to show him the way her own cousin and a man called Daphnagoras, of whom she was extremely fond'.

Xenophon set out after dinner 'and took with him, with the idea of doing them a good turn, the captains who had been his particular friends', turning away a lot more, so as not to have to give them a share of the booty. But the tower, when they got to it, 'was high and strong, with battlements, and manned by a large number of good soldiers . . . and the wall was eight earthen bricks thick'. By daybreak a breach was made, through which someone from inside ran a large spit for roasting oxen right through the thigh of the man nearest to the opening. 'Then, by letting off volleys of arrows, they

The Castle of Pitane (Chandarli)

The Gymnasium, Pergamum

The Basilica, Pergamum

The Theatre, Pergamum

made it unsafe even to get near, and . . . made signals by
waving torches, and so Itamenes with his force came to their
relief, and from Comania there came some Assyrian hoplites
and about eighty Hyrcanian cavalrymen, also in the Persian
king's pay, and then about eight hundred peltasts, with some
cavalry as well. . . . The moment had certainly come for the
Greeks to think how they could get away. They seized all
the oxen and sheep that there were and drove them off, with
the slaves too, inside a hollow square, adopting this formation
not so much because they were interested in the booty, as
with the idea of preventing their retreat from turning into a
rout, as it might do, if they went away and left their booty
behind. . . . Meanwhile, under very heavy attack from arrows
and slingstones, they marched on, forming a circle so as to
keep their shields in the way of the missiles, and, with great
difficulty, got across the river Carcasus, nearly half of them
being wounded . . . In the end they got back to safety with
about two hundred slaves and enough sheep for sacrifices. . . .
They then returned to Pergamum, and now Xenophon had
good reason to be grateful to the god. The Spartans and all
captains and the other generals and the soldiers all united
in offering him the pick of the booty—horses, oxen and
everything. So he was at last in a position to do someone else
a good turn.'

With this satisfactory conclusion—the raiders' version of
the silver salver presented as a testimonial to a government
servant at the end of his mission—the Persian expedition of
Xenophon ends; showing Pergamum as it must have appeared
for centuries before the house of Attalus softened and exalted
it—a robber nest with sharpened talons hovering above the
valley where the eye travels 'to the Lesbian shore'.

The flat lands, over which mountains hang sudden and
steep, must long have been a borderland for raiders. Two

vital roads, east and west of Pergamum,[5] make from the
Hellespont and the pastoral steppes of Phrygia towards the
fertile rivers of the south, and Cilicia and Syria beyond them.
The importance of these roads was shown later by the care
with which the Attalids kept them up, 'to a width of at least
30 feet', and the Romans after them. The eastern road from
Cyzicus (Bal Kiz) on the southern shore of the Propontis,
reached the Caicus (Bakir Chay) about thirty-five miles east
of Pergamum and, crossing a low watershed to Sardis, led
to the plain of Laodicea. Here Xerxes followed it in one
direction and Alexander, after the battle of the Granicus,
in another. The western road came from the Hellespont
through the plain of Antandros and Adramyttium to Elaea,
and followed the Aeolian coast by Gryneium, Myrina, Cyme,
Larisa and Smyrna, to Ephesus, Tralles (Aydin) Stratoniceia
and the present Marmaris in the south. The port of Elaea
has been used in living memory, and lay in sight of whatever
ancient citadel preceded the Attalid city on the hill.

  A confused continuous rumour of trouble, growing into
sharper outlines as it comes nearer, suggests how desirable
these flat lands must always have been, where they open from
the highlands to the plain. The rocks of Atarneus south of the
plain of Antandros were rich in minerals, and power politics
began early in literally a Cimmerian darkness, for Atarneus
was one of the last strongholds of the Cimmerians, who were
pushed out of it, about 570 B.C., by the help, it is said, of
dogs.[6] An atmosphere of unpleasantness hangs over every
mention of the place. The men of Chios bought it at the price
of the life of a Lydian, whom they tore from the temple of
Athena and delivered to his enemies; and for a long time no
barley was offered from Atarneus to the gods, nor were any
holy cakes baked with its corn, nor was anything that came
from that country allowed to approach a temple.[7] The most

revolting of all the stories collected by Herodotus is that of the Chian who supplied Ephesus and Sardis with eunuchs, and was caught by one of them 'on this parcel of land which the men of Chios possess'.[8] It was finally abandoned because of mosquitoes before the days of Pausanias, and it is a relief to see it vanish into the murkiness of its times.

'Pergamum called of old Teuthrania,'[9] says Pausanias, travelling among the tumuli along the Caicus road. Their origins were legendary already. The land was thought to have been once sacred to the Cabiri and this and the tumuli suggest Thracian origins, but the people held themselves to be Arcadians from before the wars of Troy, brought over by Telephus who fought 'the followers of Agamemnon when the Greeks after missing Troy, were plundering the Meian plain by mistake'.[10] There is no historical certainty—even if we forgo Callisto and the Great Bear—but a noise of confused, indiscriminate, Homeric violence. Yet the tumuli are there, beside the main road when one has crossed the windy spaces of the Bakir Chay. Apart from the bronze woman, they are the same as Pausanias saw them.

The city on the hill grew in the sight of its dead. It built gymnasiums and enlarged its walls, collected libraries and pictures, and hung its theatre out almost in space, with seats for 15,000 and the view of the valley below. It gave the word parchment to Europe, elaborating a process which allowed of writing on *both* sides of the skins of animals. The habit of writing on one side was already ancient among the Ionians; for Herodotus says that 'they speak of paper as hides by ancient custom, because in olden times for want of paper they used the skins of goats and sheep, and yet even in my day many of the barbarian peoples write upon such hides'.[11] As well as this general benefit to humanity, the kings of Pergamum freed western Asia Minor from the Gauls. In their temple, to celebrate the victory, they built an altar with ashes of the thigh bones of the victims.[12] Perhaps because they were natives of the country, their dynasty was loved by the cities of the coast.

In 133 B.C., the last Attalid king died and left Pergamum as a legacy to Rome. The new province stretched from Propontis in the north to Marmaris in the south, and Tiberius Gracchus tried, with a Roman-Mussolinian gesture, to devote its riches to the profit of Italian farmers.[13] Its history, which had been slipping along in a natural stream of normal disturbances produced by geography and predictable laws— came suddenly to a chasm; human factors, caprice, domestic problems, an absence of obvious heirs, united the two currents of Rome and Asia Minor, and shot them out through Time in a cataract of still resounding thunder.

Pergamum became the favourite winter resort of the emperor Caracalla, who was obviously bored by the society of Senators in Rome. He built the temple of Dionysus and the high terraced walk at the foot of the theatre. The city spread down the hill and overlapped towards the west; the ruins of a Roman basilica, of an amphitheatre, of a sanctuary of Aesculapius were added, and the space of the small modern town with its Seljuk mosque was probably covered with suburbs and gardens.

In the precinct of Aesculapius, where the water runs in a stone conduit and is celebrated for its lightness, the German archaeologists have restored the Ionic portico and repaired a small marble theatre. I set up my camp bed under an olive tree on the slope nearby, to rest for an hour or two, in the solitude of the hot afternoon, with the hill of Pergamum in sight. Perched so high and garlanded by walls, it is more like a hill-town of Italy built for defence or offence than anything seen in Ionia. For the Ionians seemed ever to build for their

own enjoyment: and no doubt that was why their chance
of survival was small. In the case of Pergamum Tiberius
Gracchus died before he could pinch the revenues for his
farmers; but they were soon seized even less respectably by
people like Cassius and Brutus, whom one is educated to look
up to. The province suffered till the emperors came along
and one by one preferred the cities of Asia to Rome.[14]

How pleasant it was, in the heat of September, to sleep and
wake in this panorama of history, and see how the shadows
of the colonnade of Aesculapius had moved with the hours.
The olive branches were above my head and pushed with a
present joy into the sun. Their leaves, brighter than the sky
above them, seemed beaten out of metal, so delicate and
strong. Where they curled, it was no drooping at the edges,
but a general curve all down their length, like a tiny scroll to
be held in the hand of a statue. Even in shadow, the rough
trunks were warm—scarred and friendly to touch. In its
tough beauty, drawn out of the hard pale soil, the olive too
seemed to grow for its own pleasure, invulnerable, whoever
might collect the fruit—its benefits mere incidents in the
self-contained radiance. Harvests, gathered or ungathered,
went back, year touching year, into days before the mounded
graves of the valley were thought of, before strangers landed
from boats at Elaea, days when a nymph could still find safety
by being turned into a bear. A silent contemplation, a depth
and width uncircumscribed, held all the hillside in the hot
and solitary afternoon: and the harvest, by which so many in
so many succeeding ages have been fed, was the least part
of the olive tree's secret—an exterior ornament, a shedding
during the process of life: like the undying cities, the tree
leaves the fruit it scatters to be snatched by whoever comes:
the heart of the mystery is its own.

11

Cyme

The Phrygian Mood

The Mother of the Gods too is a Phrygian.

> (Reply of the philosopher Antisthenes when taunted
> with not being an Athenian.)[1]

Musical modes are nowhere altered without [changes in] the
most important laws in the State.

> DAMON OF ATHENS, 460 B.C.[2]

Cyme, largest and best of the Aeolian Cities, The winter
refuge—after Salamis—for the fleet of Xerxes, lies an
easy quarter of a mile west of the main Pergamum-Smyrna
road. Its low acropolis holds Mytilene in sight.

It had a reputation for stupidity in its day, for it renounced
all harbours dues, and remained a free port for three centuries, and—while other cities celebrated their deeds—the
historian of Cyme merely stated that his country was at peace.
Happy Cyme![3]

It is now called Nimrut Limani, the harbour of Nimrod —but there is nothing of a port, or even of habitation about it: the country track, manageable for carts, is chiefly used by camels carrying bales of cotton or tobacco from the fields of New Phocaea out of sight. On the winding, solitary expanse there is one small house with door-posts and lintels taken from more splendid buildings. The harbour far around is swamp, streaks of water amid whose rushes black cattle wander browsing, and to whose sweet grass the flocks are led. It lies in a wide, shallow and empty basin, and from it a stream cuts a short valley passage between acropolis and hill to the sea. It must have been one of the favourite river estuaries with a safe anchorage behind it; but nothing is left except a stone sarcophagus lying divided, on either side of a casual Turkish bridge that spans the stream.

The acropolis is a gentle place, two hundred feet high at most, marked into fields by trees. They grow thickest, I suspect, where the rubble of lost buildings has interrupted the plough. At the very top, French archaeologists in the past uncovered the head of a Doric column and a few square yards of smoothly chiselled wall. It lies sunk among thorns, in the atmosphere of ruins tampered with by men. More and more, as I travelled in Turkey, I came to regret the way that archaeologists nibble at a building and leave it, so as to bring it to the notice of all the peasants who happen to be in search of stones. The fact that Cyme is far from a village, and that carts cannot reach the summit, has so far kept the little centre of its piety intact. As one walks over ploughed terraces and levels of the empty hill, the splintered earthenware, the soft black shiny Hellenistic glaze, the red both ribbed and plain, whisper with tiny toneless voices, lying thicker or thinner about one's feet according to the ancient crowding of the streets and markets that covered the hill of Cyme. In

a western embrasure, the theatre was set: a fold shows the
curve of the seats though all the stone has vanished. And at
the western bottom of the hill one comes down again to the
sea, indented, probably to a second harbour. Quaystones run
out under waves; a fluted trunk of column lies there, white as
salt; more column shafts, four of them, are laid side by side by
some later barbarian, Byzantine or Latin; they were probably
the underprops for the landing-stage to a small fortress, for
there is the dim vestige, the shapeless mound, of what may
have been a built enclosure. Under the wall of the acropolis,
with steepness between, a sea-walk ran; and its temples and
porticoes have left pieces of their columns strewn beside the
shingle.

The column is ever in one's mind in Ionia—an invention
complete in itself with the economy of perfection—with all
essentials and nothing superfluous, and the rules of beauty
observed in its careful necessities. The caryatid was invented
later; pedestals were embellished with statues by rich Ephesus devotees; fancy spirals from Asia Minor, twisted out
of the straight, are to be seen over the altar of St. Peter's
in Rome: but the original columns of Aeolis and Ionia must
have given a straightforward delight of mere roundness, size
and smoothness, as they were cut out of a local mountain and
set up, polished or fluted, to take the place of the first tree
trunks and later wooden structures in which the gods were
housed. And what country in the world has ever had so many
columns flourishing in it all at once?

The Doric capital on the hill of Cyme came to me as a surprise, for the Ionic is usual here in the land of its greatness.
The Doric belongs perhaps to Crete and certainly to the heavily timbered hillsides of Europe, the Ionic to the lighter-built
forests of western Asia, and where it first came from, whether
from Assyria or Persia, is I believe not known. Something like

it must have travelled, like many another novelty, westward along the great highways, moulding, as it went, the cruder efforts of the Phrygian tombs: for the Ionic volute exists, vertical instead of horizontal, in the shafts of Persepolis; and early forms are seen on reliefs of Khorsabad and Koyunjuk[4]; and there is a fluted example on a Khorsabad stele. The plant-like branching ornament so common in archaic Greek architecture is constantly found in Assyria; and the Assyrian 'kiosques', with primitive architrave and cornice,[5] are like the Ionic too; as it travels westward, the column appears complete in Hittite sculptures at Pterium (Boghaz Köy.) I have a private unscientific conviction of my own that the wooden props which still hold up the porches of hillside mosques in Caspian Mazanderan—flattened horizontal capitals roughly carved, which resist the push of the wooden post below—are the Ionic capital before its first transformations, used in the sort of forest country where it began.

The chiselling of it in stone had to wait till there were iron tools to cut it. *'L'ordre à volutes se développe, pendant la période Lydienne à la faveur (du fer), qui permet de découper les contours.'*[6] It recalls us to the business of the industrial age and the working of iron, to the Lydians at Sardis and the Phrygians beside them in the north.

The Phrygians stretch like a pastoral cloud behind the Greek coast-lands. They had affinities with the Greeks before their separate migrations.[7] Their legends haunt the mountains about Smyrna; and Homer saw them farther north, on the Sangarius river[8]—a coastal people whom Priam as a young man helped in war against the Amazons.

At that time the Cilicians also, to whom Andromache belonged, lived near Troy, and the drift of these peoples was to the south. They moved, no doubt, for many generations, adopting the objects (and the women) they met with—the red polished pottery in the forms of gourds found with the earliest copper, and the three-coloured decoration, black, red, and white, 'whose immemorial home is central Asia Minor'.[9]

Their alphabet, akin to Greek, the Phrygians took, Prof. Ramsay thinks, from Cyme;[10] and used it in a language which belonged in part, as did all the languages of these Indo-European peoples—Thracians, Phrygians, Armenians—to the older lands they reached and conquered, full of words resembling the place-names of Caria. Even Greek contains about 40 per cent of root words whose origin is foreign, of the sort taken over by strangers when they come into a landscape different from their own. Such names remain for a long time. The lunar god Men, brought by the Phrygians, is still recalled in the little town of Menemen on the way to Cyme.[11]

As they came down and settled on the border lands that hang above the Caicus valley, the Phrygians entered the great area of the Hittites. Their presence, and that of the Lydians, hid the very existence of this empire from the Greeks, who were now building themselves in at the far and comparatively peaceful end of the trade route, where it touched the Aegean. Here the noise of eastern events came slowly, softened by remoteness and the ease of the sea. As by a distant desert storm whose spate comes suddenly to unexpected places, the Hittite empire was broken about 1200 B.C., and the Greeks knew nothing of it, though they themselves were known and mentioned—Ayyavala,—Aeolian,—Ahhiyava,—Achaean, in Hittite documents nearly two hundred years before.[12] Far away the Hittites fell; and the Assyrian power too rose and fell and kept the inland nations busy; and the coming of iron racked the world—and in all this time the Lydians and Phrygians led their caravans to the seaboard and watched the loading of ships.

They watched the raised decks come in, and improvements in building, and the invention of the triple tier of oars for the meeting of enemies at sea. And they too, for their part, brought down their inland crafts—the gable roof of the temple was probably theirs,[13] and the art of embroidery called Phrygian in Pliny's day,[14] and—from Lydia—the stamped currency of money.[15] Others say that this was brought to her city by Demodike, daughter of an Agamemnon, a princess of Cyme, who married a Phrygian king.[16] There was easy intercourse along the valleys. At that time, while the un-walled cities of the Greeks were young, the people of the plateau brought more perhaps than they took away, for the riches that stirred the world were in their hills. A Phrygian king, Midas the son of Gordias, was 'the first barbarian to send offerings to Delphi',[17] and the Lydian soon followed, lavish with the mountain gold. Iron, the new despotism in the world, was indigenous in Turkey and used in the 13th century by the Hittites. It had been sent about this time as tribute from Syria to Egypt, and was common in Philistia. It existed in Greece before the Dorians, though sparsely. It appears under the Phrygians (Muski) at Carchemish on the Euphrates about 1150 B.C. coming from Asia Minor; from here and from Taurus (not necessarily produced there), in the 8th century it reached the Assyrian kings.

One watches it, moving like a disease or a religion, defeating the leaf-shaped sword that carried the epic world of the sea-raiders out of the age of bronze. By the time of the Hittites' fall, the new metal had spread from the high northeast of Asia minor and was worked in Syria and Cyprus, in Phrygia and Thrace.

When the Aeolian Greeks first beached their ships on the empty shore of Cyme, iron tools and weapons were already travelling in the long descending caravans. They were there among the thick-set little horses and the mules which were said to be a Mysian invention before the Persian-brought camel was known.[18]

Roads then were probably much as Newton describes a new Smyrna road in 1854, with, on each side, a footpath which 'the people of the country make little use of, as they have no wheeled carriages. The mules and pack horses have worn away a serpentine track through the bed of the road. The smart equestrians usurp the footpath. . . . The traffic is not on the road but alongside . . . to avoid the hard pavement. . . .'[19]

The men of the caravans were dressed in the costume of the plateau that seems to have been much the same from Phrygia to Kurdistan. Herodotus describes it in the march-past of Xerxes' army, worn also by the Paphlagonians and the Ligyans, the Matieni (Kurds), the Mariandynians, Cappadocians, and Armenians, 'with wicker helmets on their heads, and little bucklers and spears of no great length, and javelins also and daggers; and on their feet . . . their own peculiar boots, that reach to the middle of the shin.'[20]

So the Phrygians walked along, with clean-shaven upper lip and pointed beard of the Egyptian fashion,[21] as we see it in the later archaic bronzes all over the Aegean to Etruria in the west. They were skilled in the breaking in of horses, and richer than all their neighbours in fields and flocks. And no doubt they prodded their newly-invented animals with the short spears of their newly-invented metal as gaily as their later muleteer descendants continue to do to this day.

The iron tools built the temples; but an echo also of something more fragile and lasting than metal hangs about the Phrygian name. For their shepherds once cut reeds where the treeless level of the plateau breaks from shallow lakes to a trickle of running water, where the gradual valleys steepen slowly as they eat themselves down to the sea. The shepherds made holes in their reeds and piped, and the name of the elegy (the kindred Armenian for reed is *elegn*), came down into our world with their lament. That high thin sound of the pipe was known in Crete, but is traditionally Phrygian. It is the channel of all elegiac singing—all fugitive personal moods, delights and sorrows that ever the western world has sung. The shepherds sang, and the priests of Cybele, the Idaean dactyls, the workers of iron, took the song into their ritual and were known as inventors of music:[22] the lament travelled down to Lesbos where the poets found it, and established it for ever. As they sang, in the 7th-6th centuries, the long supremacy of the epic came to an end: 'that is why flute-players in Greece have Phrygian names like those of slaves, Samba and Adon and Telus';[23]

> 'Aristotle calls the elegy Phrygian, and thinks it too exciting for the young.'[24]

The poets remember their debt. The echo haunts all music, and the Lake Aulocrene, loveliest of names, is not forgotten, where the best reeds used to grow. Theocritus and Vergil remembered under Sicilian ilex and Mantuan poplar; and, in the English landscape, the simple swain

> sang to the oaks and rills,
> While the still morn went out with sandals grey;
> He touched the tender stops of various quills,
> Warbling with eager thought his Doric lay.
> And now the sun has stretched out all the hills,
> And now has sunk into the western bay. . . .

The Phrygian voice sings in *Lycidas*.

12

Phocaea

Decision

A city of moderate size, skilled in nothing but to rear brave men.

DIOGENES LAERTIUS.[1]

The purple handkerchief which Timas sent for thee from Phocaea.

SAPPHO in Lesbos, 6th cent. B.C.[2]

The history of the flute and the Phrygian mood have carried us inland from the cities of Aeolis, before we have finished with Cyme. For we should not go by without mentioning that the father of the poet Hesiod came from this city;[3] and emigrated to Boeotia, so that one more sprig of early laurel must be added to the wreath of Asia Minor. It is rather suitable that he should come from Aeolis while Homer—by legend—belongs to Ionia, the difference between the heroic poet and the rather plodding historian of the gods being like that between the two regions—Aeolis richer in lands, more agricultural and quietly settled than the lean, colonizing, restless adventurous cities of the south.

We have scarcely mentioned the Lydians, who belong to these early days, and—long before the conquests of Croesus—came down to the coastal Greeks, to traffic and enlist mercenaries for their wars. Just as Ephesus became the later coastal metropolis, Cyme seems to have been the chief centre for the dealings of the first Lydian dynasty, descendants of Hercules and Omphale whose end is the opening of Herodotus' story.

Ardys,[4] one of these early Lydian kings, took refuge from a sister-in-law and her lover, and settled as an innkeeper in Cyme. He made himself agreeable, and kept up a sort of Mary Queen of Scots centre of intrigue with all the Lydians who went to and fro from Sardis. He won over, with the help of a pretty daughter, the bandit sent to kill him, who took back instead of the genuine head he was sent to fetch, a block of wood tied about with the king's long hair: and when the sister-in-law's lover was bending over it with pleasure, decapitated him from behind. The bandit walked down the road, under Sipylus across the Hermus, and stopped at an inn and rashly told his story. The innkeeper, with an eye to profit, decapitated him too and took the pair of heads to the exiled king, asking for an exemption from taxes for his hotel as his only reward. So ran the legend, bearing witness at any rate to the reputation of the Lydians for sharp business and reminiscent perhaps of the fact that they were the inventors of inns (or chaffering, the word in Herodotus is ambiguous) along the trade road.

When, after centuries, the Persians came and Sardis had fallen, all the Greek cities except Miletus preserved the Lydian friendship to the last. And when all was over, Pactyes,

a Lydian refugee, took sanctuary in Cyme. The Persians sent
messengers to have him surrendered, and

> 'the people of Cyme resolved to refer to the god of Branchidae
> [Apollo in Didyma] for counsel; for there was an oracle es-
> tablished there from of old, which all the Ionians and Aeolians
> were wont to use. . . . So the men of Cyme sent messengers
> and enquired what thing they must do touching Pactyes in or-
> der to find favour in sight of the gods. And . . . an oracle was
> given them to deliver Pactyes to the Persians. And when these
> things were reported, and the men of Cyme heard them, they
> inclined to deliver him up. But when the multitude was this
> way inclined, Aristodicus the son of Heraclides a man of rep-
> utation among the citizens, restrained the people, because he
> . . . deemed that the messengers spake untruthfully. Accord-
> ingly other messengers went a second time to enquire . . . and
> among them was Aristodicus. . . . And again the god declared to
> them the same prophecy, commanding them to deliver Pactyes
> up to the Persians. Accordingly Aristodicus by design did thus.
> He went round the temple, and plucked forth the sparrows and
> all the other kinds of birds that had builded their nests there.
> And it is said that as he did so, a voice came from the sanctuary
> . . . and said:

> "'Unholiest of men, what is this that thou darest to do? Dost
> thou ravish my suppliants from the temple?"

> 'But Aristodicus was not dismayed and said:

> "'Lord, dost thou succour thus thine own suppliants yet com-
> mand the people of Cyme to deliver up theirs?"

> 'And the god replied with these words: "Yea, I command it,
> that by working iniquity ye may the sooner perish" [a rather
> poor get-away]. . . .

'The men of Cyme then, wishing neither to deliver Pactyes up and so perish, nor to keep him and be besieged, sent him away to Mitylene. But the men of Mitylene . . . prepared to deliver him up for a certain price; how great, I cannot say with certainty, for it was never paid; for when the people of Cyme perceived that this was being done . . . they sent a boat to Lesbos and conveyed Pactyes forth to Chios. And there he was torn from the temple of Athena Poliuchus by the men of Chios'

and exchanged for the accursed territory of Atarneus north of the Caicus as we have seen before.[5]

This sort of problem was constantly being brought before the average man in the city state. Like their frugal sober pleasures, the gymnastic of the will kept them in good trim, giving the spiritual equivalent of a lean and exercised body. For there was no sitting aside while governments were blamed; either your own view or your opponents' was being acted upon, with terrific and usually immediate consequence, and no doubt this explains the passions of Greek politics as well as the regardless readiness of men to take their plunges. For what can be more demoralizing than to be *vicarious*—nationally generous, nationally honourable, nationally honest, but in oneself individually—what? This vicariousness, it seems to me, makes us, admire in a nation, qualities so base and selfish that they would exile any single person from the acquaintance of honourable men. Such a pitfall of the abstract the citizen of a town like Cyme never knew, until the state grew big enough to make the individual's decision redundant: and it would be interesting to ask oneself through history if this is not the turning point of decline?

When the Persians came down the valleys with the news of the fall of Sardis running like lightning before them, the decisions of the Greeks had to be rapid and momentous. They sent a belated embassy to conciliate the conquerer, but Cyrus told their messengers the story of the fish who would not hear the fisherman piping, and then the Ionians cast up walls round their cities (all except Miletus) and sent messengers for help to Sparta in the common cause.[6]

Aeolians and Ionians came in haste to Sparta and there chose a man from Phocaea to speak for all of them; 'and he cast a purple cloak about him, to the end that as many as possible of the Spartans should hear thereof and come together, and stood before them. . . .' There is something very touching in the picture of the Greeks who had become foreign with the novelties, the woven stuffs and dyes and fashions of the Lydians, trying to impress their relatives at home. And it was all to no purpose. Yet when they left, disappointed, the Spartans sent a fifty-oared vessel to look at Ionia and the Persians. 'And these men came to Phocaea, and sent the most notable of them, whose name was Lacrines, to Sardis to declare to Cyrus that he should do no hurt to any city of Greece, because they would not suffer it.'

Cyrus, already surrounded by Greeks, asked about the Lacedaemonians, and having been informed, remarked that 'he never yet feared men that have a place appointed in the midst of their city where they gather together and deceive one another, swearing oaths'.[7] With this unintelligent contempt of the conqueror for the merchants who are soon going to manage him and his affairs, Cyrus departed, while Pactyes prepared the rebellion and hired Greek mercenaries on the coast. And after that the Greek cities were taken one by one, by Harpagus the Mede, who heaped earth against their walls and captured them, beginning with Phocaea.

Phocaea is on a bay near the tip of the northern headland of the gulf of Smyrna, and between it and Cyme ran the line that separated Ionia and Aeolis.[8] It is very isolated, cut off by mountains that end in cliffs and enclose it in a sea-world of its own. Nothing that I have ever seen is nearer than Phocaea to the heart's desire, as you look down upon it from the pass that leads from Smyrna. A little north of Menemen, we had turned from the road where the American bull-dozers are working, and we came up through cultivated lands to ground swelling into hills, where villages push out new houses under windmills falling to decay. Beyond these, thorny solitudes close down on the road from either side; we stopped to wonder by a 'Phrygian' tomb.[9]— (Shaitan Hammam)—a thing chipped out of the natural rock with a curiously modern feeling for rectangular structure: stranded like a forgotten ark out of its unrecoverable past, it still expresses the pleasure someone must have felt in smoothing out surfaces of stone with the new-found art of iron.

The Phrygian tomb holds what must always have been a pass in the opening valley. From it one climbs by an older stone-laid Turkish road overgrown with camelthorn, steepening to high slopes on olive-growing hillsides, and in their lap a solitary bay. Many little houses are here, of one or two rooms—one above the other—places where the Greeks came to tend their terraces and, like Apollo among the Hyperboreans, 'from the spring equinox to the rise of the Pleiades to enjoy their own fine weather'.[10] But it is solitude now, and every roof is broken in, and there is only one cottage, without a sign of life about it, on the exquisite edge of the sea.

We wondered if the city had been there, but the way went on, wide and well-surfaced, boldly over a still higher shoulder, and there lay Phocaea, beyond the hairpins of the road below. Great surfaces of cliffs made a semicircle round her, with cultivated lands gently descending from them to the town. Smaller, but not much smaller, than in the days of her greatness, she lay sunlit on a headland in her bay. A screen of islands floated scattered before her, and she ran out between two harbours, Naustathmos and Lampster, as she had done in the beginning, when the emigrants from Phocis built her by agreement on empty land belonging to Cyme, and took Attic kings from Erythrae and Teos, so that they might be admitted into the Ionian league.[11]

The bay, like a many-armed goddess of India, holds the town, and, beyond its islands, gives it nothing but a sun-illuminated, wind-inhabited view of the sea. The sea was the plaything of the young men of Phocaea. 'They voyaged not in merchant ships, but in fifty-oared vessels of war,' and 'practised long seafarings before the other Greeks', and colonized Marseilles and showed the way to the Adriatic and Tyrrhenia and Iberia and Tartessus (near Cadiz in Spain) where there was a king who lived 120 years, who wished to settle them in his own country, and, when he could not persuade them, 'gave them money to cast up a wall about their city, because he heard from them that the Mede was waxing in power'. From this it appears that it took the generals of Cyrus a long time to come down from the hinterland of Sardis, for 'the circuit of the wall is not a few stades, and is wholly of great stones and well compacted'.[12]

This they built, and now the moment came when they had to decide whether to sail away in their long ships or to live under the Persians, and the decision was all the harder because Harpagus the Mede offered such easy terms. Perhaps he too was touched when he reached the hill shoulder and looked down, for there lies Phocaea, defenceless as sleep, and it takes a particular hardness of heart to break something that shows itself both fragile and secure. Or perhaps it was just the economic advantage of the sea-town and its ships.

But anyway, Harpagus asked them only 'to tear down one tower of their wall and declare one house sacred'. And the Phocaeans asked for a day before replying, if he would lead his army away from their wall.

From the height above, which must always have made the town quite undefendable by land, I looked down and thought of the anguish of that day, and the coming and going while the hulls of the ships sank lower with the load of 'children and wives and all their furniture and the images and offerings also out of the temples, except what was of brass or stone or painting'. The Persian pickets lounging on the rocks in the sun must have seen it all, and brought word to Harpagus: and the next day he entered Phocaea empty of men.

But the citizens were rowed by their young men to Chios, where they tried to buy the islands of Oenussae which lie off the gulf of Erythrae; and the Chians rather prudently refused, as their own trade would have been cut out. So the Phocaeans made for Corsica and became sea-raiders, and after much trouble and loss eventually settled the town of Hyele or Elea, which is now Castellamare di Veglia in south Italy. But as they left the familiar gulfs and islands they put back into Phocaea and slaughtered the Persian garrison, and 'when they had performed this deed, they made mighty curses against any of them that should remain behind when they departed . . . and they also cast a mass of iron into the sea and sware not to return to Phocaea before that mass should appear again. Yet as they prepared to depart to Corsica, above half the citizens were seized by a sorrowful longing for their city and their homes; and they brake their oaths and sailed back to Phocaea. . . .' And Phocaea and Teos were the only two cities who preferred their liberty to their homes.[13]

This was the decision of Phocaea, and it is one which many have had to make in our day: and whether it is better to build up the land we know under a conqueror, or to try a new world and venture everything upon it, is a question that one has to answer in the strength of one's own heart. When it is so dealt with, perhaps either answer is sound, though the unavailing regrets remain.

In the Greek city state, every citizen took his part in these decisions, and so they put their passion into them, and their hatreds too: and no doubt if we could think for ourselves and be tolerant as well, we might be better than they. But it is better to be passionate than to be tolerant at the expense of one's soul. 'The most momentous thing in human life is the art of winning the soul to good or evil. Blest are the men who acquire a good soul; if it be bad, they can never be at rest, nor ever keep the same course two days together.'[14] This is what Diogenes Laertius makes Pythagoras say, and in a roundabout way it tells us how to find stability when the decision is difficult: and as there are many varieties of soul, some no doubt can become good under the Persians and some cannot: there is no Digest to describe a safe way for all. As I looked down to the little city in the sun, my heart went out equally to the young men who rowed their last out of the bay and became sea-pirates in the Sardinian sea, and to the half of the citizens who with bitterness and sorrow of parting, and the slaughtered garrison to explain, stayed to live in the Persian bondage, round the temple of Athena which Pausanias saw 'damaged by fire, but a wonder'.[15]

Nor is this an isolated story in Phocaea. About fifty years later, in 499 B.C. when Ionia revolted and united its fleet opposite Miletus, at the little island of Lade (which is now part of the mainland), the Phocaeans produced three ships, ranged between eight from Erythrae and seventy from Lesbos; but their captain, Dionysius, seeing the stakes that were to be fought for, attempted to discipline the whole of the 353 ships of the fleet.[16]

'Then every day he brought the ships out into line, and armed the soldiers on the decks and practised the rowers, making the ships sail in and out amongst their own array; and for the rest of the day he kept the ships at anchor, so that the Ionians had toil all the day long. And for seven days they obeyed him and did his commands; but on the eighth day the Ionians. . . said:

'"What god have we offended that we do this penance? Surely we were beside ourselves . . . when we committed ourselves to a Phocaean boaster, who furnisheth but three ships?" . . .

'So they said; and thereafter straightway none would obey him, but as though there were no war, they pitched tents on the island and sought the shade, neither would they enter into the ships or practise any more. . . . Then the Samians as soon as they saw the Ionians refuse to be valiant . . . counted it gain to save their temples and their houses when they had the opportunity . . . and raised their sails and left their rank . . . all except eleven ships, the masters whereof remained and fought and hearkened not unto the captains. And because of this deed the Samian state gave them the honour to be inscribed on a pillar with the names of their fathers, as having been valiant men; and this pillar is in the market place . . . But when Dionysius of Phocaea, who had taken three ships of the enemy, perceived that the Ionian cause was come to naught, he sailed not back to Phocaea, well knowing that it would be brought into bondage with the rest of Ionia, but sailed straight to Phoenicea as he was. And there he sank ships of merchandise and took much treasure, and then sailed to Sicily, where he established himself a as spoiler of Carthaginians and Tyrrhenians, but not of Greeks.'

So each man decided for himself. And some are, and some are not, remembered in the city market-place. And as for

Phocaea, she is scarred even today. For there was a massacre in 1913 and another in 1922, and the centre of the town is a heap of ruin. Phocaea and Cheshme were the ports from which the latest Greeks departed, under heavy fire; and they themselves imitated their ancestors in not leaving without doing all the damage they could. There are no Greeks left there, and their sad houses, with ornamented doorways and good stone round the windows are empty on the quay built with the ancient stones. The mosque too is empty in a charred field of ruins; and so are the warehouses where salt used to be exported that now goes by a more convenient port in the gulf of Smyrna. One can scarcely think now of Phocaea as a city that was a friend and neighbour in the young days of Croesus, and issued staters of electrum in the time of the Lydian kings.

The inhabitants, in the main street that the Turks prefer to be out of sight of the sea, rose when they saw our car with the Union Jack upon it, and bowed to it with their customary grave and pleasant politeness. They gathered in a little circle to drink tea with us in the café of their town, and told us the turns of its fortune and theirs, and showed their mosque in its ruins, with that steadiness in meeting all things which is the oriental answer to vicissitude and may become our own. We came away with no feeling that the life of Phocaea is ended: in the long slow gestures of history we happened merely on an arrested moment, or so it seemed.

> 'Not houses finely roofed or the stones of walls well builded
> . . . make the city, but men able to use their opportunity.'[17]

The words of Alcaeus came into my mind as I looked at Phocaea, where the Turks, Well-knit, mild and stubborn, looked in their slower way as if they too could make a decision if their moment came.

13

Colophon

The Position of Women

Fair Colophon in pride of strength we settled
Leading on our armies harsh and proud.

MIMNERMUS, 7th cent. B.C.[1]

It would be very casual to pass through Turkey without
a glance at Englishmen who have inhabited or travelled
through it from time to time. Many of them helped to preserve what lay there uncared for, and most of them have
been interested in one section or another of its enormous
past. In the 19th century in particular—the best of all, I
think, for travel books—a variety of tough and cultivated
people were about there, and if it be true that every country
gets the Englishmen it deserves—the deservings of Turkey
rank high.

From pure travellers, like W. M. Leake in 1800, who
found Asia Minor 'still in that state in which a disguised
dress, an assumption of the medical character, great patience
and perseverance, the sacrifice of all European comforts,
and the concealment of pecuniary means, are necessary to
enable the traveller thoroughly to investigate the country,
when otherwise qualified for the task by literary and scientific
attainments, and by an intimate knowledge of the language
and manners of the people';[2] we pass to charming amateurs
like Sir Charles Fellows, whose learning came to him for fun,
and whom we shall often meet riding about the hills of Lycia.
We come to a whole series of erudite clergymen in the steps of
St. Paul: to the Navy, mapping out the coastline and enjoying
its adventure: to engineers like Mr. Wood who devoted six
years and the whole of his income, and discovered the Arte-
misium in Ephesus at the end: to Prof. W. Ramsay and his
disciples in (almost) our own day: and to the consuls who
were particularly stimulated in an age when 'on receiving

this appointment from the F.O. . . . ' they were instructed 'to use such opportunities as presented themselves for the acquisition of antiquities for the British Museum, and with this object' . . . were authorized to extend their researches beyond the limits of their Vice-Consulship.[3]

Although they were apt to 'vegetate at Cyprus and Rhodes for twelve long years without ever asking for a furlough', their travels were surprisingly facilitated by 'stray Ionians' (inhabitants that is of the W. Ionian islands). 'Wherever there are Ionians there is litigation, and litigation is sure to come, sooner or later, within the action of the Consul. It is for these reasons that Consuls can so easily make their way in the most inhospitable villages of the Levant, where unprotected travellers might be left to starve.'

I think with very warm gratitude of Consuls. Apart from D. B. in Smyrna, there was. Mr. Wilkinson, whose qualifications as a traveller would have satisfied even W. M. Leake. He is related to the Whittall family—one of those private dynasties that pushed out into the Levant and handed the reins of its commerce from father to son for generations. Their greatness is over, but they still live in discreet affluence in Victorian houses, retired with classic stucco pediments in walls and gardens, in pleasant villages on the outskirts of Smyrna; and though Mr. Wilkinson is too conscientious to leave his office and travel about (since the F.O. in this century no longer encourages the collection of antiquities), yet there is little he has not studied in the history of Asia Minor, and very few places that he has not investigated in his district. To me he was patiently kind, and I am glad to take this occasion to thank him, in the natural course of my touring, for we visited Colophon together.

We left in the afternoon, as it is no more than twenty-nine miles from Smyrna, with Ahmet and nephew in the taxi, and turned to the right from the Ephesus road. The dust in the lanes was deep, the surface excruciating, and brambles hit us from the sides; but a memory of luxury pervades the expedition because of Mr. Wilkinson's tea-basket. Even eau-de-Cologne was included in it. In their hey-day, the government of Colophon hired female musicians to play for an official salary from dawn to dusk;[4] the eau-de-Cologne seemed an echo, very diluted, of those perfumed days.

There is a feel of country about the landscape, due perhaps to its deep freshness under high trees. The village of Deghir-mendere is almost invisible in the summer luxuriance, its mud walls melted away from sight by tangles of shadow and sunlight, the glossy surfaces of mulberry and darknesses of pine. There is none of the openness of Ionia and the sea is forgotten. The writers who describe it talk of inland things. 'Lofty Colophon,'[5] said Athenaeus, and: 'One comes to the mountain Gallesius,' says Strabo:[6] and Pausanias mentions, with the ash trees of the grove of Apollo, the river Ales, 'the coldest in Ionia.'[7]

There are still panthers, and their cubs can be surprised in crannies of the rocks: and no doubt the deer still swim from the Coracian mountain to the island of Artemis to give birth to their young;[8] for it is all wild and mountainous and few people live between Colophon and Lebedus, which was a military area and forbidden.

Of the ancient city nothing, not even the name, is left — except a few dim heavings of disintegrated walls on a steep and ruinous hillside thickly overgrown. Even in history, there is a vagueness about it different from the other Ionian cities, who keep their clear-cut crystal quality however little of their story may be known. In Colophon, the press of events is dense as the multitude of leaves today, but the events themselves elude one, fugitive as shadows that beckon and are not there.

Why for instance is Colophon alone of the Ionian cities so far inland from the sea? And who were the Cretans under Rhacius who first settled here among the Carian holders of the land? What were they doing so far from their ships and the sea-roads of their friends?

Many things must have happened, and perhaps it is as well to stick to the legends; they will tell as much of the detail as we are likely to know. They say that Manto, the daughter of the blind prophet Tiresias, was brought a prisoner to Delphi from Thebes; and thence crossed in one of the ships sent by Apollo to found a colony in Asia. As they landed at Clarus, the Cretans came against them and carried them to Rhacius, who married Manto and allowed her shipmates to inhabit the land; and in course of time their son Mopsus (later to reappear in Cilicia, and reach Ascalon, and throw the goddess there into her own lake), drove the Carians away.

The place is thick with prophets, both male and female. Calchas, coming on foot on his way from Troy, is said to have died of grief here when he met Mopsus, a prophet better than himself.[9]

My own idea, for what it may be worth, is that Colophon was more ancient than most of the Ionian cities, and the sea-coasts not yet safe for any sailors, Minoan or others, at a time when some tiny boat-load took refuge among the Carians, Leleges and Lydians of the shore. It was only when later waves of Greek colonization began to pour across, that the balance of the population turned in favour of the Greeks, as the exploits of Mopsus record. There is an air of age about the legends, of earlier and perhaps matriarchal people, under priests who were Lydians of the mainland, keeping their office into historic times[10] when the city itself had long become Ionian under an Ionian king, and had taken to the same language as Ephesus, Lebedus, Teos, Clazomenae, and

Phocaea. Colophon founded (and was therefore older than) Smyrna: and we have seen how she was already a firmly established city when the Erythraeans had not yet chosen their site.[11]

What is certain is that, in the days of the Lydians, she was rich, powerful, brave and luxurious. '. . . the rich . . . superior in numbers . . . as formerly at Colophon, for there the majority had large possessions before the Lydian war.'[12]

In the 7th century B.C., she was attacked and taken by Gyges, the Lydian usurper of the Herodotus story,[13] possibly because of some attachment to the older dynasty to which the Colophon priesthood belonged.

Whatever mixture of races they came from, the Colophonians had taken to the Lydian way of life. Xenophanes describes them, their cloaks of purple, their scented hair.[14] In war they were famous like the Lydians, and unlike the Greeks, for their cavalry, 'in which they were so far superior to the others that wherever, in wars that were hard to finish, the cavalry of the Colophonians served as an ally, the war came to an end; whence arose the proverb: He put Colophon to it—which is quoted when a sure finish is put to any affair',[15] and still survives at the end of our books, put to a different use.

Alyattes, the great-grandson of Gyges, who drove the Cimmerians out of Asia and took Smyrna, hired the Colophon cavalry, and,—becoming afraid,—persuaded them to leave their horses in the camp outside Sardis and to enter the city, with promise of double pay and bounties; and there the Lydian troops butchered them. The inner history of this drastic act is lost in time, and may have been no more than a Lydian way of dealing with strikes.[16]

The women in Colophon seem to have managed their affairs more diplomatically than the cavalry, and expressed their personalities in a great variety of ways—from Manto the prophet's daughter and the sybil Herophile, to Arachne who was turned into a spider by Athena: a later legend makes her the daughter of a Colophonian dyer, and her son, according to Pliny, invented spindles.[17] Among male Colophonian musicians and poets, like Polymnastus, or Histiaeus, who added a ninth string to the lyre, and Mimnermus and Xeno-phanes, is a poetess called by the ugly name of Gongyla, a disciple of Sappho. One should pause a little beside Xeno-phanes, who was a great man, a satyrist and mocker of the anthropomorphic gods—but I am enticed by the women of Colophon. Archeanassa, for instance, the courtesan loved by Plato: 'Even upon her wrinkles', he sang, 'there rests a bitter passion. Ah, ye wretches who encountered her youth in its first course, through what hot flame did ye pass?'[18]

It must surely be to a woman rather out of the ordinary that a sonnet of this kind is addressed? And Alcman too, 'fell immoderately in love with a poetess who was able to attract lovers to her by her conversation'.[19] One is always being told that love with the Greeks was entirely physical as far as women were concerned; I would never believe anything so unlikely, and prefer to remember Pericles, who never left the house without twice embracing his Aspasia.

The female character, among the Greeks of Asia Minor, seems to have kept two streaks distinctly—one from the east, and one from the north-west and the sea. The Lydianized Ionians, for instance, secluded their high-born women, while nakedness was admitted by the Dorians:[20] 'To put off her shift and play the Dorian', Anacreon sings in Teos.

The dress, too, varied, for the Ionians wore the discreet tubular eastern gown, called Carian by Herodotus, still worn in Kalymnos, Egypt and Syria,[21] 'A motley gown, a fair Lydian work, reached to her feet';[22] while the Dorian was open down the side, with a long history behind it, leading back through the Minoan skirt and jacket of Crete to a prehistoric past.

Pausanias wonders when die Graces first shed their dress: he remarks that the older artists of Smyrna and Pergamum put clothes upon them.[23] And here is a purely oriental pur-dah touch from a timid well-brought-up woman of the 6th century, who says: 'I hate a bad man, and veil my face as I pass him, keeping my heart light as a little bird's.'[24]

The Greeks in fact were late-comers to the coasts of Ionia, not mentioned there by Homer, to whom even Miletus is 'Carian, uncouth of speech',[25] and they brought no wives with them, 'but took Carian women whose menfolk they had murdered. . . . For this murder,' says Herodotus, 'these women made them a law . . . that they should never eat together with their husbands nor call them by name. . . .' It is a general oriental custom for men and women to eat separately,[26] and Herodotus has given the gist of the matter a legendary twist.

The annexing of wives is the most ancient process by which civilization is preserved: captured women bring their needles and their ovens, their cooking-pots and all the mechanism of domestic life, and cover the hiatus produced by a new set of men. Nothing is more alluring than to follow some single object among these domestic utensils—the pierced stone or piece of clay for instance, that weights the woollen thread as it falls rolled from the hand of the spinner, such as the young nomad girls use today in the mountains of Caria, walking ahead of their camels with the leading string tucked under their arm, spinning as they walk: the same instrument is found in layer upon layer of human habitation, through iron and bronze ages and copper, to the neolithic flint. Looking upon it, one wonders if the most important female function in history is not that of marrying the invader? And if this is so, what comes of our female education? And the W.R.A.F.s, and W.R.A.C.s, and W.R.N.S.? In the animal kingdom, the female stands aside from the fighting and goes off with the conqueror. And presumably our cooking-pots would be of a much inferior pattern if women had not continued to do so through most of the human past.

The local women in Colophon were not less influential than any others. Their land was the land of the Mother Goddess; the Amazons' footprints are everywhere about it; we have seen them in Smyrna, Cyme, and Myrina. Priestesses apparently, their rites, their weapons, their fawn-skins wrapped around them, created the legends: and the priests of the Lydians had to dress like women (and were very often eunuchs). While the matriarchy of the Lydians is not as explicit as that of the Lycians in the south, there are traces here and there that allow it to be inferred. When the mistress of King Gyges of Lydia died, 'he reared the monument which is to this day still named after the Companion, raising it so high that when he made his royal progresses within the region of Mount Tmolus, wherever he chanced to turn, he could see it, and it was visible to all the inhabitants of Lydia';[27] furthermore : 'the tomb of his son was a tumulus which I have seen on the edge of the lake in sight of Sardis, and the largest portion of it was built with the money of the courtesans.'[28]

Whether or not the acceptance of the courtesan as a respectable woman is an advantage or no to the feminine position as a whole, I am unable to say. It is anyway engaging to see them employing their money to good purpose. The Athenian prostitutes in the army of Pericles before Samos dedicated a temple to Aphrodite (when their earnings were sufficient);[29] and in the last war, the Governor of Aden was approached by the lodgers in the street of prostitutes begging that the embargo might be lifted which put them out of bounds to the British Army, and pointing out that they had made, in proportion, the largest of all the contributions to King George's Fund.

'No wonder there is a shrine to the Companion everywhere, but nowhere in all Greece is there one to the wife,' says Philetaerus in *The Huntress*. This seems a pity; and there are plenty of wives in Greek history to make it seem unjust: but as for the Companion, whatever our modern code may think of the profession, it is surely a sign of liberality to allow good and gentle actions to be within reach of all. The box of ointment, so surprising to the puritan Hebrews, would apparently not have astonished either the ladies of Aden or of Lydia.

14

Clarus and Notium
Xenophanes and Reason

But without toil he sets everything in motion, by the thought
of his mind.

XENOPHANES, 6th cent. B.C.[1]

As we left the lanes of Colophon and skirted the pine-
clad mountain feet towards the temple of Apollo at
Clarus, the country opened from its high look of mythological
aloofness; the liveableness of Ionia began to reappear. Dry
steep beds showed where the streams had run in winter and
in spring. A *sebil,* like a shrine, offered its spout of water
by the lonely and beautiful wayside. The lane wandered up
and down under tall trees and among olives, the echoes of
its centuries gathered as if into a bunch of quiet, smothered
perhaps under the autumn dust.

"I know of no other Greeks who are accusomed to sacrifice
puppies except the people of Colophon," writes Pausanias.
And goes on to say that they immolate a black bitch to the

Wayside Goddess, at night.[2] But, as we drove, the sun's fingers streaked the hillside under the tree stems and water from hidden recesses came spinning out into the light; the earth rested on its strength, like Hercules on his club, after the turmoils and movement of the year; and even the darkness of the underworld seemed nourishing and kindly, giver of moisture and feeder of roots, more concerned with the living than the dead. Like the clear Ionian voice out of obscure mythologies and the groping of mixed peoples, the thin thread of water, the wayfarer's perennial refreshment, came lightly out of the earth.

"There are no bridges left to us from the early centuries of Greece," Mr. Wilkinson told me as we made across torrent layers of gravel towards the lessening hills, "for no religious Greek would have liked to offend a river god with anything as shackling as stone."

As the hills sank, folding into each other in the rather monotonous way they often have near the sea, we came by the last jerk and heave of a lane not meant for cars to Ahmet Beyli, a village of Bulgarian refugees who grow tobacco here in the shade of great fig trees. The valley then opened to a gentle bay, with the 'coldest river in Ionia' silting through it under tamarisk and rushes and sycamores. The temple foundations stand on the eastern edge, with their columns shuffled by earthquakes into slices symmetrically laid, like a French roti, one overlapping the other. They faced east, and had a peristyle of fluted Doric columns, repeated from early patterns in a later day. And they are being excavated by Professor and Mme Louis Robert and M. Martin, happy in a grant from their country guaranteed to continue till the work is accomplished—in another ten years or so. This not only allows the archaeologist to work in peace, but also makes a finished excavation possible with no loopholes for villagers to quarry stone; and permits of a site where beauty can be considered and not information only, with a column or two set up again, and a few trees planted, in the interests of landscape as well as learning. So M. Robert promised, a happy man, living his bronzed and absorbed summers astride of Time.

He showed us the propylaea uncovered, and the steps and narrow passage that led (probably) to the oracle chamber, now green with seeping water; and the bases of statues of Pompey and Lepidus and the Romans of the day. The grey marble had come out of the earth preserved and brightened with a film of yellow mud; this vulgarly strident colour and the fact that practically every surface was coated with letters produced an astonishing newness, and—with the wordiness of the inscriptions—gave a temporary illusion of bustle not unlike a newspaper office and probably much nearer the original temple atmosphere than the dreaminess of ruins. The venerable age of the oracle, which the people of Colophon asserted, is hidden; what the present temple reproduces, with interesting completeness, is a century of Asia Minor under Rome, with visitors even from Russia in the north, and the day-to-day problems of a 'personal column' in a paper. The most human of the inscriptions is a waspish answer to a deputation from the rival oracle in Ephesus, refusing to help those 'who are not in the habit of coming to ask here'.

At less than half an hour's walk, by a 'sacred way' now vanished, the town of Notium, the seaport of Colophon, stood on a hill above the sea. Its theatre, too, is shuffled into ruin, and looks inland to the folded valley-hills; and from the headland's summit, where a city temple stood, the coast is visible on a wide arc from Samos and the twin peaks of Mycale, to Ephesus, on a sea-bay then, but now marooned

in marshy flat lands green across the dark water, like beetles'
wings in the sun.

From Clarus Mopsus is said to have colonized Cilicia.
Close by, the fleet of Alcibiades (in his absence) was defeated
by Lysander the Spartan admiral;[3] a little farther eastward
along the coast Alcidas, the Spartan, landed so as to butcher
his prisoners.[4] About that time, about 426 B.C., the Colophonians deserted their inland city, captured by Persians
called in during a party quarrel.

Thucydides describes the restlessness of that time:

> 'The refugees, after settling in Notium, again split up into fac-
> tions, one of which called in Arcadian and barbarian mercenaries
> . . . and formed a new community with the Persian party of the
> Colophonians who joined them from the upper town . . . Their
> opponents . . . invited Hippias, the commander of the Arcadi-
> ans in the fortified quarter, to a parley, upon condition that,
> if they could not agree, he was to be put back safe and sound
> in the fortifications. However, upon his coming out, they put
> him into custody, though not in chains, and attacked suddenly
> and took by surprise the fortification, and putting the Arcadians
> and the barbarians found in it to the sword, afterwards took
> Hippias into it as promised and, as soon as he was inside, seized
> him and shot him down.'[5]

The city was then given up to the anti-Persian party, and
settlers sent from Athens, and the place colonized again according to Athenian laws, after collecting all the Colophonians round about. Then, in the 3rd century, Lysimachus transported the dwindling populations of Colophon and Lebedus
to furnish his new-walled Ephesus; and those of the citizens
who resisted were 'buried . . . left of the road to Clarus'.[6]
Colophon disappears, and Notium, pillaged in 85 B.C. by
Cilician pirates, flickering into the last light of a visit from

Germanicus, sinks undistinguished into the prosperity of Rome.[7]

'Pride destroyed the Magnesians, and Colophon and Smyrna,'[8] a poet sings. It is easy to say so after everything has happened.

But Xenophanes is the poet of Colophon. Out of the superstitions, the municipal violence and treasons, the long tussle of Carians and Leleges and Lydians, Cretan wanderers and expelled Pelasgians fleeing from the Dorians—out of this earth of luxury, forgetfulness, and defeat, the clear Ionian spring-water rises. And a tiny cup of it remains in the verses of Xenophanes, familiar and intimate as if spoken in a room where the centuries cease to be.[9]

'Three score and seven years have tossed my careworn soul up and down the land of Hellas; and there were then five and twenty years from my birth'—he sings of himself as an old man of ninety-two, looking back perhaps to the breaking of his youth when Harpagus took the towns.

The facts of his life are the least thing about it—whether he joined the Phocaean exiles in their colony and founded the school of Elaea; or whether—more likely—he spent his last days with other 'intellectuals' at the court of Hieron in Sicily; or whether he wrote a philosophic epic as well as those which described the foundings of Elaea and of Colophon. All are lost, and these are puzzles for the expert. But the poet is clear. In the few pages left, he himself comes down the aisle of time towards us, with the clarity, the humility, the curiosity, the steadfast repose of moderation—the perfume of Ionia.

'Let these be taken as fancies, something like the truth': so he pauses, with this hesitation on his threshold.

To his Ionian interest in weather,

'The sun swinging over the earth and warming it,'

'The mighty sea, father of clouds and of winds and of rivers,'

he adds an infinite seeking, of a mind pacing with immortal eagerness beyond what it can know:

'The gods have not revealed all things to men from the beginning, but by seeking they find in time what is better.'

And as he turns from the darkness of the old mythology— the sacrifice of the black bitch at night and the intrigues of the oracle at Clarus, 'Homer and Hesiod have ascribed to the gods all things that are a shame and a disgrace among mortals, stealings and adulteries and deceivings of one another,' he looks as we all do, for 'one God, the greatest among gods and men, neither in form like unto mortals nor in thought.'

'And he abideth ever in the selfsame place, moving not at all; nor doth it befit him to go about now hither now thither.'

'He sees all over, thinks all over, and hears all over.'

In a few lines, mellowed by age and goodness, the artist appears, proud and disillusioned, who has seen the fall of cities and felt the hardness of exile.

'Far better is our art than the strength of men and horses . . . Even if there arise a mighty boxer among the people . . . the city would be none the better governed for that . . . ' 'If a man win victory in swiftness of foot . . . he will not deserve . . . so much as I do.'

And he turns, as we all do if we are wise, to our one link between the attainable and the unattainable—the beauty of everyday:

'Now is the floor clean, and the hands and cups of all; one sets twisted garlands on our heads, another hands us fragrant ointments on a salver. The mixing bowl stands ready, full of gladness and there is more wine at hand . . . soft and smelling of flowers in the jars! . . . Nor would a man mix wine in a cup by pouring out the wine first, but water first and wine on top of it. . . . Brown loaves are set before us and a lordly table laden with cheese and rich honey. The altar in the midst is clustered round with flowers. . . . Then after libation and prayer made that we may have strength to do right—for that is in truth the first thing to do—no sin is it to drink as much as a man can take and get home without an attendant, so he be not stricken in years. And of all men is he to be praised who after drinking gives goodly proof of himself in the trial of skill, as memory will serve him. Let him not sing of Titans and Giants—those fictions of the men of old—nor of turbulent civil broils in which is no good at all; but to give heedful reverence to the gods is ever good.'

This gentle harmony of living where the seen and unseen are united, where knowledge is loved and humility never forgotten, has blossomed under the pines of Colophon out of its dark and violent past.

15

Sardis

The Commerce of Sardis

Ancient Sardis, abode of my fathers, had I been reared in you,
I should have been a maund-bearer to Cybele or beaten pretty
tambours as one of her gilded eunuchs.

ALCMAN, 7th cent, B.C.[1]

All the chariots and armoured footmen of Lydia.

SAPPHO 6th cent. B.C.[2]

My elders who saw him rout the serried ranks of the Lydian
cavalry in the plain of Hermus, rout them with a spear.

MIMNERMUS, 7th cent. B.C.[3]

The first mention in history of the name of Asia is that
of 'The Asian mead by Caystrios' stream'.[4] Homer saw
the wild swans settling there: and Strabo says it is a meadow
with a 'hero temple of Cayster and a certain Asius, and the
Cayster river that streams forth near by'.[5] This is now the

plain of the town of Ödemish, in a south-west bay of Tmolus mountain, with the village centres of Tire and Bayindir inside it: and Tire appears to have been the original fief of a Lydian dynasty which began with King Gyges in the 7th century B.C.

The earlier Lydians, living under kings descended from Heracles, were known to Homer as Maeonians: 'And those Maeonians that beneath the mountain Tmolus sprung . . . '[6]

Even Assurbanipal the Assyrian, who had a long ancestral alliance with them, complained in an official document, about 650 B.C., that he had never heard the Lydian name before.[7] The new dynasty therefore, whose origins Herodotus treats with a certain aristocratic, disdainful picturesqueness, seem to have been upstarts in their day. But their predecessors, the descendants of Heracles, trace back through six centuries before them: and Heracles himself is a wanderer from the East, whether myth or human. By Tyre or Ascalon, or more probably direct from Mesopotamia, he travelled, and left his children established over the Thracian-Oriental tribes scattered in the 'best of all plains', around the slopes of Tmolus.

Here they flourished, and developed their stretch of the great trade route under the Hittite empire, till the Hittite empire fell. Sardis their capital, the Shardana of Egypt, is mentioned in hieroglyphs as early as the 15th century B.C.[8] and many things—the great earthenware jars for burial and household, the wheeled cart of the 4th millennium from Elam,[9] the 20-stringed harp[10] and the metal helmet, and probably the art of casting in bronze[11]—came travelling along the military road to be worked upon by skilled craftsmen and women at its gentler end.

'As when some woman of Maeonia or Caria staineth ivory with purple, to make a cheek-piece for horses, and it is laid up in the treasure chamber, and many a horseman prayeth for it to

wear; but it is laid up to be a king's boast, alike an adornment
for his horse and a glory for his charioteer.'[12]

The very structure of their aristocratic government was
oriental—a prime minister,[13] a band of 'King's Friends',
the priest-king himself with the family name of Sandon,
which belongs to the Assyrian Heracles: and Semitic epithets
like Alyattes, or Sadyattes, transformed into names. But the
people themselves were of mixed origin, and their Thracian
tumuli for the dead are scattered about the Hermus valley to
this day: and Thracian names of towns balance the Semitic
names of gods and kings.[14] Their language, still spoken at
Cibyra in Strabo's day—akin to Phrygian and Mysian, and
akin to Greek—is said to have given us the word *Tyrant,* from
Lydian 'tyra' or 'teira', a fortified place—related to Pelasgic
Tyrsis, and Tyrius—and to the tribe Tyrrhenos which lived
at the foot of Tmolus, and was described by Herodotus as
embarking for Tuscany and the future Tyrrhenian Sea. The
word is found in Lydia, in an inscription at Kula, as an epithet
of the gods Zeus and Men; and Archilochus first uses it in
Greek in the time of Gyges, whose brilliant and successful
usurpation set a fashion in 'tyranny' throughout the coastal
world.[15]

A middle-class commercial revolution took place with the
dynastic change.

The descendants of Heracles seem undistinguished men,
beset with quarrels. Ardys, whom we saw in exile in Cyme,
had an army of 30,000 cavalry and reigned through the mid-
8th century for 70 years. The butterfly light of history shows
him for a mere moment, an old man carried in a litter to the
Assembly in Sardis, to curse the murderers of his favourite
minister. His son was among the murderers, and expiated the
crime voluntarily, by three years' exile at the friendly court

of Babylon—and then became king—Meles, Alyattes—in his turn.[16] But the widow of the victim, with her little son, fled to the Black Sea coast and there, at Sinope, in the third generation, in 716 B.C., Gyges her grandson was born. Some among the learned held him to be a Solar Myth, until Assyrian tablets proved that he existed. Nicholas of Damascus, in the most reasonable version of his story, tells how he came back at the age of 18 to his family lands at Tire, to stay with a grand-uncle who was childless and had obtained leave to send for the family from exile. The father of Gyges was an Ardys, and therefore probably belonged to a branch of the royal Herculean stem.[17] However this may be, the young man stayed in Tire, which seems to have been the family centre of his clan. Here, in Ephesus and Caria nearby, the good mercenaries were to be found. Here too he might come into touch with the Ephesian bankers, such as the house of Melas, who were to help, and marry into, his dynasty for the next 150 years.[18]

After a time Gyges made his way at the court of Sardis. Candaules the king was an easy-going man, with a fondness, as Herodotus depicts it, not only for his women but also for his pictures, for he is said to have bought one for its weight in gold. He came to love Gyges in spite of the jealousy of nobles who feared the 'hereditary enmity'. He made him his minister, and sent him, in the royal chariot, to fetch a Mysian princess to whom Gyges on the way made proposals of his own. Being repulsed, and in danger, and warned by a serving maid, he killed King Candaules-Sadyattes in his bed. When the dawn came, he sent for the 'King's Friends'; eliminated those he was not sure of; and with the rest presented himself to the Assembly: where it was agreed, as in Herodotus' story, to ask for a final decision from the oracle at Delphi.[19] In the year 687 B.C. Gyges became king, or 'tyrant' of the

Lydians, and the fashion of 'tyranny'—the type of Renais-
sance despot—spread all over Ionia and Aeolis, while the
old families, the Neleides of Miletus, Basilides of Erythrae,
Androclides of Ephesus, Codrides of Phocaea, and Penthe-
lides of Mitylene were deposed. The epidemic reached the
mainland of Greece in the ages of Pisistratus and Periander
and Polycrates, in Athens and Corinth and Samos.

All this was a part of the commercial prosperity. Under
the Hittites at first and then on their own account the Lydians
had been the organizers of the trade-route;[20] and as their
trade widened, their attention turned increasingly from the
East to the opening markets of the sea.

A new world was setting its currents, with new dan-
gers. Unknown barbarians, the Cimmerians, threatened in
the north; and the loosely-knit, oligarchical, feudal people
needed a leader. A young middle class, not interested in the
'landed provincial gentry' of Lydia, was active in the seaboard
towns; and almost every year a new colony was founded along
the Aegean or Mediterranean shores.[21] The long Maeonian
subservience to Assyria too was irksome. When the Cimmerians descended, pouring across the plateau to Taurus,
Esarhaddon in 678 B.C. defeated them and the Lydians turned
to him by necessity, but they dropped the alliance again as
soon as their northern horizon cleared.[22] Then they set to and
developed tributary roads for their commerce on the great
highway; to Cyzicus and Dascylium (Bursa) in the north;
through Cibyra to Cilicia and Syria in the south.[23] They collected their tolls at convenient cross-roads, of which Sardis
was one;[24] and made a cadastral survey for tribute, which the
Persians later took over. They organized the caravan traffic
with the institution of inns at regular stages (unknown in
the time of Homer); and a few generations later Xenophon,
marching in Cyrus' army, noticed how food and fodder could

only be found in the Lydian markets. A proverb made a synonym of publican and Lydian. The name of Ankara, transformed by the Greeks, is a Lydian word which denotes a
station on the way.[25]

Wealth, pouring in from many new sources, made the
opening of other markets necessary; and the opening of markets brought the Lydians to the coast. Gyges took Colophon,
and attacked Miletus and Smyrna; his son took Priene and
attacked Miletus; his great-grandson, Alyattes took Smyrna
and failed before Clazomenae; and was succeeded by Croesus,
who besieged Ephesus and planned to conquer the islands.
The pretexts mattered little: 'bringing one charge against
this city and another against that. And those in whom he
could find greater offence, he charged with greater faults,
but some he charged with trifles.'[26] The change of dynasty
no doubt shook a number of old friendships and loyalties;
and made the road from Sardis to Cyme less used, and that to
desolate Smyrna scarcely at all in the next 300 years; but the
traffic increased through Tire to Ephesus over Tmolus, and
there was no basic change. The new masters acted as the old
trading partners had done for generations. All they cared for
was that there should be no hindrance at the outlets to the
sea. The Lydians in fact helped the Greek cities when they
could:

'Having received no benefits at our hands and knowing us
not at all, they gave us 2000 staters.' So Alcaeus wrote, of
Mitylene.[27] And the Greeks of the coast who—like the Ephesian Eurybates—joined Cyrus against Lydia, were looked
upon by their own people as traitors to a common cause.[28]

Gyges had a warrior's life, fighting the Cimmerians. As
these came south, the friendly Phrygian king committed
suicide, and the lands of Adramyttium north of Pergamum
were lost. The Cimmerians probably found allies, for their

later commander Lygdamus has a Carian name. Under his attack, in the second invasion, the town (but not the citadel) of Sardis fell. Magnesia on the Maeander was sacked in 652 B.C., the year of Gyges' death,[29] and the temple in Ephesus burnt and the lands harried; until Artemis from her swamp sent pestilence, and Lygdamus died in Cilicia, and the invasion came to an end.[30] Then Ardys the son of Gyges ruled, and his son and grandson after him, for about a century to the reign of Croesus, the last of the Lydian kings.

During this time, one of the corners of history was turned by the invention of money. This came out of the meeting of the overland traffic with the highways of the sea. In Homeric days, when commerce was mainly sea-borne, barter could suffice—for the sea needs exchange of merchandise if ships are to travel with full holds; but the land needs a currency, and bills of exchange and the payment for goods with metal had long before been thought of by the Sumerians.[31] The Lydians now put a government stamp of a lion or a fox on their discs of electron from Tmolus; and the Ionians, swiftly taking to the new invention, worked the designs into beauty by lifting them from their sunken stamped sockets into high relief: and the business of modern currency was born. The Greek words for money—talent, mina—had long ago travelled from Asia down the Eastern road: but the first date of the government-minted Lydian coins is not before 680 B.C. in the reign of Gyges—and almost immediately Aegina followed with coins of silver.[32]

I have spent a long time over this background of Lydia, because of its importance in the Ionian world: for Sardis was at its apogee at the moment when the Persians came. 'Of later date than the Trojan times, yet nevertheless a great city, and old, and has a strong citadel,' though much shattered

with earthquakes; and Pactolus stream; and Tmolus, 'a blest
mountain, with a look-out on its summit, an arcade of white
marble, a work of the Persians—whence there is a view of
the plains all round, and particularly the Cayster plain.'[33]

This is Strabo when the days of its greatness are over and
Pactolus no longer carried gold: but in the 6th century, before
546 and the fall of Croesus, it was the lodestar of the cities of
the coast. 'There came one by one to Sardis, which prospered
and was wealthy, all the wise men of Greece that were alive
at that time.' It was visited as Paris came to be visited in
Europe, by the jewellers, the bankers, the musicians, the
mercenary soldiers, the engineers like Thales of Miletus, the
political refugees from the mainland of Greece.[34]

'One can see that you have never been to Sardis, if you
don't know what a pelisse is,' says Aristophanes.[35]

And the relation with Greece was well established. Gyges,
a hundred years before, had been 'the first of all barbarians
that we know of, except Midas . . . king of Phrygia, who
dedicated offerings at Delphi'.[36] He had Corinthian friends,
and probably arranged to know beforehand what the oracle was likely to decide when he referred to it for his right
to the throne of Lydia.[37] This routine, in the Levant, is
surely as old as the Mediterranean sea! The Corinthian and
Clazomenian treasuries in Delphi gave friendly lodging to
the Lydian offerings that followed so satisfactory a conclusion: Apollo conceded freedom from taxes, seats of honour, citizenship: the dazzle of Lydia reached the mainland of
Greece.[38]

Meanwhile, in Asia Minor, the changing and mixing of
Lydian and Ionian went on for a hundred years under Gyges'
successors. The brightly painted archaic earthenware for
roofs and pediments came through from the East, and the
tombs of Sardis were sculptured with colour, red and black.[39]

Sardis (Sert): Door-Post of the Temple of Cybele

Sardis (Sert): In Winter: The Acropolis

Sardis (Sert): The Temple of Cybele, and Pactolus Beyond

Sardis (Sert): The Temple from the Acropolis
Sardis (Sert): Byzantine Wall of the Acropolis

'The art of the large vessels,' great drums of terra-cotta, still lay by the temple of Artemis in 1882, seen by Gregorovius.[40] The blocks in the funeral tumuli of Sardis are laid as the best Greek craftsmen laid them, and the workmanship is indistinguishable.[41]

Industry too was very much the same for Greek and Lydian. Sardis worked in leather and Colophon made shoes; and the saffron of Tmolus 'croceos ut Tmolus odores',[42] was turned into scent in Lydia as in Ephesus and Smyrna. There was weaving and dyeing, in purple and many colours, both for linen, flax, and wool; and the Sardis carpets, still famous today in Ushak and Gordes, were so fine that the Persians kept them for the private apartments of their kings.[43]

In their personal intercourse the same interchanges appear. Priesthoods are shared,[44] and the patrician daughters of Ionia, long before the conquest, married the Lydian princes.[45] The old-fashioned in Sardis wore the oriental mitra, but the young tied their hair with the circlet and wore purple tunics of the Aegean embroidered with gold. When the Lydian troops marched past Xerxes, another century later, their round shields and their dress and their spears were not to be distinguished from the Greek.[46]

'Cities of Ionia, strong and many-peopled, where the Greeks and barbarians mingle,' says Euripides, bringing the Bacchantes' chorus of women from 'holy Tmolus', and making Dionysus declare that 'Lydia is my home'. Aristotle goes so far as to give Homer an adopted father, a royal Lydian, in Maeonia.[47] The father of Croesus had one Carian and one Ionian wife.[48] Only in their horsemanship, their skill with chariots, their complicated cookery, in their love of parks and gardens, and their predilection for eunuchs (characteristics which the Persians seem to have taken over), the Lydians differentiated themselves from the coast.[49]

Rumour of their riches comes down the centuries in a still vivid atmosphere of admiration, disapproval and envy. It is the background to Plato's rejection of the 'Lydian mode' and Alcman's music 'issued from lofty Sardis'.

The Lydians had the touchstone for gold in their possession, and sent rings and earrings to be sold across the sea. They turned from agriculture to dig in their mines for ore, like that millionaire—Pythios of Celaenae—who offered a ` fortune to Xerxes.[50] Yet the greater, though less sensational, revenue, came from the trade route. And the Persians—a poor people—inherited it, and were fabulous for riches in their turn.

Croesus surrendered, and the Greek coastland mourned, yet there seems to have been no intrinsic change. The Persians took over Ionian engineers and Lydian business men with the whole of their organization as it stood. All they seem to have added was the system of posts, a necessary military precaution along what is henceforth called the Royal Road. The cities of Ionia could settle into much the same kind of situation as before. The decision that was taken in this century was not between Persian and Lydian, but between East and West. A generation after Salamis and Plataea, a treaty[51] forbade any Persian to come within a day's journey of the sea; by the Athenian empire's monopoly, the great trade route was maimed; though traffic always continued, yet, through the rest of history, shifting and menacing like the base of a tornado and never altogether removed, the barrier has remained, and a separate world grown up on either side. Many efforts, conscious and unconscious, have been made to undo this act. Alexander nearly held the whole trade route, but died; and Rome kept her portion for a long time, but never really held the Euphrates: and no conqueror from the East has yet come to live easily with the sea. Byzantium nearly succeeded; she was placed midway, in much the same situation as Lydia and on a larger scale, and the Latin betrayal which defeated her, is, for this reason mainly, one of the tragedies of the world.

One would gladly be independent of commerce, yet the evidence of history seems to mark the transcontinental highways as the thread which the life of the world as we know it must spin. The weight of this necessity is so great that it forces a way through the enmities and stupidities of nations and a wraith of the huge traffic has continued. But the steady flow, the wide safety, the exuberance of the result, have gone, though for thirty centuries the mapping of the great highway has scarcely changed. Sardis, whence Brutus and Cassius set out for Philippi, which Tamerlane destroyed completely, in 1675 was 'reduite à un pauvre village où il y a pourtant un grand khan . . . où les voyageurs sont comodément logés. C'est le grand passage des caravanes qui vont de Smyrne à Alep et en Perse'.[52]

Even they have ceased, and the village has dwindled even more. The acropolis, half eaten away, slopes like a truncated wave over the plain from the south, as if about to break. Its inner sides of petrified conglomerate have been washed down and their ruin covers, in sweeps of rain-fed grass, theatre and stadium and merchants' houses on the slope below.

As we drove there, in the steep shadow of Sipylus, by Manisa and Turgutlu, the valley widened and narrowed with bays and islands, and kept Hermus hidden by many screens of trees. The whole flat space was glowing with the metal-bright leaves of the small seedless sultana vines; with golden poplars in groups of three like Graces, and the foil of the jade-green olive; so that it looked as if the hidden river were flowing through a tapestry of a bright, repeated pattern, mile after mile. The road, dotted with new metal bridges and about to be dealt with by American bull-dozers, still had muddy patches: and little horses struggled with high carts brightly painted, their shafts joined by an arch above their shoulders in the central-Asian way, their bogged wheels turning in a smooth paste of mud.

The little towns we passed had domes and minarets in the places of their temples; cobbled streets and painted wood-trimmed houses; new cement buildings in the suburbs; and here and there in the fields, but very rarely, cottages, 'of reed or with roofs of reed', like the houses of Sardis burnt by the Ionians, when the crews of twenty Athenian ships walked over Tmolus, and the rebellion against Persia, and the trouble, began.[53]

After Turgutlu, a fair-sized little town, the valley widened into flat stretches surrounded by hills. The heights on the right lowered to an eroded labyrinth washed from Tmolus. The road, with ponds of rain-water and browsing flocks, took a turn, and showed the far high outline of Sardis, that the Lydian cavalry must have looked for often, as they quickened their paces and cantered in from summer warfare across the plain. Close by—under a poor village on high banks—Pactolus flows grey and loose among gravel, with ribs of water like any other stream. But in its upper reaches its course was visible down Tmolus, outlined through dark hillside shadows by golden maple against the pine. Where the hill slackened and it smoothed its waters, in a pastoral bay out of sight of houses, the temple of Cybele was excavated by Americans thirty years or so ago. Grass has had time to blur the ugly mounds that, on three sides, cup the ruin. They seem to hold its forgotten rites in a triple silence. The rectangular stylobate, the two columns seen complete by earlier travellers, the half-columns of the peristyle along the south, and half the great great entrance door, are there. The Lydians, if it was the Lydians, built it

with a Grecian respect for the landscape's meaning, so that
it seems to live at peace with the quality of the rocks and the
slant of the skyline, the roots of trees and depth of waters.
Surely the love of the Greeks for landscape is proved by their
care with all they ever placed in its foreground? One catches
one's breath when one comes upon the temple of Sardis in
the bay of Tmolus, as if afraid of disturbing that quietness,
that certainty known long ago and transmitted, so fragile
and so persistent that with any roughness it may vanish, but
will return when the visitor goes, when the temple and its
landscape reunite.

So we thought, and lunched respectfully, seated on blocks
of the wall among camomile flowers in the peace of the
sun, and then climbed up the slopes for an hour, to a grassy
ridge about 900 feet up that connects the acropolis with
Tmolus; and thence to the citadel under what is left of a
depraved Byzantine wall piled high with chunks of columns,
inscriptions, cornices—a massacre which Time in his turn is
eating, eroding the earth of the hill bit by bit and leaving the
wall's foundations in the air.

The Persians of Cyrus camped by the lower town here in
sight: and the fortress felt secure, for the image of a lion (long
before in the reign of Meles) had been taken round the walls
to safeguard them, in every place except the steepest. But a
Persian saw the way by which a Lydian soldier climbed down
the furrowed pudding-stone to pick up his helmet, and the
stronghold was taken in fourteen days.[54] Xenophon tells of
a feint, and a night climb to the acropolis led by a Persian
who had been a slave, and Cyrus entered in the morning,
about the middle of November, in 546 B.C. Croesus sent him
a message from his palace; and a guard was despatched as a
protection.[55] And this version of the story is more probable
than that of Herodotus who believes that Croesus was to

be burnt by his captors. The Persians were fire-worshippers and therefore not likely to pollute their purest element with the flesh of their enemies: but it is possible that he himself might try to end himself, and the fourteen noble Lydian youths with him, in the semitic tradition of Heracles, and Sardanapalus, or the later Dido. However this may be, and whether the pyre, if there was one, was put out by rain, or at the request of Cyrus—Croesus lived long enough to be a friend of the Persian king's with a bodyguard of 5,000 horsemen and 10,000 archers, and the revenues of Ecbatana[56] (Hamadan).

There is nothing left by which to picture the fortress in its greatness. All that remains are steep descending slopes whittled to ridges, where a block or two of white stone held askew waits for the winter rain to wash it down. Below the hollow ruin of erosion, green terraces lie where the town is buried; the road, the ancient and the modern, straightens across flat land towards eastern passes that make for Ankara. The plain lies fifteen miles or so across, with Hermus winding in loops from the pale lake of Gyges. At its eastern corner, near Adala village, the decisive battle with Cyrus before the siege was fought.

On the lake's near side and even paler in the sun than its waters, are the mounds of the Lydian kings. They make a hill landscape of their own, small as a map, on a sloping strip beneath widening mountains, under the same lake-coloured sky. There is no heap so eloquent as tumulus, for no farewell is quite as definite as that of the grass-growing earth.

From these ramparts, while the Persian sentries walked where now the sweet air scented with hay is blowing in empty space, the Lydian must often have looked across his valley, and seen the great mound of Alyattes and the many lesser ones about it, and thought of Croesus exiled in Ecbatana: and looked down and seen the uninterrupted caravans of Asia padding with the new-fangled Persian camel along the old road, halting at the end of the day at the same stages, that never faltered till they reached the sea.

16

Ephesus

Commerce and the Unexpected

Smyrna was an Amazon who took possession of Ephesus.

STRABO[1]

They were devoted to dancers and taken up with pantomimes, and the whole city was full of pipers, and full of effeminate rascals, and full of noise.

APOLLONIUS OF TYANA, 1st cent. A.D. by Philostratus.[2]

Few places can minister like the site of the temple in Ephesus to the triumph of Time. The process of building, ever richer and more magnificent, went on through centuries, till the stream of religion changed its bed, and offerings which had raised the second temple in the age of Alexander (or the third or fourth as the case may be), failed after the looting of the Goths six hundred years later.[3] Yet for eight or nine hundred years the riches of the faithful were brought to a shrine where an ancient goddess and her priestesses had become transformed into the Grecian Artemis with Amazons; and the final ruin when it came was less due to foreign barbarians than to Christian zeal, to the collector's fervour, and to Justinian, who transported what marble he could to Constantinople.

What is now left of one of the richest of sanctuaries is sunk in a swampy hollow: and indeed nothing is left except an ideal shape floating with known dimensions in the mind and anchored to a single block of existing masonry, the moulded base of the podium, by which alone the two latest floor levels of the temple can be defined. 'The whole of the altar, filled, one may say, with the works of Praxiteles';[4] the pillars given by Croesus;[5] the 127 pillars, some with figure-sculptured bases, the gifts of kings; all must be attached in the mind's eye to this poor piece to reconstruct what was once one of the Seven Wonders.

The tourist agency will tell you that it is not worth visiting; nor is it, if the tangible alone is to count in this world. But if we treat history as a friend, and ease its facts with love and knowledge, the imagination can supply much of truth; as in a palimpsest, the ghost of the temple of Artemis will stand in the swamp. Sad hillocks of archaeological mud surround it, where fig trees grow on the bare ground and a man is ploughing the earth of lives long past. A wandering cow rubs herself and flicks her ropy tail against the single stone, passive now with its meaning and purpose forgotten, yellow and delicate as an old woman's hand that lies idle among shapeless draperies of age. Every other vestige the restlessness of man has carried away, or the swamp has eaten: and the solitary podium itself was buried deep until Mr. Wood—building railways—became interested and started at the Magnesia gate, where the Sacred Way was known to go; and followed

Ephesus (Seljuk): The Great Street
From the Serapium in Ephesus (Seljuk)

Ephesus (Seljuk): The Church of St. John

Ephesus (Seljuk): The Walls of Justinian

The Coastline of Ephesus: Mt. Mycale in the Distance

it with excavation, until he was stopped by a field of standing corn. He could not wait till the harvest was over, but with a lucky guess found the road again on the farther side, and was led to his site and made his soundings. Six years he worked in a frock coat and pork-pie hat through the malarial summers, while a devoted and—luckily—well-to-do wife distributed quinine to the peasants—until the temple was found.[6] Its marbles had long ago been built by Justinian into the basilica of St. John on the hill nearby; and then again been taken in part by the Seljuks[7] for the smooth, mellow, windowless outer walls of their mosque a stone's throw below: and the ruins of the three faiths are in sight all together, on the slope of a small isolated hill.

D. G. Hogarth noticed that there were no traces of an Aegean civilization[8] when he excavated the oldest, 7th century, temple floor; and indeed the impression of Ephesus is more that of the Asiatic mainland than of the sea. Her fertile lands made markets or colonies abroad unnecessary, and she had the trade route and the goddess to bring her all she needed. When besieged by Croesus, the city on its little hill attached itself with a rope to the temple below, and surrendered and was spared;[9] and in his turn Lysimachus, when he burned the ships in harbour, saved the citizens and exempted the goddess from taxation.[10]

She is lost in Time. Pindar says 'that this sanctuary was founded by the Amazons during their campaign against Athens and Theseus. . . . But [it] was founded earlier by Coresus, a native of the country, and Ephesus, thought to have been a son of the river Cayster. The inhabitants of the land were partly Leleges, a branch of the Carians, but the greater number were Lydians. Others dwelt there for protection, as some women of the Amazons. But Androcles the son of Codrus [who led the colonists from Greece] chased the Leleges and Lydians from the higher town. Those who dwelt round the sanctuary had nothing to fear; they exchanged oaths of friendship and escaped warfare. . . .'[11] So Pausanias quotes, with a slight hesitation over the parentage of the founder: and even the mere possibility of a river-god as father shows a family well established.

For some reason now unknown, after the century and a half of friendship with Lydia, Croesus feared and attacked Ephesus; Pindar Melas, the then representative of the leading banking family, retired to Greece; and the citizens were removed from their defensible acropolis of Coresus (now a hillock on the plain close by the ruins of a later gymnasium), and were settled on the low land round the temple, at the foot of the old Lydian city on the hill. Here they stayed till Lysimachus in the third century, by flooding their houses with the city sewage in the rainy season,[12] induced them to move into his new town, built close to their earliest centre, where the chief ruins of Ephesus are spread, down a shallow quiet valley. Justinian shuffled them back to the Lydian hill, and built his walls with square towers and round, and the basilica of St. John where the saint lies buried. It was known as Ayyasoluk, or Altoluogo to the Genoese,[13] when they came to traffic in the Middle Ages, and was the centre of a small Seljuk dynasty, and never quite deserted. In 1306 the Catalans drove out the Turks, but in 1375 they were back, and wrote their date over the mosque built by Sultan Isa II of Aydin. And now the Byzantine walls and marble gateway; the white church-piers with the pink marble of smaller, older church walls visible between them; the tomb of St. John accessible but neglected down a subterranean passage under a slab of corrugated iron; the great Seljuk minaret and mosque with domes like eggs, smooth against the hill's slope below—all are tightly clustered together, like the landscape in a medieval book of hours. And that indeed is what it is, though the hours are centuries, and the book written on the transformations of earth.

Commerce and religion, feeding each other, seem to be the keynote of Ephesus altogether. Even now a new road is winding up the hill behind the walls of Lysimachus, and a hotel running up to shelter pilgrims who visit the house where Mary, seen by Catherine Maria Emmerich in a vision, is said to have died. A nakedly restored chapel over ancient foundations[14] nestles under a plane tree, in a bosom of hills, from which nothing is visible but high sunlight on sea: and the Mother of God must have been extremely robust to get up here through roadless scrub at the age— presumably—of ninety or near it. But it is all in the tradition of Ephesus, where the divinity of Christ was first proclaimed (in 431) and Mary first hailed as the Mother of God, and the first church dedicated to her was built while the temple of the Mother Goddess still stood. Religion was profitable and acrimonious. In the 8th century, during the iconoclastic controversy, 'many monks in the public square of Ephesus were given their choice of marriage or death'.[15] The scene of St. Paul and the goldsmiths is what one would expect, and fits with the history of Ephesus, which continued to be fanatical but international too. In the 9th century the Emperor Michael III gave permission to an Arab scholar and guide to visit the cave of the Seven Martyrs (Sleepers), which is still being visited today.[16] Two centuries later, the founding of monasteries was greatly encouraged by Lazarus the monk who lived for years on a pillar: and I think the habit of the Stylites was the result of a feeling for *economy,* since the numbers of pillars lying about and doing nothing must have been colossal. To touch religion here, both before Christianity and after, was to touch commerce, and therefore dangerous, since most people resent being threatened simultaneously in this world and the next.

In Ephesus indeed—what with the want of the Aegean influence noticed by Hogarth, and the strength of the eastern trade which flowed through Sardis, and an Asiatic preponderance both in population and religion—that Ionian miracle, the balance of East and West, seems to have been dangerously strained: an eastern hieratic rigidity prevails more and more.

Perhaps Pindar, son of Melas, felt this, when he retired from politics to the Peloponnesian independence:[17] and Heraclitus[18] felt it undoubtedly, speaking out of a bitter depth against the perverters, the 'night-walkers, Magians, Bakchoi, Lenai, and the initiated'—those who practise the 'unholy mysteries', and pray 'to these images, as if one were to talk to a man's house, knowing not what gods or heroes are'. 'They vainly purify themselves by defiling themselves with blood, just as if one who had stepped into the mud were to wash his feet in mud. Any man who marked him doing this would deem him mad.'

Heraclitus is the first of the bitter philosophers, and I think the reason is that the Lydian tinge in Ephesus was too strong for him. He turns his back on the delightful quality of the Ionians—their attention to the variety of life as it comes, with theory and practice together. To attain this quality one must live, after all, in a world which understands it, since it requires the intercourse of men. The ideas of Miletus were familiar to him, and Pythagoras and Xenophanes were not much older than he; yet he stood apart—not in ideas, but in his conduct of life. He renounced his ancestral kingship in his city, and washed his hands of those who sing ' the shameful phallic hymn', and found his truth in the solitude of hills. And though this has been attributed to a morose temper, it seems to me that it is just as probably explained by an uncongenial atmosphere in a town given over to a Lydian commercial religion. (And it may be noted that Sardis, entirely Lydian, was unable to produce a philosopher at all.)

Heraclitus, like his own Sybil, '. . . with raving lips uttered things mirthless, unbedizened, unperfumed, reaching over a thousand years, thanks to the god in him'. His theory taught a fundamental Unity, kept straight as it were by the continual pull of opposites, a harmony produced by tensions—as the note of the lyre is sounded by the holding and pulling in opposite directions of the string. Where this strife stops, is stagnation and death. And we may use this picture for the East and West tensions that produced Ionia: and left her to collapse when, through the preponderance of either, the tension failed.

> 'Men do not know how what is at variance agrees with itself. It is an attunement of opposite tensions, like that of the bow and the lyre.'

> 'God is day and night, winter and summer, war and peace, surfeit and hunger; but he takes various shapes, just as fire, when it is mingled with spices, is named according to the savour of each.'

> 'It rests by changing.'

> 'Even the posset separates, if it is not stirred.'

There is a note of passion and greatness in all that Heraclitus has left. His mere meteorology is wrapped in a universal atmosphere, a spiritual robe.

'If there were no sun it would be night, for all the other stars could do.' Whatever he meant by it, the whole of love and life is in the phrase.

> 'The sun is new every day.'

'The sun will not overstep his measures; if he does, the Erinyes, the handmaids of Justice, will find him out.'

It is a quality of great writing that it adapts itself to more than was ever in the writer's mind—and perhaps that too is an illustration of the philosopher's fundamental Unity. But in any case it is a mistake to think, as one is apt to do with the classics, or the Elizabethan English, that some inevitable *luck* made their language: for words are but drops pressed out of the lives of those who lived them.

'The limit of dawn and evening is the Bear; and opposite the Bear is the boundary of bright Zeus.'

However far we may now look beyond that boundary, the concrete simple radiance remains, and could never come from someone who has not looked at a horizon.

And so it is in the deeper snatches of Heraclitus, that bring down to us, brokenly, the passionate, selfless seeking, the faith in the ever-living fire, the reconcilement of unity and strain, the 'thought by which all things are steered through all things'.

In the fire, into which all passes away and is born, where 'the way up and the way down is one and the same', and 'mortals are immortals, and immortals are mortals, the one living the other's death and dying the other's life', equilibrium and change are kept and produced by continual tension, so that 'strife is justice and all things come into being and pass away through strife'.

'Homer was wrong in saying: Would that strife might perish from among gods and men! He did not see that he was praying for the destruction of the universe; for, if his prayer were heard, all things would pass away.'

And it follows that 'To god all things are fair and good and right, but men hold some things wrong and some right', and 'would not have known the name of justice if these (injustices) were not'.

Beyond this universe of strain, the eternal unity existed in his mind, but how the two were joined I cannot make out, not being a philosopher—and probably it is just that the right fragment has not reached us. Yet: 'the wise is one only', and 'wisdom is apart from all'. One divine law feeds all human laws, and 'prevails as much as it will, and suffices for all things with something to spare'; and therefore 'those who speak with understanding must hold fast to what is common to all, as a city holds fast to its law, and even more strongly'. In this Unity we are awake or living; and asleep, or dead, in separation:

'For the waking share[19] one world, but the sleeping turn aside each into a world of his own.'

It is the basic foundation of mystic faith, and Heraclitus shares the passion of the prophets; and also their singular impatience with human deficiencies—which he himself, after all, has been explaining as a part of the essential, universal strain. Just as if he had not been warning us that we may stop the whole machine by all being good at once, he inveighs against those 'knowing not how to listen nor how to speak', who are 'estranged from that with which they have most constant intercourse', whose 'eyes and ears are bad witnesses . . . if they have souls that understand not their language'. This is less the voice of Ionia than of the Hebrew prophets, of Ruskin too or Carlyle: all embittered by the business-like quality of the civilization around them.

Material prosperity clung to Ephesus under one domination after the other through centuries. She issued electron staters of her own as early as the reigns of Croesus' father and grandfather: and Croesus himself, as a young prince, came here to find his mercenaries and borrow their pay from Pamphaes of Priene.[20] The Phrygian merchant is described by Hipponax, in the 7th century, venturing down from the interior (where the Greeks rarely went to trade)—risking capture down the long Maeander road. 'And if they catch the Phrygians, bargaining in pidgin lingo, they sell them for slaves.'[21] Hipponax was born in Ephesus: its mixed language, Greek-Phrygian-Lydian-Old Anatolian, breaks through in his lampoons. He has no illusions over the commercial quality of his religion. As early as the 5th century B.C. the holy temple was receiving deposits on account, and lending money secured by mortgages in Sardis.[22] Priene and Miletus declined, but Ephesus continually flourished. In 499 B.C. the harbour was silting so heavily that ships bringing troops to attack the Persians in Sardis were unable to disembark them in the port: but, liberated from Persia by Alexander in 334 B.C., the city fell to his general Lysimachus, who made her the capital of Asia Minor for half a century and forcibly altered the site of the silted harbour. She was Sulla's headquarters, and the station where Caesar, pursuing Pompey, stayed to receive the submission of Asia: and Mark Antony wintered here with Cleopatra, having extracted ten years' taxes from the city in advance.[23]

In the early days of Christianity she was still 'the largest trading centre in Asia this side of Taurus',[24] as St. Paul had found her; famous, like Sardis, for perfumes and wool, and for the first Christian church, mentioned in the acts of the council of Ephesus.

These later histories are beyond my journey, but one cannot avoid feeling them in Ephesus, for the lightness of Ionia has vanished: it is ever Lydia, or Persia, or Rome. All is luxury,

The Northern Slopes of Mycale (Samsun Dagh)
The Site of Panionium: Samos to the Right

Priene (Gülbahche): The Theatre

and Anacreon's simple garlands are forgotten. Timotheus, even in the 4th century B.C., for his ode to Artemis, was paid 1,000 pieces of gold. And an ancient brutality continues to flourish under the Roman peace. The first gladiator show in Asia Minor was given here by Lucullus (in 71–70 B.C.);[25] and Timotheus, describing the barbarian foeman, 'dweller in the pasture-lands of Celaenae'—held up by his long hair, praying for mercy, and for leave to go home to Sardis, Susa or Ecbatana, makes him invoke Artemis of Ephesus as *his* goddess and protectress.[26]

With this, there is a comfortable, an imperturbable security among the ruins in the valley where the city of Lysimachus slopes down under the vestiges of Rome. Even the view is not, as in the other cities of Ionia, a creature of the imagination, a vision to catch the heart with what can never be seen: enclosed and pastoral, the outlines of trees are in the place of the waves of the bay now filled by the delta of Cayster. The gymnasiums, the theatres, the library built with double walls (against damp), fastidiously by the son of Celsus in memory of his father; the agora with gate dedicated by his freedmen in gratitude to Augustus; the half-excavated colonnades two columns deep and the small squares of shops; the paved road, 40 feet wide, the widest in Asia Minor, laid to the sea with statues and porticoes by Arcadius while the shadow of Alaric hung over Rome; the steps in which it ends, and the theatre, the huge Serapium, the capitals and drums of columns spread like limbs of a dead Goliath on the ground—one would spend weeks among them, dreaming contentedly, asking few questions, for it is the human world, the Italian world enriched by Asia—built with money and tangible religions, easy shows (the theatre holds 25,000 spectators), and the Roman comfort of baths. What is missing? Curiosity perhaps? The world shut out by too many lifeless objects? The early magic, the

morning dew, has gone. Heraclitus knew it, walking embittered among the scented hills, laying his works on the temple
altar for posterity, dying alone. That tightness which he saw
holding all things in tune, the balance of soul and body on the
watershed of the universe, had slipped in his own city: and
the notion of the final readjustment comforted him as little as
it does most philosophers when the matter is brought down
to every day.

'It is hard to fight with one's heart's desire. Whatever it
wishes to get, it purchases at the cost of soul.' So he writes,
loosening his hold of the travelling world; and adds that 'every
beast is driven to pasture with blows', thinking no doubt of
the wooden-headedness of the Ephesians. But the Ionian light
plays and glitters through the cracks of his darkened door.
'If you do not expect the unexpected,' it says 'you will not
find it; for it is hard to be sought out and difficult.' Perhaps
that is the secret; comfort and commerce grew thick and the
unexpected was hidden, and life ceased to glow—and he who
has the Unexpected on his side is happier than the Ephesians.
Beyond life itself it beckons with 'such things as men look
not for nor dream of'. Ill at ease in his days, Heraclitus is
the most modern of the philosophers. His unhappiness and
his modernity come, I think, from circumstances very like
ours. Us too the tension of life has tilted dangerously towards
the material side of the watershed, disabling the balance of
our soul; so that we are constrained at intervals to leave the
social structure of our time, and turn away for our stability
to breathe in quiet, hoping for the Unexpected.

17

The Panionium

Symbols

The Seven Sages: 'Some make them meet at the Pan-Ionian festival.'[1]

The rainy season had started when I crossed from Ephesus to the Maeander. Every day, waves of blackhearted clouds with ragged plumes came tumbling from the west, stretched themselves on the smooth invisible floor made by the draught of the valley, and hid the heights of Messogis, Mycale and Samos, the bony finger of the hand of Tmolus. Towards evening, however, a lift would often come, darkness would wrap the slopes reflected in an angry hyacmthine sea; and daylight passed out like a Mrs. Siddons of the sky with the lightnings of tragedy about her.

Mr. Wilkinson kindly took me from Ephesus along the coast, and we lunched at Kushadasi, the medieval Scalanova, which is the only bathing resort of all the incomparable beaches of the coastline south of Smyrna: and it is a very

unobtrusive little resort at that—a tiny Turkish town with
the odd reminiscence of an English High Street produced by
bow windows, and a Turkish gatehouse closing across it. It
is built on what, in the days of Herodotus, was still open sea;
but by the 14th century A.D., the port of Ania had grown
up close by and was a centre for Byzantine and Latin pirates.
The Seljuk and later Turkish conquerors of Ephesus presently
followed their example on a grander scale. The Catalans and
the Genoese and Pisan ruffians *'de Lombardia per discordia ex-
pulsis',* sided with the Turks, and established another pirate
centre, also called Altoluogo.[2] There is still a Genoese or
Venetian castle, on the 'Island of Birds' which gives the town
its Turkish name, and a fine dilapidated khan with double
tiers of arcades in a Latin battlemented shell. But the Turkish Altoluogo (the ancient Lydian-Byzantine city of Ephesus)
remained the headquarters of commerce, which one could
reach by donkey from the coast, and where, in a bazaar in the
church of St. John, one could visit the saint's tomb by pay-
ing. When Sir Charles Fellows rode through Kushadasi a little
over a hundred years ago, he found the harbour tenantless,
and the town, then one of the largest in the region, beautiful
but isolated by the plague.[3]

The great bay of Mycale has the lands of Teos and Notium
on the N.W. skyline, and Samos in the west. Another Latin
castle, now but a mound with poplars, breaks the flat
shore.

As we made for the southern arm, we left history medieval
or modern, and came towards the centre of Ionia. The solitary
headlands of Mycale tilt down in forest to deep water, and
somewhere on their northern flank the twelve cities that
stood between Miletus and Phocaea built their temple and
gathered by sea or land round the altar of the Heliconian
Poseidon.[4]

Herodotus in his driest manner observes that 'to say that these [cities] are more Ionian than the others, or a whit better born, is great folly, seeing that not the least portion of them are Abantes from Euboea, who have no part even in the name of Ionians, and that the Minyae from Orchomenos are mingled with them, and Cadmeans, and Dryopes, and a portion from Phocis, and Molossians and Arcadians [who are Pelasgian], and Epidaurians [who are Dorian], and many other peoples. And even those who set forth from the town hall in Athens and consider that they are the highest born of the Ionians, brought no wives with them to the colony but took Carian women. . . . Howbeit, seeing that they cleave to the name more than the other Ionians, let them be called the pure-born Ionians' . . . [5] It is like a conversation by Jane Austen, and there is indeed a sort of county flavour in the care of the Greeks for their descent. But the fact remains that the Heliconian Poseidon had shrines in both Miletus and Teos, and had been worshipped in Helice of Achaia before the Ionians, leaving their first Peloponnesian home, reached even Attica, let alone Asia Minor. [6]

Out of the questions I should ask Herodotus, if I could have an hour's conversation with him, his real opinion about foreigners would be among the first: and I suspect that one might find it to be a very English opinion, that is to say that he would be interested in what is remote, and pleased with its variety, and safe in the consciousness that his own was best. If one's own lot is not best, one ought obviously to have altered it long ago: and as the Greeks spent so much time and energy in discovering the good life, it would be depressing for them to think that other people, with less mental effort, had succeeded in finding a better. One should therefore, I think, look upon this quiet confidence as a virtue, though dangerous, dangerous because it easily slips from the rightness of self to the wrongness of others, forgetting that every creature, including oneself, can have a different rightness of their own.

While, therefore, we are not necessarily better than others, it seems to me equally narrow-minded to think others unreasonably better than ourselves, and this is the fault of a governessy, an ethical, a falsely theological simplification, the conceit that only one black and one white exist. By an intrusion of ethics where they are not required, we are put into the absurd position of assuming the Absolute to be within our reach.

From such impoverishment the existence of many gods, but especially divine Curiosity, preserved the Ionians; for the object of curiosity stands in an atmosphere of its own, firm in its rights, a creature whose particular laws of being are recognized, whether good or bad. The respect which curiosity inspires makes it more welcome than charity. It makes us not only in love with, but also interested in our neighbour; and if we cannot be both, then interest is the more important, for that will prevent our doing things for him not in his way but in ours. And curiosity is of course the negation of missionary zeal: for we cannot wish to alter, or do more than move in its own direction the thing we truly care for.

Once divested of missionary virus, the cult of our own gods gives no offence. It would be a peaceful age if this were recognized, and religion, Christian, communist or any other, were to rely on practice and not on conversion for her growth.

And if one had to distinguish the chief ingredients of distress in the modern world, I think I should point to this impassioned desire to convert, which makes us forget that our business is the exercise of our own faith and nothing more. Whatever intolerance the Ionians may have indulged in (and all one reads in Greek literature points to a serene and unruffled contempt of the foreigner), it was not made bitter by the wish to proselytize the opinions of others, nor made ridiculous by the neglect of their own.

They fostered their symbols, and hedged them about and made them exclusive, realizing them as cups for the sacredness and happiness of life, wrought for them by their fathers through uncounted lives and fitted by many changes not for anyone in general but for themselves. After the battle of Plataea, 'when the Greeks enquired of the Oracle what sacrifices they should make, the god replied that they should build an altar to Zeus Eleutherius, and not sacrifice upon it till they had extinguished all fire, as being defiled by the Barbarians all through the country, and kindle a pure flame thereon from the common hearth at Delphi'.[7]

And though their civilization grew, as ours does, and every other, by the addition of novelty, yet they made even that their own by limiting it to times and places and occasions. Out of the Phrygian music and primitive dances of god and shepherds, they built the dithyramb and invented a new chorus to dance round the flute-player and the altar where the bull was sacrificed with ancient rites. Then three winners would carry away an ox, a jar of wine, or a goat anointed with wine-lees; while the chorus grew till, gradually, in the day of Simonides and later, it numbered fifty men or more, becoming instrumental, with less of dance and song, spreading and enriching itself, from its earliest 7th-century fragment in Ionia[8] to the great Athenian tragedians.[9]

Symbolic too were the daphnephorica or laurel-bearing songs adopted by the Mytilenians and Simonides and Pindar—written for processions led by a handsome boy, the chosen priest of the year, followed by maidens who carried the pungent branches. These maiden songs with the scent of their hillsides still about them and the pleasant freedom of women, were common to Aeolian, Ionian and Dorian.

The laurel too presided over the Athenian paean, when the wine was mixed with water in three bowls and a ladle of each poured to the ground, to Olympian Zeus, to the Heroes, and to Zeus the Saviour: and each man sang it, holding a twig. If the feast went on, and a fresh bowl was required, the paean was sung again; and sometimes again at the end, by the host alone; while a hired flute-girl played.

Not feast days only, but every pattern of daily life was shaped with its appropriate ritual and song—'the pipe notes fit for herds of cows and oxen, or what agreed with the goats, what were pleasing to flocks of sheep . . . : the dance of the wine press, the cutting and gathering . . . carrying of the baskets, then the treading . . . in the press, the tunning of the wine into the butts. . . .'[10] There were the mill-songs and weavers' songs, the reapers' and herding songs, the bath-men's song, and one for women winnowing, and lullabies and songs of wailing: and at Athens they used to sing, over the wine, the laws of Charondas.[11] So they were able to say that the life of a city was altered by the altering of its songs: and this pattern one may still find among simple and imaginative people—among the Beduin for instance, with the ritual of their coffee-making, or the things they croon to their camels. "We help them," I was once told, "when they are tired, with our song." Even with us, the habit of grace before meals, the taking off of hats when a funeral passes, dressing for dinner, the opening of doors to women, are all small details made to enhance the sacred quality of living.

This was the background to the gatherings of the Panion-ium, surrounded by many picnics on the grass, and gaiety of a non-religious sort. Anacreon there, tipsy, has come down to us, with a wreath on his head, stumbling against and abusing a nurse who carries in her arms the future ruler of Rhodes, one of the seven Sages, the beautiful Cleobulus, the Carian. His grave is on the headland of Lindos; and his daughter, Cleobulina, was like him, a poetess famous for riddles—a poor claim to fame—but she is more interestingly praised by Thales of Miletus for 'admirable judgement, a political mind, a sweet disposition, and her father's rule is the lighter for it'.[12]

Mostly the Panionium has come down to us as I saw it with storms about its headland—for here the Greeks gathered when in trouble. Here they decided to send envoys to Sparta under the first threat of Cyrus,[13] and again when Harpagus had conquered their cities, and Bias of Priene advised them to sail all together to Sardinia and found one free city for all.[14] Here again they gathered, in the revolt of Miletus, before the battle of Lade, and determined to fight it out by sea.[15] Until the Athenian Empire interrupted them, through good and bad fortune they continued round the altar; until the danger from their constant wars became too great and the festival was removed towards Ephesus in the early 4th century B.C. Alexander reinstated it, and it was still held in the Poseidon temple—though in an intermittent way—when Rome came to Asia Minor.[16] But as for its beginning, little is known, except that between the 9th and 8th centuries Melia, an Ionian city on the slope of Mycale, was destroyed by Miletus, Priene, Colophon, and Samos; and its lands were partitioned and the temple erected,[17] causing a dispute between Samos and Priene of over 500 years, eventually settled by Rome.

And now the very site is only vaguely known, and even Mr. Wilkinson had not visited it, and Mr. Cook, who had explored it from Athens, said very little about it. The promontory finishes in steep, lonely slopes of bear, pig, and panther, which the soldiers explore, and gaze across the narrow strait at Samos. Two villages only are there on the landward side, Davutlar and Güzel Chamli, and with them the flat lands end that are fit for ploughing. And the only modern guide I could find was Ximenes, who mentions the temple site as being close to two chapels, St. Nicholas and Panaghia, in ruins; while another cloister, Panaghia Kourouniotisa, is described on a ridge of Mycale, where the track from Priene runs.

It would be fun to walk or ride from Priene, four or five hours, over the shoulder of Mycale (the Samsun Dagh), and to drop from monastery ruin to ruin along what must have been the Pagan as well as the Christian pilgrims' road. But I had a jeep and a driver from Kushadasi, and we took off doubtfully on a rainy day, down a dripping hillside from the pass where the main road tops the ridge above one of the finest bays in Ionia, between the Cayster delta and the Maeander.

The wind darkened the sea and made the olives of the slopes look like aigrettes of silver. It also reminded me with every puff that the jeep had been carrying fish. The driver was new, obliging, and gay, but not expert like Ahmet with my Turkish, which is a tabloid language where every word has to be expanded by the listener. It was soon better not to use words at all down the track we followed, shared with a stream new-born the night before. The slopes around were trickling with these wrinkled little water-courses, crumbling the substance of the hills to the deltas below. The hillside was luckily too steep for mud. Hawthorn, wild pears, bracken and broom and brambles, cyclamen everywhere, were glistening with raindrops; and the scent of the earth came, sparkling, whenever the strength of the fish would let it.

We sank steeply to Chifarli Köy, and straightened out across three or four tottery wooden bridges to Davutlar, surrounded among hedges by a landscape like the Highlands —gloomy slopes ascending into cloud.

The village peace was shaken by the arrival, on a rainy day, of a woman without a language alone in a jeep and asking for ruins of which no one knew the existence. The inhabitants gathered from the doors under plane trees of their muddy little square and took me to a very young Müdïr who spoke French. He came from Stambul and was interested in Civilization in an abstract way, and in a new rifle, but not particularly in ruins; and we were drifting towards that deadlock so hard to bridge, the meeting of two worlds that will not mingle, the official and the gypsy—when a Friend appeared, strolling into the office and picking up the new rifle with a caressing hand to examine its markings.

He was evidently of some local standing. He had a firm mouth, frequent in the villages—not full and unreliable nor yet closed thin in a bitter line over its own weakness, but a manly, natural, reassuring mouth of the sort that women like because they know it is going to get its own way without any fuss. With my eye upon it, I punctuated the Effendi's Turkish stream with such monosyllables as I thought might help, and the Friend presently left and reappeared with the oldest inhabitant, who said he remembered a cloister on the way to Güzel Chamli in the days before the Greeks were destroyed.

I was hampered by Strabo who is not very helpful about the Panionium because he mentions so many sites in the same neighbourhood, all of which are now unknown.

'After the Samian strait,' he says, 'as one sails to Ephesus, one comes, on the right, to the seaboard of the Ephesians; and a part of this seaboard is held by the Samians. First on the seaboard is the Panionium, lying three stadia [about a quarter of a mile] above the sea. . . . Then comes Neapolis . . . then Pygela, a small town, with a temple of Artemis Munychia, founded by

Agamemnon and inhabited by a part of his troops; for it is
said that some of his soldiers became afflicted with a disease
of the buttocks and were called "diseased buttocks" . . . and
that the place thus received the appropriate name. Then comes
the harbour called Panormus, with a temple of the Ephesian
Artemis [whence Hadrian used to be rowed in his barge]; and
then the city Ephesus. On the same coast, slightly above the sea,
is also Ortygia . . . the mythical scene of the birth [of Apollo and
Artemis] and . . . above the grove lies mount Solmissus where,
it is said, the Curetes . . . with the din of their arms frightened
Hera . . . and helped to conceal the birth.'[18]

All this was not really helpful, and if what is now Davutlar
was possibly Pygela, the less said about its origin the better, even if my Turkish had been equal to explaining it. I
looked round the piazza, with two Byzantine marbles from
the monasteries but nothing earlier under its trees; and sat
passive while the Müdür, and the Friend, the oldest inhabitant and one or two more climbed into the jeep, and we
drove towards Chamli along foothills keeping parallel to the
swampy shore.

There was not a vestige of the monastery which the oldest
inhabitant remembered; but one could see what remained of
Kourouniotisa high up on a spur above, and make out the
track which was doubtless used by the citizens of Priene, as
they travelled from the south slope of Mycale to celebrate
the sacrifice which was their city's prerogative. The great
slopes were clear now, blue as ink and sodden with rain,
with Chamli tucked into the last gentleness of the ground,
a small village under plane trees, with a Greek-built house,
now the mayor's, finely decorated, and a poor minaretless
mosque to show its present poverty and past well-being. After
some searching and enquiry, the two ruined Greek churches
mentioned by Ximenes were found, some ten minutes farther

on where the track ends in a patch of rubble overgrown by brambles, on the very edge of the sea. It is the site of the temple, or very near it, for the flat ground ends here; a terrace, where a new house lodges a lieutenant and some guards, looks at Samos across a sea that lies most of the day in shadow, under the steep wooded cliffs of Mycale.[19] Perhaps a few of the church's stones are old; the top bricks of a Byzantine arch show just above the level of the ground; the lieutenant's horse was feeding in a ruined apse, livid as a wound, which he hesitated to let me enter, out of delicacy for what my feelings about a sacred place might be.

We were a poor little company brought together without cohesion in a historical setting twice emptied of its meaning; nothing that mattered, either Pagan, or Christian remained. But we sat over coffee and talked to the mayor, and presendy another old inhabitant appeared, and remarked that he could lead us to a *pillar,* only fifteen minutes' walk away.

I know these fifteen minutes, but the afternoon was young; and we climbed again into the jeep, and left it in Chamli, and—adding the mayor and the lieutenant to our party— walked due south up a fold of Mycale, climbing steadily for half an hour, till we came to an easing of the slope, and to cornfields strewn familiarly with the red potsherds of a past habitation, all held by a dip in the slant of the mountain, as if it were a bay. Here somewhere the pillar must be, in a place covered with the thickets that grow out of fallen houses.

The two villagers, scattering and hunting, went into the labyrinth and shouted at intervals, and another half-hour went by. Nothing but worn indistinguishable stones were found, and the basin of a fountain that might have belonged to any place or time. The site was probably a monastery village along the pilgrim way.

The afternoon was now wearing and we were about to give up, when a shout of victory came from the tangled woods. I followed the voice, pushing over half-buried stones and under boughs, and there in a green twilight reached a chapel, with roofless apse. The pillar, grey mottled marble, more ancient than all that surrounded it, lay aslant, half out of the ground, smoothly bright and alien in that place where, for centuries, only twilight and darkness had marked the changing of its days; and it moved me strangely. It too was a symbol, forgotten even before the stones that surrounded it were ruined, and now doubly lost, yet it still shone with its self-contained completeness, while its meaning, transformed, unrecognized but alive in innumerable columns, serving new faiths and unexpected races, was out and efficient in the daylight of the world.

18

Priene

Greatness in Art

Virtue consists, not in avoiding wrong-doing, but in having no wish thereto.

DEMOCRITUS OF ABDERA, 5th cent. B.C.[1]

Men perish because they cannot join the beginning to the end.

ALCMAN OF CROTON, early 5th cent. B.C.[2]

Eight miles from Söke, a little town blossoming with prosperity and cotton, along a road that once followed (with a few old paving stones left), the ins and outs of the Latmian shore, and now keeps beside the flat delta of Maeander—what remains of Priene lies high up in the sun. I climbed and entered the little city by its eastern gate, and walked along a level, above the ruins of its houses.

The entry to the theatre is so unobtrusive that one scarcely notices it. Without preparation, it is there. The straight stone shafts that support the proscenium are standing; there is a round base for a statue; a ramp of grey stone slopes down with seats fanning out in something more than a semicircle—the Greek and not the Roman fashion; and one steps suddenly between the seats and the proscenium, into the orchestra, a small grassy space light with daisies, enclosed in a semicircle where six stone arm-chairs for the most important people are evenly spaced with an altar among them. The seats behind rise in their tiers; the narrow shallow steps of gangways cut them at intervals; and I felt that I was interrupting—that actors and audience, like a flight of shy birds, had fled in the very instant of my stepping across their threshold with my feet still shod in Time. I felt this with a power and a strangeness not to be described; with tears on my cheeks in a sudden pang of surprise and excitement and wonder; and I lingered in the little theatre as if I were a person in the legend, who is given one glimpse of a world which appears to last for seconds only, though all the expanses of time are packed there.

There was perfect quiet in the theatre. The carvings on the stone were so sharp and delicate that the hand that worked them still seemed alive. They were simple patterns of alternate ivy leaves, placed only where they were required, on the piers of the entrance, on the six chairs with their arm-rests and cushions and footstools cut in stone. There was no seeking for praise, through things worked upon beyond their own necessities for their effect on other people—where the superfluous begins; for nothing here was superfluous. The whole city was built in the flower of the Hellenistic age, and to that its rich austerity belonged.

What was the secret? *Respect* perhaps, so closely tied to love? Respect for what gives itself, and is therefore vulnerable, whether it be a human being or a piece of stone?

A gratitude that inspires fastidiousness, a longing to keep intact in its own dignity the object or the being that has helped one to create and to become?

That so subtle a scruple can transmute itself into stone and stay there, is magic; and no conscious effort of the craftsman, nothing but the feeling itself, can leave that mark. Where it exists, it is definite, and every true artist will recognize it across any bridge of time. Without it there is neither sincerity nor greatness. It is a sharing partnership, both giving and taking—a marriage in terms of human life—a tender thankfulness for a benefit received and a forgetfulness of self in the interest of another; and it reaches through the depths of being to that which Heraclitus thought of as Fire and we think of as Love.

The Greek walls whose blocks are finely cut all round so that even what is hidden is beautiful; the backs of Venetian palaces carved with marble cornices and mouldings on narrow blind canals where no one goes; the Greek siting of their buildings fitted to the unevenness of the land as they found it; the rich cloth that is mended because it cannot be replaced; the road that winds about with the landscape instead of cutting through it, however uneconomic or inconvenient— all these make an intercourse and harmony between two things that contribute to each other, the creator and his creature, the receiver and giver, the artist and his stone.

The enchantment of Priene continued all over the hill shoulder where, high up under the sheer cliff of its acropolis, in the 4th century B.C., the little town was built.

Even by the end of the 5th century the silt of Maeander seems to have made the older Priene inaccessible to warships; a century later the inhabitants moved several hundred feet up their hillside and constructed, apparently with Athenian help, the city that now remains.[3] A port was given by Alexander, some three miles south-west of the town, where many people settled: and Alexander also commuted their tribute from ships to money,[4] and helped with the finishing of the great temple to Athena—admired by Pausanias.[5]

The first Priene was said to have been founded in the 10th century B.C., by Aepytus the son of Neleus (from Athens and originally from Pylos) and later by Philotas who brought colonists from Thebes. From its very beginning it was surrounded by trouble. Ephesus helped it against the Carians, the Lydian Ardys captured it, its citizens were carried off by Mazares to Persian slavery, its boundary on Mycale was a constant subject of dispute with Samos. The new city too was almost immediately a prey to a local tyrant, and attacked by Magnesians and the 'natives of the neighbourhood'[6] from whom Lysimachus liberated it; and a long dispute went on for decades with Miletus over the Maeander channel, eventually decided in favour of Priene by Rome. The chief source of trouble was always the Maeander river of whose two streams the northern one flowed nearby. Its irresponsibility was so clearly recognized that lawsuits could be brought against it, for damages to the riverain fields, payable out of the toll of its ferries: and as early as the 2nd century B.C., a passage had to be cut for both Miletus and Priene through the mud.[7]

The river now flows down the southern side of its wide bed, in sight yet far from Priene, wandering among marsh and cotton, with patches of water or shadows. Miletus lies on flattened ridges, and beyond—on the Carian hills—are the clouds' rounded thrones. The sea, which in the days of Strabo was already four miles, is now ten miles away.

Priene declined, but still existed as a bishopric in Christian days, and the names of its bishops appear in the early Councils.[8] It must always have held its quiet perfection. In the 2nd century B.C., the record of one of its diplomats shows him

Priene (Gülbahche): The Theatre

Priene (Gülbahche): The Council House

travelling to Miletus, Magnesia, Samos, Tralles, Alexandria in the Troad, Ephesus, Mylasa, Erythrae, Sardis, Colophon, Alabanda, and as far as Syria on the city's business;[9] and the Artists of Dionysus were established here by Mark Antony and Cleopatra in the winter which they spent before Actium in Ephesus and Samos.

The town—in the 4th century, and later—was built by Pithios, inspired by Hippodamus of Miletus. Its buildings were painted, and everything, even statues, were coloured.[10] The private houses, climbing up the hill, with steep steps or lanes to divide them, opened to inner courts approached through a corridor or colonnade from the front door. Sometimes a vestibule was built with columns, and the three chief rooms at the back of the court—for living, dining, and sleeping, opened on to it in the shade. Cooking was usually done on a portable stove in the vestibule, and there were livingrooms above, on the second story, and sometimes smaller rooms on the other three sides of the court. Plants and herbs and blossoming trees grew in spaces between the slabs of the courtyard floor.[11]

Thanks to the labour of German archaeologists, who excavated about 340 houses in Priene, one can move intimately up and down its tilted streets in the full eye of the sun. One can climb to the temple of Demeter, the highest of all, with only a piece of its south-east corner standing—sheltered under pines, and the acropolis sheer above, with the zigzags of paths still visible, cut in the rock face. From the vast platform of Athena one can look down and see the whole town, the west gate where the road from Alexander's harbour came in, flagged with white slabs of stone between the richer houses, to the wide expanse of the agora, its shops and a first row of column bases still before them. There the main street turns to the corner of the Prytaneum, and an altar burned continuous fire; and nearby is the meeting-place of the city council, a rectangle of stone seats descending as in a theatre, with gangways at the corners and an altar in the midst. Here again is the intimacy, the strangely moving quality of Priene: the city fathers might barely have risen and left, so strong is the sense of their presence, though the grass grows in the crannies of the seats.

In the gymnasium the washing troughs of yellow marble are still there; and the marble mouths of lions through which the water spouted. In a long stadium below, the spaces are marked for the discus throwers, and the seats are in the enjoyment of the view, facing out from the landward side. Stripped to their very essence, like the music of Bach, shreds of walls of the temple remain, and of the town—with blocks laid double and a hollow space between. There are three gates, unobtrusive and discreet with no Roman grandeur, made for what they are asked to do, like everything else in Priene.

The battle of Mycale was fought close by, on the afternoon of the same day as the battle of Plataea in 479 B.C.[12]

The Persian fleet had put in from Samos, anxious, before the Greek navy overtook them, to join the 60,000 landsmen stationed on the promontory. Under a temple of Demeter they 'drew the ships up and surrounded them with a fence of stones and of timbers from garden trees which they hewed down; and they planted sharp stakes round about the fence. And so they were ready for a siege'.

But the Greeks, vexed not to find them in Samos, made towards Mycale, and Leotychides, the Spartan commander, 'sailed along in his ship, as close to the shore as he could keep, and made proclamation to the Ionians by means of a crier, saying: "Men of Ionia . . . when we join battle, let each of you remember freedom first, and secondly the password, which is Hera."' And:

'the Greeks brought their ships to land, and went forth upon the shore, and set themselves in array. And when the Persians saw the Greeks preparing themselves for battle, then first they took from the Samians their weapons, because they suspected that they favoured the Greeks, for indeed, when Athenian captives . . . were brought in the ships of the barbarians, the Samians ransomed them all, and gave them provision for the journey, and sent them back to Athens. . . . Moreover, they [the Persians] appointed the men of Miletus to keep the passes which led into the mountain tops of Mycale . . . so that they might be out of the camp. So by these means the Persians guarded themselves against those Ionians who they deemed would surely do some mischief if they got the power: but as for themselves, they joined their plaited shields together to make a fence. . . . So the Greeks and the barbarians were eager for battle, seeing the isles and the Hellespont were as prizes offered'.

The battle was fought some four or nine miles west of the later Priene,[13] where the shore was evidently gentle, for the Athenian wing faced a plain: the Spartans higher up, crossing a torrent, came more slowly over mountainous ground while their allies were already engaged.

'As long as the plaited shields of the Persians yet stood, they defended themselves and had nowise the worst of the battle: but at length the Athenians and their neighbours . . . thrust asunder the plaited shields, and rushed all together upon the Persians, who withstood them and for a great while defended themselves, but in the end fled within the wall. . . . And when the wall was taken also, the barbarians thought no more of resistance, but turned to flight, all except the Persians, who yet fought, here a few and there a few. . . . But the Samian soldiers in the Median camp, whose weapons had been taken from them, when at the outset they saw the battle doubtful did all they were able to help the Greeks. And when the other Ionians saw that the Samians had made a beginning, then they also rebelled and fell upon the barbarians. And the men of Miletus who had been appointed by the Persians to keep the passes for the sake of their escape . . . did the very contrary of that which was appointed them: for they guided them in their flight by other roads which led among the enemy, and were found in the end to be their bitterest foes. And thus Ionia rebelled for the second time against the Persians.'[14]

No doubt the people of Priene—wherever in the neighbourhood their town may then have been—had men stationed on the vantage-point of their later acropolis, and watched the Persians cutting down their fruit trees, and followed with hopes and doubts the turns of the day. When it was over, they went out with the others, and stripped the dead bodies on the shore and the treasure in the camp of the stockade. They took their fortune as it came to them, as it comes to us all, out of its great distance. Among their many buffetings, they kept a steady hand, and chiselled in the hard world the record of their life, with that regard for the matter it is made of which renders it beautiful: sure in their human dignity that the greatness of art is not what we have, but what we want and long for, and recognize but never see in men's hearts or in the substances of earth. So they dealt carefully, not smirching with vanity the things they used, but respecting in each its own secret; and transmitted it in stone for as long as the stone may wear.

19

The Oracle of Didyma
Ecclesiastical Tradition

But since Fate has so far advanced us in time that we must obey
others as rulers but must suffer the consequences ourselves;
and when the worst results are not the work of heaven or fate
but of our administrators, then it is necessary to speak.

LYCOPHRON THE SOPHIST, early 4th cent. B.C.[1]

M r. and Mrs. Sime, managers in a liquorice factory,
entertained me kindly in Söke. The liquorice, in case
others are as ignorant in this matter as I was, grows as the
root of a bushy shrub all over the Maeander valley and its
lower hills; and is an ugly unsociable plant, refusing to adapt
itself to cultivation. As the wild parts of Turkey diminish,
the liquorice is likely to diminish too: but for the present it
is still gathered profusely, and Mr. Sime rides from village to
village to collect it, and sees it into the steaming vats from
which it eventually emerges, fit for the smokers of American
cigarettes, who like it in their tobacco. The picturesque days a

century ago, when Messrs. MacAndrew and Forbes could order a special train whenever they wished to travel to Smyrna,
are over—but the modest, blackened factory chimney is still
a respected landmark, and the managers' houses pleasant in
a garden under trees; and remembered with gratitude by a
great many people as well as myself for their comfort and
hospitality.

No kindness however could make the November climate a
good one for travelling about the Maeander valley, and days
passed while storms shifted and jostled, knotting themselves
in a tangle of lightnings and cloud, and never clearing from
the roof of Mycale. Sitting in Söke, on the edge of the flatness
of the delta, on whose far bay just visible Miletus rested with
Caria behind her, all this business of the heavens—'black
rain and fire and hail' and an occasional rainbow, clearing here and there only to concentrate somewhere else like
those old-fashioned landscapes where things are going on in
the corners—made one feel as if one were sitting at a theatre
with the play in a foreign language, and very long-winded at
that. At last a blue rift appeared, and a message came from
Halil Bey Özbashi that he was going to try to get across in a
lorry in fifteen minutes and would take me if I could be ready
in time.

The Özbashi brothers, belonging to Söke and educated
at Robert College in Stambul and at Princeton, are among
the pleasantest people one could meet anywhere, and the
kindest. They own great patches of the delta land, and a
fishery on the other side, where the fish swim up into nets
from the lake of Bafa and are packed into boxes and driven
across the flats in lorries for the markets of Söke and Smyrna.
Halil Bey was used to friends who wanted to look at Miletus
and Didyma, and even—rarely—at Heracleia under Latmus,
and he offered me the hospitality of a flat in the fishery, from

where I could be taken in all weathers. Meanwhile it was not certain that we could get across Maeander at all.

A road is planned for two years hence, and a bridge, and one will drive in an hour or two at most from Ephesus and no longer realize what a river delta means: and in eight more years they plan to 'control' the Maeander waters in their upper reaches, and the river god will no longer be free to toss and turn in his wide territory, and tear the fields and smother the cities, and will indeed no longer be a god at all, but a regulated product in a regulated state as we all are. But meanwhile he still does as he pleases, and the winter helps him, liquefying his soft estuary into one sea of mud.

"These are the last cars to be used till the summer comes," said Halil Bey, turning our truck at a quick and expert angle from the hard-surfaced Priene road into the delta. "When the mud gets beyond lorries we use tractors; and when it is impossible for tractors, then horses; and finally camels: and at last get round by sea."

A sort of retreat from Russia landscape lay around us, a surface sweeping southward where wheels had plunged, seeking firmer, ground, and made a bog. Their shapeless ruts gaped, filled with water, reflecting the stormy sky. The valley, five miles or so across, had to be taken slantingly, at three times its width. Its flatness undulated into imperceptible mounds, visible only by coarse grass, tamarisk 'which grows best by the Maeander',[2] or liquorice emerging sodden out of more sodden dips of mud. On either side, for stretches at a time, the fields of cotton spread their rain-wet seed-pods like votive rags on the bushes; and the peasants were out picking, women standing like pictures by Millais with their heads tied in bright kerchiefs, waist-high in the wet crop, and the men in high jack-boots and jodhpurs, their peaked caps worn over one ear on the windward side.

This used to be the best sheep grazing in Turkey—and we could still see a few nomads (Yürüks), though most of the black tents had already made for the winter hills. "At the moment," said Halil, "this is the richest land in the country, and produces forty million tons in one year. Next year there will be no Yürüks; it will all be under cultivation."

"Two years ago," he told me, "I could point to every tractor by its owner's name: now there are two thousand in the delta alone; and the farms you see"—three or four widely scattered among plantations—"have been built within the last three years." The land here all belongs to the local people—extremely rich now; and yet the cotton future is not too secure, since the same land continues to be sown over and over again and is liable to turn sour.

Cooking our pilau
8.11.52

Priene (Gülbahche): The Temple of Athena and the Maeander Delta

Didyma (Yeronda): Temple of Apollo with Small Oracle-Door

Didyma (Yeronda): Temple of Apollo Peristyle

Didyma (Yeronda): Temple of Apollo

A storm came tilting from one side of the valley to the other, across our path, and Halil turned into a farm which stood alone on one of the rafts of solid ground. It was small, built with four rooms and a high shed roofed with tiles; and an old African slave woman lived in it and cooked for the labourers. She had once been marooned for a month by the winter rains.

She was squatting over her fire enveloped in her gathered trousers like a deflated balloon of innumerable folds. A wooden platform with mattresses, two chairs and a small table, some blackened pots, a large and a small amphora for water, rags, bottles, two cats, two dogs, an enquiring flock of beautiful black-and-white turkeys, were all the furnishings; and when we had sat down, the old woman began to move about in her slippers in a slow stiff way, dealing with a fowl in a saucepan and wrinkling her small eyes with affection, tight-lidded as a Chinese, whenever she looked at Halil. She had fine hands, brown-black as ebony, and high polished cheekbones, and a look of pleasure with every little thing that came in her way, which made her face young, like a wrinkled flower. The rain lashed down in a sudden attack, and when we had eaten our pilaf and given and heard the news, the storm had passed.

It had done for us, however. At the next little bridge—invisible under its mud—our lorry stuck. Even Halil, who had woven in and out like a darning needle in a stocking, gave it up and called to a tractor. The tractor in the delta has a Homeric quality. It is what the fifty-oared galley must have been in the days of the heroes, ploughing the sea between Miletus and Priene. It came now, churning mud from the strong chisel teeth of its wheels and took the ditch beside us at a run, like a beetle in a bath. The mud was too strong, and drove it back time after time; one of the tough men in jack-boots disappeared into the landscape and returned after twenty minutes or so with a spade; the ditch was filled in; the tractor ground its way over and pulled at the lorry; Halil was able to turn round, settled me on the tractor, and we parted. I could not get across that evening, but would find shelter with Nazim Bey in his farm half-way across.

This was a welcome solid place to arrive at, in the late afternoon. The ground, though uniform mud, looked hard, and small trees were beginning to grow reluctantly round the whitewashed buildings. A platoon of tractors were grouped like an army waiting to attack but immobilized for the moment, with dogs and farmyard animals about them. In the house, there was pleasant country domesticity and comfort. Nazim had a beautiful charming young wife and they welcomed a stranger as if they had known and expected her for years; a room and the bathroom were ready; the evening passed with the relaxed leisure which the weatherbound country possesses, when nothing particular to do is within reach and there is more time beyond every little milestone of time. The elder little girl was handed around to amuse us. In the sitting-room, in a box slung from a pulley in the ceiling, the latest baby was rocked—a little despot whom no mere cradle could satisfy: she swung nearly to the perpendicular, and gave a small but peremptory moan whenever, for a moment's rest, the swinging stopped. The parents and members of the household took it in turns to work day and night at this perpetual motion, fostering no doubt a subconscious feeling of omnipotence, for the little creature, staring from her woollies into space, evidently knew that a small noise was enough to set all the world in motion to the accompaniment of a wavelike, wordless, two-note lullaby.

Next morning, a yellow cart was tied to a tractor for the last part of the way. Well rested, I was settled between sacks of cotton and, with a heave as if into a stormy sea, we plunged into the mud again. The sun was shining; the labourers were out, picking their fifty kilos or so a day even now at the end of the season. In the drying air, the thick contours of the ruts began to show lighter edges, and to look like architecture of a debased period in huge heavy folds. Camels, moving slowly under sodden bales or standing in groups on legs aslant to rest them, looked at us with tilted heads and heavy-lidded eyes, like Eternity looking at Time. We plunged in and out of our furrows. At every little bridge, the tractor driver looked back to see if I was still there, and smiled.

We reached Maeander. It was flowing to the top of its banks, 120 feet across, a yellow stream that carried the melting hills. In the middle, the strongest current was filled with hurrying eddies. The ferry was the oldest of patterns, a platform and low parapet, and an upright rod of iron revolving against a chain, at which they pulled to cross the stream. It had been mended with quite thin wire, and was attached to two poles on either side, already slanting with the strain. On the far bank, a hut of reeds, a bench and an amphora for water, two bits of marble column emerging from mud, made the ferryman's shelter, and he himself was an old feeble man to look at. I wondered if we should drift down to sea and end perhaps at Samos. But two waiting camels were coaxed down the slope and embarked, and we followed, and were presently safe on the southern shore. The fishery, the Dalyan, was only a few hundred yards away, long and low among trees, with roofs of rush and tiles and a concrete house in the middle: and here the factor, a silent grey-haired Turk in thigh boots, received my letter with a certain grimness, called Fatalism to his help, and took me up the stairs of the house where the

Özbashis have a flat of three rooms and a sitting-room ready
for their use whenever they cross the valley.

Here I spent three days, and came to feel at home with the
rugged men and their kind, silent ways. The fact that I was a
woman, and could only fling out single and unassisted words
by way of conversation, probably added to the silence; and
also the fact, which I gathered from the headman in a day or
two, that I had come when there was no female servant about
the place. Ismail, who cooked for the fishery men, did his
best, and appeared with a grilled fish and a mug of tea at odd
intervals between ten a.m. and five; on the second day, being
wet through and cold, I made my way into his kitchen and
found him squatting over a fire of sticks concocting a soup
or potatoes, mutton fat and pepper, in water, in a frying-
pan—modestly pleased to be complimented by the epithet
of 'cook'. As soon as it was seen that I liked the kitchen fire,
a friendliness grew up around me.

When the day's fish had been lifted and packed, and twenty
camels, each with a box on either side of its saddle, had
started, tied in long lines, with a slow, loose, public school
stride for the ferry and the nine hours' crossing beyond—the
men would come in one by one, and hang up their tarpaulin
coats, and cut a slab of black bread from Ismail's store, and
warm themselves and go away. The two lorry drivers lived
in a little apartment of their own; and Emin Effendi, a good-
looking young Circassian who sighed for his wife and home in
Söke and did the accounts, took particular care of me, with a
few sentences of English here and there. The headman began
to smile. I felt I could easily live here for weeks, occupied
with that endless arrangement of small necessities not yet
reduced to order which people miscall the simple life.

A cloud like blue ink still hid Mycale, with a rainbow
arched against it—but the south wind now blew strong and

kept our side of the delta clear; and on the morning after my arrival the drivers were ready to take me in a lorry to Didyma, where a hard road, made for the fishery to the bay of Kovela, carried enough of a slope to make it possible in all weathers. As the wheels bit on it, I realized how we depend on the solidity of earth: when it quakes, or even quivers superficially in bog or mud, it is a threat to all the stability we know.

We were climbing now, not high, but on to wide un-dulations of uncultivated scrub, the limestone emptiness of the Ionian promontories gay with the sea-winds and the sun. Here and there a cistern for water, roofed with a dome and old, showed it to be a way long-used—probably by the an-cients when they drove from Panormus into Caria, for the Mylasa track branched off from ours a little way above the fishery.

Now the Maeander was forgotten and Miletus out of sight; and after twelve miles or so we descended by low troughs of valleys to where the Sacred Way took off from Kovela, a little harbour still marked by an upright broken column shining white in the sea. Nothing else had been built on the water's edge except, on a more westerly-facing inlet, a cottage and a small Turkish guard-house under trees.

Emin did his business here while the drivers talked to a skipper from Samos buying fish, whose caïque reared in the bay against the steep little waves of the south wind. We soon left, and retraced our road through the few vines and pomegranate patches of an invisible village, and turned south for the two miles to Didyma. Here along the ridge, in 1854, Newton saw 'a continuous line of wall in front of which a number of statues are placed at intervals. The figures are seated in chairs, their hands resting on their knees . . . all draped in a chiton or tunic to the feet, over which is a mantle.' They can be seen in the British Museum now.[3]

More scientific excavation has since been done by the Germans. The temple, now wholly uncovered, soon appeared with its stones ranged orderly around it, standing by the wide open street of a village which is still called Yeronda (Hieronda from Hieron), though the name is now—regrettably—to be changed.

The Greek atmosphere persists, though the Greeks have gone. The village has a happy openness of low-walled gardens, where almond and peach and cypress trees over many acres of ground imitate with their small curves the large curves of the bending landscape. A few miles away over the headland, on three sides, is the band of the sea, filled with light. The church is wrecked and its western door in ruins, but it faces away and—from the temple—still looks like the centre of a hill-clustering little town: and perhaps because of this inland, upland quality, the Turks have not turned the place from its meaning as they do with the seaboard, but continue to use the straggling wide road and *maidan* in a diminished way, and to sit at a wooden café in sight of the Oracle.

This was Branchidae, so-called from the family which administered it, descended from Branchus the son of Apollo —a temple, in the Augustan age 'surpassing all other Greek oracles except Delphi'[4] and still seen standing in the 15th century A.D. by Ciriaco d'Ancona.[5] It was older in its worship than the Greeks and their gods[6] and only a late legend marked it as one of several places where Apollo and Artemis were conceived.[7]

Its fame spread early across the Aegean Sea; Menelaus, on his way home from Troy, here dedicated his shield, seen by Hermotimus (in the 7th century) 'so rotten through and through that the ivory facing only was left'.[8] Necho, king of

Egypt, who killed 120,000 labourers in the first attempt at the Suez Canal,[9] sent here a dress he had worn in a victorious battle in 608 B.C. against the Jews.[10] In the deep ruin of Miletus, Didyma too was burned by Darius. Its statue, the work of Canakhus of Sicyon at the end of the 6th century, was carried to Ecbatana; and the sacred spring thought to flow under the sea from the heights of Mycale, dried up till Alexander came. The wisdom or prudence of the Oracle, after 150 years of silence, foretold the victory of Issus and secured the conqueror's support; and Miletus began to re-build it. Antiochus brought the statue back from Persia. He presented a toll-gate for the collecting of funds. With in-terludes of pirates the reconstruction continued, till—in the reign of Caligula and with the coming of Christianity—the still unfinished temple declined.[11]

Meanwhile roads had been made. The early approach was by sea; but as their own harbour silted up, Trajan built a land road for the Milesians to Panormus, to join the Sacred Way. In the 4th century A.D., four miles of it were relaid by Julian, and the Oracle declared him a prophet. In the time of Pausanias the tomb of Neleus, who had brought the Grecian colonists from Athens to the Maeander valley, could still be seen not far from the south gate of Miletus, on the left hand, along the temple way.[12]

This is what Strabo wrote about the temple, shortly before the Christian era:

'Next after the Poseidium of the Milesians, eighteen stadia inland, is the oracle of Apollo Didymeus among the Branch-idae . . . who gave over the treasures of the god to the Persian king, and accompanied him in his flight in order to escape punishment for the robbing and betraying of the temple. But later the Milesians erected the largest temple in the world, though on account of its size it remained without a roof. At any rate the circuit of the sacred enclosure holds a village settlement and there is a magnificent sacred grove both inside and outside the enclosure; and other sacred enclosures contain the oracle and the shrines. Here is laid the scene of the myth of Branchus and the love of Apollo. The temple is adorned with costliest offerings consisting of early works of art. Thence to the city is no long journey, by land or sea. . . . [13]

The sacred groves have vanished, but the feeling remains of a temple and village united. But for this ancient sanctity, Hieronda and its inhabitants would probably never have cut the limestone into gardens, and the promontory would be one among the many empty headlands of Caria. As it is, the Sacred Way ends where it always did, by the long north temple wall, and one turns beside a lion of marble, found on the wayside, whose mellowed flanks, with shadowed ribs and lithe shape exquisite and ready, show the meeting of Asia and Europe in the long intercourse of craftsmen.

Three columns only remain standing, and one is unfinished, still unfluted under the trailing clouds: but the bases and half-columns are there to make a glade of marble on the peristyle, between the steps of the vast platform and the door. The marble is light grey, brittle and elegant, so that its immense size, the polygonal carved bases and fat laurel leaf cushions above them, the deep incision of the flutings and rich Ionic volutes against the sky, seem normal to the size of men: it is the human walking among them who feels enlarged and exalted, as if suddenly made capable of a new dimension. And this sensation is strangely deepened by the greatness of the door, carved posts of eleven yards resting on a nine-yard block of marble, beginning waist-high so that the tremendous opening is not for crossing but for looking only, and the majesty and the remoteness are enhanced.

Didyma (Yeronda): Lion from the Sacred Way

The Theatre of Miletus (Balat)

Within, surrounded by the fine jointed wall with capitals on pilasters along it, is a wide inner stairway and a space roofed from the beginning by the sky. One enters across the peristyle by two small side doors and passages about three feet wide; steeply descending, smoothly vaulted, with swastikas carved on the stone ceilings, and bosses signed with a mark or letter left rough for the handling of the stone—by this devious twilight the Oracle was approached.

Like the Church of Rome, the Oracles constantly remind one that the art of government is in the management of people's *feelings*. Our essence is religious; intellectual appeals tickle the surface, but the permanence of government lies in religion too. Another similarity with Rome is a delicate combination of the local and universal, which is helped by a diversity of gods. The Apollo of Didyma was not the same as he of Delphi, and yet they were the same; and so with many a saint and even higher. It is doubtful whether early Greek or European civilization could have come into being at all without this dovetailing of the two strongest pulleys of the human heart, the familiarity of habit, and the lodestar of mystery.

With what diplomatic skill, in early days, Lydian and Phrygian and Egyptian kings are drawn into the orbit of Apollo! He had twenty-nine oracles altogether, and nineteen of them were in Asia Minor: and the readiness with which even Delphi responded to the Lydian gold seems to have shocked the more respectable mainland Greeks. The god, however, did not think for himself alone: he worked with a team spirit and, when Alyattes the Lydian warred against Miletus and accidentally burned the temple of Athena, the Pythian took advantage of the king's illness to make him rebuild it. The policies of oracle, Greek statesmen and foreign kings are interwoven.

'For when Periander [the tyrant of Corinth] heard the oracle
that was given to Alyattes, then because he was passing friendly
with Thrasybulus who was tyrant of Miletus at that time, he sent
a messenger and declared it to Thrasybulus, who . . . devised
as followeth. All the corn that was in the town . . . he brought
together into the market place, and proclaimed unto the men
of Miletus that . . . they must all drink and make merry . . . so
that the ambassador from Sardis might see a great heap of corn
poured out . . . and bear word thereof to Alyattes; the which
also came to pass . . . and Alyattes built two temples instead of
one to Athena, and himself recovered of his sickness.'[14]

An intelligent support of established governments is another
resemblance between Oracle and Church. In the Persian war,
Strabo suggests[15] that Didyma made a slip and backed a loser;
and that Xerxes, retreating defeated, carried the priests who
had given him the temple money safely away from Ionian
vengeance into Persia. There, in a little town of Sogdiana
their descendants a century and a half later welcomed the
victorious Alexander—and were all killed in memory of
the ancient crime.[16] The story is, it seems, a baseless slur
on ecclesiastical diplomacy: even if true, the Oracle soon
retrieved its error, got itself a new generation of priests,
made a lucky guess before Issus, and came again into harmony
and a happy financial relationship with the Government in
Power, as all sensible Oracles do.

20

Miletus

The Aegean

Miletus, the town of a twelve-walled people that is chief
among the Achaeans.

TIMOTHEUS, 4th cent, B.C.[1]

But Nastes led the Carians, uncouth of speech, that possessed
Miletus and the mountain Phthires, of leafage numberless, and
the streams of Maeander and the steep crest of Mycale . . . And
he came, forsooth, to battle with golden attire like a
girl—fond man—that held not back . . . grievous destruction.

ILIAD II.[2]

M iletus, outstretched where the Carian hills ebb to Maeander, had now been for days and nights in my dreams.
From the Ephesus road over the pass, from Söke and Priene
and across the delta plain, and from the windows of my fishery, I had been watching it, and a blue strip of the Aegean
behind it whenever a rise in the ground occurred. The lowness
of the Maeander valley caused the horizon to be outlined as it
were by the limbs of the city, relaxed on gentle slopes from
south to north: the flatness of the oldest acropolis dropped
to the body of the town and rose again to the solid mass of
the theatre, where a snout of land once ended in sea. The sun
illuminated it against the darkness of cloud that hung upon
Mycale, so that it shone with varied light under the arch
of the day—shone indistinct in its brightness as it shines in
history—the last splendour of the Aegean world of bronze.

Miletus was colonized by the Cretans from their own
more ancient Miletus,[3] and lies there—not hidden from
the mainland like Phocaea but prominently defenceless and
open—built for a sea-laced world where traffickers could
flit with their brittle wares round little harbours, in the
safety of a sea supremacy, from welcoming islands to empty

promontories, drawing in their wake—like some fine vintage through a tiny spout—the uninterrupted civilization of the Mediterranean.

There is no break in the East Mediterranean between the neolithic and the copper and the bronze.[4] Their history fans out in a sea-distance, as if it were the earliest whiteness of the pathway of the sun. Men appear, moving from south to north, from east to west, with implements of stone; inhabiting the Cyclades islands, linking them with Caria,[5] bringing to the seashores 'the hinterland of Asia',[6] peopling their world with little fat idols of marble or clay.[7] It is the men of the Cyclades, and not Cretans, that first begin to paint the human figure on their vases.[8] They inhabit easy shores and scatter their sea shells, advancing from stone to copper, chipping for centuries and centuries, into the age of metal, the sharp flukes of obsidian in Melos;[9] transmitting to their successors their two great treasures—the pattern of the spiral and the use of bronze.

Bronze, and copper before it, came from the north-west, through Troy; and was mined in Anatolia early in the third millennium—the latter also in Cyprus, as the name implies.[10] When the neolithic ended, Cretan islanders already wore copper daggers. They lived collectively in decorated houses, and stored their goods in stone or painted vases,[11] and offered in their shrines small clay models of boats,[12] symbols of their prosperity and how it came. But the greatness of the island began, about the middle of the third millennium, with the bronze trade, and went on for a thousand years at the crossroads of the sea. For Crete stood midway, between Egypt and Peloponnesus and Asia and Troy by way of the Cyclades;[13] and it was her monopoly to trade for centuries in the most precious substance that her world possessed— as it might be uranium today. When time had passed and the Nordics had come down from their highlands, raiding or settling and contributing their barbaric nobility and timber-built rectangular houses; and the Achaean branch had spilt into Asia, and the glory of Crete was over; and Achilles held funeral games for Patroclus beneath the walls of Troy: even then, after centuries of such commerce, a bronze tripod was valued at three times the price of a woman.[14]

Neither bronze, nor geography and the nymph Economics her handmaid, who explain most things in history between them, can quite explain the miracle of Crete. For here everything that other civilizations plod at, with centuries of monotony and repetition, blossoms not only into beauty but into unexpectedness and variety, as if the fountain of life were pouring from one of those egg-shell vases[15] painted with radiant and accurate fancies by fishermen and hunters, or watchers of the bull ring—craftsmen in some neat flat-roofed two-storied brick house, timbered and plastered as the faience tiles show them,[16] with painted door and windows, on a street that climbs, with shallow steps and paving stones and a drain for rain-waters beside it, in the shadow of a palace on a hill.[17]

There, through a sparkling variety of changing fashions, was shaped the pattern of the world we know—unknown before—of urban, middle class, productive life, of colonizing commercial dealings and peaceful settling of artisans across the sea. The quick, clean-shaven, wasp-waisted men were met all over the Aegean, with sun-burned naked torso and loose curls, with a loin-cloth or mere sheath for garment and a dagger at the belt and woollen cloak when needed, and boots for out-of-doors of white leather still known in the island now.[18] The women with their gay insubordinate profiles and sophisticated hair-do, their many-coloured skirts flounced or divided, their half-sleeved short boleros, transparent bodices, audacious breasts and thin gold wreaths of leaves and flowers, and hairpins and Parisian variety of hats—sent their fashions to decorate the walls of Tiryns and fill the dim hearts of Nordic wives with complicated female longings which are the preludes of civilizations or wars.

In the fine climate of the Aegean the Sumerian East was transformed:[19] seals, and clay tablets with the art of writing; the metal helmet and the shapes of weapons; the socketed axe and the four-wheeled cart that preceded both horses and chariots; coffins of clay, shallow carving, imitation in pottery of the shell inlay of Mesopotamia in stone; the very origins of their art travelled and were changed when they reached the sea: and the mud palace round a courtyard in the plain of Babylonia was transformed into a tumble of terraces, a play of light and shade, painted walls and polished gypsum floors for shoeless feet, pleasant windows and columned doors placed cunningly and casually for air, the perfect drainage, the easy stairways and unsymmetrical liveableness of the Cretan palace.[20]

There were great fortifications, but that was in the early centuries, about 2,000 B.C. when the heads of equal clans fought each other in the island and—long before Priam— the second city of Troy was burning. The first quiet, rural Ionians were then beginning to trickle into Greece.[21] Three hundred years later, in some unremembered revolution and all together, the palaces of Crete were burned to the ground. A new opulence under the house of Minos came to reign unquestioned for another three hundred years, protected by its navy; and in that security the greater, unfortified palaces were built.[22]

Every roadstead of the Aegean world would now be visited by Minoan traders. The name of Minos was given to cities in Delos and Amorgos and Paros, Siphnos and Laconia and the Syrian coast. The Achaeans, new settlers in Greece, were pouring southward, learning the pleasant arts of life, the cultivation of vines,[23] and the secrets of navigation; they were establishing the Homeric world in Mycenae, Corinth, Argos, Thebes, Orchomenos, and in Pylos on the routes of tin and amber.[24] They too now began, in high-prowed ships with oar-shaped rudders and anchors of bronze,[25] to export homemade wares copied from the island patterns. Cretan and Mycenaean jostle each other in trading stations of the islands—Kos, Kalymnos, Karpathos and elsewhere—where their potteries are found.[26]

This is the time of the early, half-legendary settlements in Ionia, when 'Oenopion sailed with a fleet from Crete to Chios'[27] and the 'son of Rhadamanthus founded Erythrae'[28] and Cretans were remembered in Colophon,[29] and the colonies of Rhodes and Miletus were founded. And Herodotus describes, in a probable way, the smooth relations of the Sea power and the aborigines—Carians who 'of old were subject to Minos and possessed the isles, being called Leleges; and they payed no tribute, as far as I am able to discover from report, but manned the ships of Minos, whenever he required. Therefore, because he had conquered much land and prospered in his warfare, the Carian people was at that season the most notable by far of all peoples'.[30]

All this ended, as more and more migrations came pouring from the north. Chaos overtook the Minoan age of peaceful trading. Somewhere about the year 1400, suddenly as with a thunderclap, the palace of Knossos and the supremacy of Crete were destroyed.[31] Phrygians in Asia Minor, Achaeans in Thessaly came pressing southward. 'Fighting to fill their bellies daily', the sea-raiders attacked Egypt;[32] the Philistines settled in Palestine; and already, and probably long before the 13th century, the Aegean spoke Greek.[33] New men, under

Homeric Idomeneus, take over what is left of the palaces of Crete; no paintings are ever seen on their walls again; and the northern megaron, the rectangular hall of the Achaeans with its hearth-centre, first appears on the island.[34] Piracy, now an honourable trade, serves to keep the Cretan arts of navigation from being forgotten. And the waves of people, pressed outward, now begin to reverse their motion and pour from west to east: the Aegeanized Ionians and Achaeans set out from Greece and settle where the Cretans had traded, along the Asiatic shore,[35] while new Dorian invaders press down from the north. The stream—west to east now—brings the coast of Asia Minor into history. Somewhere about the 12th century the siege of Troy is recorded, three generations after the fall of Crete.[36]

'The islands were without rest',[37] and the Dorians came, with iron in their hand. Even the echo of the golden days disappears—even the little that Homer remembered— 'Knossos and Gortys of the great walls, Lyktus and Miletus and chalky Lykastus and Phaestus and Rhytion, established cities all; and all others that dwelt in Crete of the hundred cities';[38] the intercourse between Crete and Sparta; and the first of all theatres 'which once in wide Knossos Daedalus wrought for Ariadne of the lovely tresses. There were youths dancing and maidens . . . their hands upon one another's wrists . . . And now would they run round with deft feet exceeding lightly . . . and now anon they would run in lines to meet each other. And a great company stood round the lovely dance in joy . . . ; and through the midst of them, leading the measure, two tumblers whirled'.[39] All vanishes, like the splendour of Nastes, 'attired like a girl'; and Glaucus in his golden armour from Lycia, who thought so little of it that he exchanged it with Diomedes for bronze.[40] The echoes wander round the black-hulled ships and are lost when the

Dorians come. And Miletus alone is left on the coast of Asia to remember.

She too was re-settled in the latest migration, by Neleus whose family, from Pylos, took refuge like many other Ionians in Athens, and came to rule there 'though they were strangers'.[41] Now Androclus, the king's son, led the last of the Ionian migrations, whereby the twelve cities of Herodotus were inhabited; and among them Miletus, already 'founded and established by the Cretans above the sea', on the flat acropolis where Strabo saw the ancient houses. Pausanias, agreeing in his account of the Cretans, and their friendship with the earlier Carians, and the coming of the Athenians under Neleus—adds that when these 'had overcome the ancient Milesians they killed every male, except those who escaped at the capture of the city, but the wives of the Milesians and their daughters they married'. And he pointed out the grave of Neleus 'on the left of the road, not far from the gate as you go to Didyma', which, he says again 'is older than the Ionian immigration'.[42]

This continuity in the history of Miletus, with whatever incidents of rape and murder there may be, is borne out by pottery, found in unbroken series from Mycenaean times. But apart from all this, and from the witness of legends encrusted with the very old lichens of time, there is a size about Miletus which carries its own conviction, though all that was old in the days of Pausanias—except a few stones on the Cretan acropolis, the Kalabek Tepe—is lost or destroyed.

If someone were dropped blindfold and ignorant on the height of Akköy village, it is just possible that, taking off his bandage, he might look with indifference across the low hills. But it did not *seem* possible to me, as I jolted out between rainstorms in a lorry from the fishery, with Mustafa and Salim both to drive me—delighted to look at antiquities instead of dealing with fish. We kept to the rising ground of what was once the indented Latmian shore, where we knew there was stone beneath the mud, unlike the flat delta below us; and having left the village, and the pleasant house of the German archaeologists now ruinous too on its hill, we began, with nothing old around us but this feeling of awe, to descend through the vanished city, which was said to be bigger by a third than the one that followed,[43] whose later Roman vestiges stand round the four landlocked harbours today.

It was a dreadful afternoon. Rain poured, not steadily but with paroxysms, never stopping, but throwing its heart at intervals into the effort to get worse. The low tussocks be-tween the harbours slipped about our ankles, teasing them with wet grasses, sodden with delvings of so many civiliza-tions all ending liquefied in mud. Mustafa and Salim turned up their collars and took what came with silent amiability, and we plodded by the quaysides of the harbour, beside the base of a triumphal monument or pharos, up the agora street, where a long portico once hid baths and gymnasium, to the square with the propylaea of Aesculapius and the circular council chamber, where fine Roman lettering glistened in the rain. We came to the theatre built by Trajan, humped in the landscape with Hellenic grace but with a Roman vastness, a feeling of crowds moving or loitering under shadows that lost themselves in arches, under the immense vomitoria.

Even in later days, when Miletus had recovered from the Persian destruction of 494 B.C., and the Peloponnesian wars that followed, and Alcibiades and Tissaphernes, and the massacre of 300 democrats in the agora in 405 B.C.;[44] when the bravery of Alexander's siege was over and 'democracy' returned in 334;[45] and Demetrius in 287 was forgotten; and Philip V[46] of Macedon in 201;[47] and the war with Samos in which Pericles fought;[48] and Miletus had become a provincial

city where the Empress Faustina built baths in the Roman
peace—even then, as the thirty thousand spectators poured
out from the tiered semicircle, the Past, like a deeper shadow,
must have hung among the shadows of those archways, seen
perhaps for an instant by some young dreamer, who carried
in his slim agility and curling locks and pointed features the
memory of several thousand years.

Not many later shadows have accumulated. The silting of
the delta has taken history away and the two couching lions
no longer guard the entrance to the Lion harbour. The great
theatre, seen—perfectly preserved—in the 15th century by
Ciriaco d'Ancona,[49] has a Byzantine castle in shoddy ruin,
like a barnacle on its back. There was a flicker of nobility in
the third century A.D., when the Goths attacked, and a wall
was built, and Macarius, an Asiarch, repulsed them.[50] In the
6th century, Isidore of Miletus was one of the architects of
St. Sophia.[51] Christianity had come, and remembered the
leave-taking here of St. Paul and his Ephesians; and in 1369
the place was still a bishopric, till the Emirs of Mentesh took
it,[52] and it disappeared from the Acts of the Patriarchs, and
Palatia village grew up, miserably shrunken, on the long low
stretch of the town where the foreign temples stood. Here,
with the ancient marbles, inlaid in red and blue, the gem of a
Seljuk mosque was built,[53] as perfect in its way as the theatre
of Priene.

The rain came pouring down, and made even the River god
spread out on the floor of a gymnasium look unhappy: and
we took refuge for a time in an arched tomb, thankful for the
smooth 2nd century joining of stones which remained intact
when the rivets of bronze had long been hacked away. It is
remarkable how vertical every ruin except an arch appears
to be in the rain.

Just opposite, not more than a stone's throw away to all appearance, and landlocked in the delta, the mound rose which was once the island of Lade, where in 494 B.C. the naval battle was fought and Miletus, mother of more than sixty colonies, the greatest city of Asia Minor, was destroyed.[54] With prestige and diplomacy she had survived the Lydian wars and the conquest of Cyrus unharmed; and now the Persians came 'by land and sea, digging under the walls and bringing up all manner of engines';[55] and the city, built in the days of a forgotten security, built for the sea on a low peninsula round rich harbours, the nursling of the Aegean and only inheritor of Crete since Crete had fallen, famous for ancient arts—painting, ceramics, and weaving—the centre of the late Aegean world, was wiped away.

These were the facts of Miletus.

But as we stood in the shelter of the tomb, with rain like the streaks of a drawing before us, and the landscape blurred behind, it seemed to me that the reality was different and that everything we had been looking at—the solid Roman, the Byzantine, the Seljuk, my own self included—were phantoms hiding with dull illusion a brilliance extricated from Time, free and operative for ever: that Miletus herself had survived her defeats and brought victoriously to port an argosy richer than any that her ships had carried, a history safely landed from the histories that went before it, neolithic and bronze—landed in spite of the Persians, into the Future— into the waiting arms of Athens and Augustine and Dante, Stratford and Rome.

The real Miletus, invisible and bright and separate from its ruin, appeared to me as a bridge where the heirs of the most ancient Mediterranean were passing, safely to our side as we waited in our tomb in the rain—not I alone from England, but Mustafa too and Salim, unconscious, from their Turanian steppe; the gaiety and beauty were moving towards us all. There were the learned and the adventurous, Cadmus the first Greek historian,[56] Phocylides and Timotheus, musicians and poets, and sculptors and the painter Bularchus whose picture was bought by Croesus for its weight in gold.[57] The father of Pythagoras was there, the gem engraver from Samos[58]—and the Samian youths 'with their hair combed out behind, wrapped in fair garments; they touched the ground with their snowy tunics and wore golden brooches like grasshoppers, with plaited bracelets on their wrists, and their hair floated in the wind in its golden bands'.[59] Among them perhaps is Thargelia,[60] who took an interest in politics through fourteen influential lovers and was recommended as a pattern to Xenophon's wife by Aspasia, also a Milesian born: for though they no longer drive chariots or leap the bull's horns,[61] the females of Knossos, easy and charming still, come, arm in arm with philosophy, across the Aegean bridge.

Hecataeus was there, historian and father of maps,[62] who tried to dissuade his city from the revolt against Persia and 'when he could not persuade them, then he counselled them so to do that they should have command of the sea' and of the treasure of Didyma too—but they would not hear him.

There were engineers in the great Minoan tradition, like those who built the tunnel in Samos and bridged the Bosphorus.[63] And Thales, engineer, mathematician, statesman, philosopher, who advised the federation of Ionia under Teos, and foretold an eclipse;[64] credited with the thinking out of almanacs, and with the Greek system (different from that of the Phoenicians) of steering by the pole star instead of by the plough.[65]

Two Ionians follow Thales, Anaximander and Anaximenes, teachers or disciples to one another in the century
when the Persians came.[66] Anaximander also was a political
man and the leader of a colony in his lifetime, and a statue
was put up to him on the road to Didyma; but it is not the
political things of their day that we remember but the fact that
these three first looked at the world in a universal light, and
carried across to us, in the scanty bundle of fragments that are
saved, the whole of western philosophy. The empires of the
East had fallen, and the Nordics had shaken and dethroned the
Mother Goddess herself and the neolithic gods of the Aegean;
but in Miletus, while she still flourished on her coastlands,
these three were able to think with clarity and freedom, and
stepped out in the quest that still continues, for what may be
abiding beyond the tides of the world. This advance, almost
as important as that of life from matter, as Promethean in its
essence as speech or fire, was first attempted, as far as we
know, by the Milesian school.

With the eyes of their mind, with varying but astonishing
degrees of truth like blind men with sensitive fingers, they
touched the objects within their reach. They realized from
the first that there is no difference in substance between the
heavens and earth, and Thales thought to find the general
origin in water.[67] Anaximander sped swiftly to 'the Infinite,
he being the first to introduce this name of the material
cause.[68] He says it is neither water nor any of the so-called
elements, but a substance different from them, which is
infinite, from which arise all the heavens and the worlds
within them'. 'He says that this is eternal and ageless', and
that it 'encompasses all the worlds'!

Believing in a plurality of worlds, the Milesian cosmologists
held that there was a boundless body outside the heavens:[69]

and that the earth, separated off from the infinite, was shut up in fire, which moved in rings about it, showing—through interstices in its sheath of air—the sun and moon and stars. One hears the voice of Dante, handing the echo on.

Anaximander saw that the earth swings free,[70] held in its place because it is equidistant from everything; and the sun was a wheel around it 'twenty-eight times the size of the earth, like a chariot wheel with the felloe hollow, showing the fire at a certain point through an orifice, as through the nozzle of a pair of bellows'.[71] For him, the solid vault of the older heavens had vanished, and he looked into the boundless substance where a multitude of vortex worlds sped whirling: and saw, in our own world, 'living creatures rise from the moist element, evaporated by the sun'. For he said that 'man was like another animal, namely a fish, in the beginning', and 'had he been originally as he is now, he would never have survived'.

Such was Anaximander, noticing by Necessity the survival of the fittest and the adaptation to environment, and the fact that the higher mammal could not be the original type of animal. And Anaximenes followed with another vital discovery, basing his universe on air[72] 'that differs in different substances in virtue of its *rarefaction and condensation*'. By this he made it possible to derive from one substance only the diversity of things: rarefied or condensed, the presence of less of the infinite or more made the variety—and it extended to men: 'Just as our soul, being air, holds us together, so do breath and air encompass the whole world.'

The Persians could now dig away as they liked at our bridge of Miletus, setting their engines to separate them from a world already ancient in their day. When the bridge fell, the discovery of the infinity of man and his universe was safely on our side: Pythagoras and Empedocles, Athens and

Rome, the Fathers of the Church and the philosophers, even to the dividers of the atom, were waiting in their turn to receive and to transmute it: and we have ever felt that the only thing that matters had become safely ours.

But the people of the 5th century saw the whole shining structure of their past go down with Miletus. They could not guess that a few fragments would suffice to feed the future; and they mourned with an anguish that can still be felt. They wept in the theatre in Athens: and when the later Carians looked for allies, the Oracle of Didyma answered them with a cry that still echoes, bitter with desolation, saying that: 'There was a time when the Milesians were brave.'[73]

As we drove back by the Latmian shore, the sky cleared at last behind the acropolis and Lade, and the translation of an ancient Ionian game kept singing itself in my mind:

> Turtle, turtle, what dost thou here?
> I'm weaving a web of Milesian rare.
> And how comes thy bantling a corpse to be?
> He drove a white horse and went splash in the sea.[74]

I was watching the waves close over the painted terraces of Crete.

Byzantine Islet on Lake Bafa

Heracleia (Kapa Keri): Lake Bafa from the Temple of Athena

21

Heracleia

The Myth

Next comes the Latmian gulf, on which is situated Heracleia below Latmus, as it is called, a small town that has an anchoring place . . . At a slight distance away from it, after one has crossed a little river, there is to be seen the sepulchre of Endymion, in a cave.

STRABO.[1]

The savage and remote outline of Latmus belongs to Caria, and to the Marsyas river that tumbles among gorges in a world of rocks, where the victory is recorded of Apollo over more ancient gods. A main road to the south runs there without softening the solitude; the chaos of boulders, smoothed and flattened and eroded, keep their primitive hostility; till the last of them, on the side of Ionia, leap like the attack of a breaking wave into the crests of Latmus above the lake of Bafa.

The Turks call it Besh Parmak, the hill of the Five Fingers, from its many summits, and it is visible from far away on the Maeander, and across the delta of what was once the Latmian bay.

Here, as the moon increased, I watched her climbing in the south, hidden by the five crests and re-emerging as she went from one to another, and appearing, by a trick of the light, to stoop between them as she did so; till she swam out again, far above the gentler Ionian headlands, into the limitless translucent westerly spaces of the sky. I watched her with an incredulous, tremulous wonder, riding the heights with her silver reins, and shedding, as if into the darkness of moonlit chasms, the shackles of time. For what else did some shepherd see in his earlier day, but the Goddess bending from rock to rock as I saw her, till in that high and barren chaos above the height of trees she looked down on a more fortunate shepherd, Endymion asleep? So the legend began. And whoever it was who first made articulate that loveliness and ecstasy of the night—he was my brother while I knew the thing he knew, whatever ages might lie between us. It was strange to share a secret with someone so long forgotten, who may have existed before even the art of writing was thought of, and saw what I saw and felt as I felt when he looked on the radiance stooping among the Latmian rocks.

Meanwhile I waited in my fishery through another long day of rain, hoping to reach Heracleia; and the Maeander rose, and nothing on wheels, not even a tractor, could circulate about the delta. But the third day shone clear and fine, and the old overseer thought the lake might be reached on horseback. Emin, the Circassian clerk, came with me; and we took bread and figs in our pockets, and descended from the last of the slope, already drying, to the sodden grassland squelching water; and then went gingerly, for nearly an hour, slithering as if through glue above the fetlocks, in a world of diluted mud.

Sari Kemer, probably ancient Pyrrha,[2] a little township on a rise and the only bridge in the delta, lay away from us on the left; and a two-hours' ride beyond, but out of sight and inaccessible in marshes and quite deserted, was Myus, or Afshar Kalesi, one of the twelve Ionian cities. There, in the 5th century B.C. two hundred warships could ride at anchor, when the place was given by the Persian king to Themistocles, to supply him with fish. But it declined, and Strabo found it already added on to Miletus, and only attainable by going 'inland for three miles in row boats'; and Pausanias, in the 2nd century of our era, describes it as an Ionian city taken from the Carians and abandoned because 'a small inlet of the sea used to run into their land. This inlet the river Maeander turned into a lake, by blocking up the entrance with mud. When the water . . . became fresh, gnats in vast swarms bred in the lake until the inhabitants were forced to leave the city. They departed for Miletus, taking with them the images of the gods and their other movables, and on my visit I found nothing in Myus except a white marble temple of Dionysus', of which today a few scanty Doric remnants above some scraps of polygonal wall are all that remain, under a ruined Byzantine castle on a hill.[3]

That is what happens with the Maeander, and here we were, immersed in the process so to say. The ponies knew it, and walked with their heads down, grateful for a firm hand on the rein that held them when they slid. And the mud, risen now about ten feet above its ancient level,[4] rearing its ridges and small heaps from the more liquid flatness and shining sterile and aimless in the sun, seemed to melt without a dividing line into the white, sealed-off waters of lake Bafa, as it had once melted into the condemned seas of Myus.

A little cabin of dried boughs on eight crooked poles serves as a waiting-room in the solitude to a landing-stage of a few loose bricks and faggots islanded on the strand. Here boats come across from the very ancient Mylasa track on the opposite shore, out of sight. Flat-bottomed boxes are loaded with passengers and cargoes and pushed out to embark in deeper water, by boatmen who, with clothes rolled to the thighs, wade from the scarcely shelving shore. A car, a day or two before, had almost reached the landing-stage and gone back, leaving a gay curved trace like a fine flourish of the mechanic age: but now the mud had conquered, and the day's travellers—a family from Sari Kemer—arrived in the old way, pillion and horseback, with young women cheerful and safe in lavishly pleated trousers, but rueful over their city-heeled shoes. While they were leaving, our ponies were taken off to bring tins of petrol, and a small boat was found to take us to Kapa Keri, which is built in the ruins of Heracleia on the northern shore, and not served by any traffic that passes to and fro.

A wild enchanting feeling of sanctuary broods over this lake, solitary in the folds of Latmus and sacred still, surely, to Artemis. Even as one approached, it became apparent that every untamed creature felt at home. On a strip that was neither land nor water, a hundred or more pelicans loitered, with a look less busy but no less important than that of the United Nations in an interval of the Assembly. The pelicans had the advantage that they could loiter in the sun. Beside the landing-stage, his bristles in the ooze and his four feet gathered trimly beneath him, still dapper and pathetic as any plump little trifler whom death has overtaken, a small boar, over-trustful of Artemis or men, lay shot. And the whole near surface of the lake was covered with a pattern of black water birds—coot—so careless that they scarcely moved till the boat was upon them, but floated in galaxies, in triangles or circles, rising separately or all together, and then flapping, like hens running, legs faster than wings, scrabbling the pale water up in little Dantesque spurts, like flames behind them; and all the lake was full of the flashing of their flights. Beyond them, as we passed out from banks of reeds into the deeper water, black cormorants were diving, and eagles sailed round the wooded clefts of the shore.

Nor were these the only fugitives who had found refuge here. In the first half of the 7th century, monks from Sinai and the west Arabian coast settled in the almost deserted Heracleia. Their hermitages and monasteries are clustered over the folds of Latmus and all the little islands of the lake, and their oldest paintings show the Pantocrator south of Heracleia in a cave. They seem to have been the first Christians settled here; and they were overrun by the Saracens, and revived a century later, and flourished all through the 9th century and the 1oth—when Priene, Magnesia, Tralles, and Amyzon in Latmus were all fortified bishoprics, and Miletus was known as the 'polis' to the monks. Even the tiny Thebes of Mycale (where the great battle had once been fought) had a church life of its own.[5] The name of Latmus was changed by the monks to Latros,[6] or 'worship'; and two great pilgrimages a year visited St. John in Ephesus, passing by Myus under the Byzantine castle. It was probably under Saracen attacks, between A.D. 830 and 840, that the first monasteries were fortified.

In A.D. 863, a Byzantine victory brought a long spell of peace, and the communities flourished and the saints and abbots multiplied.[7] Thirteen names of monasteries are known, and St. Acacius was buried in a cave, and St. Arsenius was

the most famous of the abbots. But the best-known in Latmus was St. Paul Junior,[8] who died in A.D. 955 in the
monastery of Jediler, east of Heracleia. He was born at Elaea
near Pergamum, and his father, a naval officer, died young
from wounds inflicted by Arab-Cretan pirates off Chios. His
mother took her two sons to Mysia, where they were educated in a monastery, and Basileus, the elder, grew up to be
a monk on Mycale. But Paul remained so poor that he was
forced to be a swineherd until his brother sent for him. The
journey to Maeander at that time was dangerous, and the village people tried to dissuade him from going, fearing that he
might be sold into slavery. From Mycale he came to Latmus,
and lived for eight months in a cave eating the thorny scrub-
oak acorns, anxious to settle on a pillar. His abbot, sensibly,
pointed to the high rocks all about him, and remarked that
they would do as well; and he chose the most inaccessible of
the caves, and lived there—mentioning earthquakes among
his trials—until his holiness made him too popular, and he
left Latmus altogether and settled in the old 'cave of Pythagoras' in Samos, where three Arab-destroyed monasteries are
still to be traced. But his monks from Latmus found him,
and induced him to return, and pilgrims came from Crete,
Russia, Bulgaria, and Rome. He visited Samos once more,
travelling by night for fear of pirates; and died in the middle
of the 10th century, as we have seen.

In A.D. 1045 a battle of Zahra is mentioned as a Saracen
victory.[9] The Emir of Smyrna built a fleet about 1080; and
Melaundion (Melanudium), the chief fortress of the district
(probably Myus), was taken with siege engines brought from
the Saracen ships. The abbot Cristodulos abandoned his 'Sty-
lus' monastery in the Latmian rocks, packed off the library
to Constantinople safely by sea, and himself in A.D. 1080
founded the monastery on Patmos. In A.D. 1090 Ephesus

was taken, by Tungri Parmak, for several years, and Smyrna and Nicaea, Samos and Rhodes were captured for a time; till the Crusaders' victory at Dorylaeum in 1097 liberated western Asia Minor. Then the monks returned to their wrecked monasteries, and the second Crusade passed on its way; until the defeat of the Emperor Manuel in 1176 again swung the pendulum over the harassed lands. The flocks and herds of the monasteries were plundered, and the Mentesh Emirs ruled in Mylasa; but Latmus, and even Melaundion-Myus, remained in Christian hands; until Salpakis the Emir took Tralles and all around it in 1280. He lost it temporarily with his widow and treasure inside it, but the Seljuk victories continued; and by 1307 Ephesus and all the west were in the Muslim power.[10]

*   *   *

The pale waters of the lake, whiter than blue, fanned out from our boat like ribbons through a hand, making no break of foam but satin undulations. The sun shone on the far outline of Miletus, straight in the gap of Maeander. The wooded southern shore, the slopes of 'Phthires, of leafage numberless',[11] showed a hamlet or a ruin or two, here and there in a clearing. On the north, the wild rocks slanted like descending torrents; the trees grew singly in narrow cracks; the pathless shore opened to small edgings of white sands, unmarked by human feet. With great dark folds and high sunlit triangles of rock, the majesty of Latmus spread its morning shadow, where two little monastery islets lay off it in the sea; a brick arch and fine carved marble lintel were still in place in the roofless church, and the patterns of the trees were drawn by the sunlight on small-stoned Byzantine walls laced with brick courses, and amateurish battlements above.

Round a bend, in the solitude, the fair Greek stones, the walls of Heracleia appeared. Grey like the mountain, they climb through the chaos of boulders high up the mountain shoulder; they lose themselves and reappear among rocks like a swimmer in waves. Round or square towers at intervals bear the straightforward doors and windows whose sides and lintels are cleanly cut, each from a single stone.

Nowhere in this region can one see the plain courageous beauty of the Greek walls better than in Heracleia. Like those of Priene, and of Lysimachus in Ephesus, they were built about 300 B.C. The siege methods of Philip II of Macedon had shown the weakness of battlements without mortar, easily overturned; and a closed wall was therefore invented, economical of men, where sentinels could walk hidden behind a curtain; the only look-outs were arranged at vulnerable points; and the towers were roofed like tents; and this fashion became uniform over the Greek world until mortar was adopted.[12] At Heracleia, the great blocks of the walls that climb up and up regardless of labour were cradled in foundations carved in the rounded, huge, weather-pitted boulders of the hillside floor itself.

The whole city, within the triangle of its walls, sloped down the great derelict avalanche of Latmus. Two unobtrusive late gates in the east are simply arched, and the wall continues by a south-east spur to a Byzantine castle on the lake, which is built with remnants of older material. The wall then turns and follows the lake shore, a course or two only remaining, shadowed by olives and enclosing fields of cotton or tobacco. It swings uphill again at the south-west corner, beyond an islet with monastic battlements, anchored like a ship in a roadstead, where cormorants in a row sit looking down for fish. We ran our boat in by the remains of a little port; pilgrims must have stepped ashore before us, under a window by a gateway and steps. On a clear space above, the agora had been held up by great foundations, where a neat

new admirable Turkish village school is building. The forty
houses of Kapa Keri were beyond, their red roofs decorated
with white arabesques in the modern Carian way. The stream
of life in Heracleia has come murmuring down into our day,
but so shrunken that it scarcely interrupts the strong voice of
the ancient stone. Proudly aloof from ornament, immense in
labour, severe in its devotion, the wall is there triumphant
in a wilderness where one would never expect to find the
victories of men.

The life of the free and ancient city can still be followed,
sometimes emerging and sometimes barely covered in the
ground. The Temple of Athena stands smooth and clear, on
jutting foundation courses, overlooking the lake; slabs of the
marble pavement are still there—as are those on the wide
grassy stretch of the agora floor with a row of shops complete
below, with windows and stone cornice. Farther, across a
brook, is the city's council house, a square building with
broken columns; and the theatre above; and the sanctuary
of Endymion nearby, with fluted drums of columns and one
smooth bole standing. He was, says Pausanias, 'the son of
Aethlias and Protogeneia, children of Deucalion and Zeus,
and the Moon bore him fifty daughters. . . . Others, with
greater probability say that he took a wife Asterodia . . . but
all agree that he begat Paion, Epeius, Aetolus . . . ' who ruled
the Aetolians. As to his death, 'the people of Heracleia near
Miletus do not agree with the Elaeans; for while these show
a tomb, the folk of Hercleia say that he retired to Mount
Latmus, and give him honour, there being a shrine.'[13]

As one walks over the ruins of Heracleia, one becomes
curiously uncertain as to where the confines of reality end or
begin. The very folds and wrinkles of the ground, starred
with a yellow crocus[14] and miniature scented narcissus,
are not earth at all but buried wall or columns, suddenly

Heracleia (Kapa Keri): Foundations of the City Wall

Heracleia (Kapa Keri): Agora Building and Mt. Latmus

Heracliea (Kapa Keri): East Wall and Lower Gate

Magnesia on the Lethaeus River: Roman Gymnasium

recognizable, like shapes under water. A kinder slant, down some great boulder, has been chipped long ago, to make an easy path from one vanished house to another. On an eastern slope, under olive trees so drenched in the afternoon sun that they seemed wet with light, the city necropolis shows its strange tombs—square or rectangular holes cut on the tops of boulders, with a lid of the stone roughly flattened on its under surface. They are ugly enough to make the whole hillside look like a canto from Dante. The Ionian or Carian, who built his great walls beautiful, was too practical to spurn a ready-supplied sarcophagus mass-produced by the hill.

What was the old connection between Endymion and the mainland of Greece? The Maeander river, according to a tradition, emptying at Miletus reappeared as the Asopus across the sea; and 'when Marsyas met with his disaster, the river Marsyas carried the flutes to the Maeander; reappearing in the Asopus, they were cast ashore in the Sicyonian territory and given to Apollo by the shepherd who found them. I found none of these offerings in existence,' says Pausanias, ' for they were destroyed when the temple of Persuasion (in Corinth) was burnt'.[15]

Such is myth, a little more blurred than history, but alive.

It was now two o'clock, and we left, through the smooth pale water in the sun; and mounted our horses and rode home across what looked as if it had become part of the lake since the morning, for the Maeander was now spilling over in shallow wet slabs of light.

Next day Emin took me back across the ferry. In the muddy waste, I found a Corinthian capital with a marble shaft half submerged beside it to mount from: the old ferryman had used it to weight his cable across the stream. The mud was drying on the rises and deepening in the hollows, but Nazim Bey, when we reached his house, was preparing to venture a tractor load of cotton sacks for Söke, and I was piled on top, on a soft precarious ledge. I knew the Maeander weather now and wrapped a towel round my head before we started, and the rainstorms poured down on us and passed. A man climbed on by the ropes and squatted beside me, murmuring Allah when we lurched; and we reached the stone-built road of the northern shore in safety.

22

Magnesia on Maeander
The Persian Administration

But a good man is sometimes bad and sometimes good.

PLATO,[1]

He could also excellently divine the good and evil which lay in the unseen future.

THUCYDIDES.[2]

The Maeander valley, when the delta is left behind, lifts itself gradually on to the uplands of Anatolia, with wide fertile expanses, a royal opulence, a stable multi-millennial prosperity. It is clothed with fig trees whose generations there have been as regular as the generations of men, and, with the olive, have built civilizations for longer than men remember: before Pythagoras, the athletes trained on them, with wheatmeal and soft cheese,[3] and the 'three-leaved' fig which Strabo mentions[4] in the valley grows there still.

D. B. and I picnicked in Magnesia, in country which at last was no longer delta, but had been solid agriculture for ages.

Some Greek-speaking Muslim settlers from Macedonia had taken us to a corner fortress of the city, and had led us by a slit between blocks of stone, to stairs and narrow rooms, hidden and airless in the rough Roman thickness of the wall; till we had to turn back because of a meeting of the British Council in a town nearby, which loomed with archaeological intervals in D. B.'s mind. Out of sight and quite ruined, we were told, a theatre lay in the lap of a range of hillocks, over which the town once extended. We could not go so far, but rested near the high road. A black wooden bridge of sixteen arches spanned a Maeander tributary, the ancient Lethaeus. D. B. complained that my conversation made him puzzle the inhabitants of his district with names unknown there for 2,000 years, and the fact is that I have forgotten the modern name of Lethaeus: but it was a pleasant prosperous river, trickling small in a vast gravelly bed in the sun, and the carts forded it and kept their fine bridge for the winter floods. The city walls came down to it in the empty landscape, with only an inner cement core of rubble left them; the once fine temple, attributed to Hermogenes, like that of Teos[5], lay in a shapeless tumble of stone and column nearby; and a Roman gymnasium gave us shade to rest in, with huge arches unroofed and purposeless as the skeletons of mastodons. Enclosing us, the rim of the valley rippled high and gentle against the northern sky; the foothills rose to it one behind the other indistinguishably, as if they were the tiers of a shallow theatre, so cultivated and overgrown, so varied with willows and poplars and olives, that their sharp stony structure was all underground, out of sight. We rested in the centre of a rich, agricultural, unpolitical, basic peace.

Settled traditionally by Thessalian Aeolians; destroyed by pride according to Theognis and Callinus,[6] but much more effectually by the Cimmerians in 651 B.C.;[7] captured by the Persians;[8] warred on by Miletus and then Ephesus; moved to the river Lethaeus where we sat, some three miles north of the Maeander at that time, under the protection of a more ancient shrine to Artemis Leucophryne;[9] and founded here a second time, about 400 B.C., by Thibron[10] (who took over Xenophon's Ten Thousand when he left them at Pergamum):—the city of Magnesia constantly recovered and carried its prosperity into Roman times.[11] The reason lay in the fertile gentle soil and in the fact that all the traffic from the Latmian gulf and from Ephesus, across Messogis, passed here along the 'Southern Highway', which led south and north and east, to Cilicia, Byzantium and the Euphrates, 'a kind of common road constantly used by all who travel from Ephesus towards the east'.[12]

This strategically commercial position gave to Magnesia as to Ephesus a more Asiatic complexion than that of the sea-cities of Ionia. 'Lydians and Carians were mixed with Greeks',[13] with a coarsening of taste. Here

'Hegesias the orator, more than any other, initiated the Asiatic style, as it is called, whereby he corrupted the established Attic custom; and Simus . . . he too . . . corrupted the style handed down by the earlier melic poets and introduced the loose Simoedia song, just as that style was corrupted still more by . . . Cleomachus the pugilist, who, having fallen in love with a certain obscene cinaedus and with a young female slave who was kept as a prostitute by him, imitated the style of dialects and mannerisms that was in vogue among the cinaedi. . . . As for Anaxenor, the singer to the lyre, the theatres exalted him, but Antony exalted him all he possibly could, since he even appointed him exactor of tribute from four cities, giving him a bodyguard of soldiers. Further, his native land greatly increased his honours, having clad him in purple as consecrated to Zeus . . . as is plainly indicated in his painted image in the market place. And there is also a bronze statue of him in the theatre, with an inscription from Homer. . . . But the engraver . . . left out the last letter of the second verse, the base of the statue not being wide enough for its inscription; so that he laid the city open to the charge of ignorance. . . .'[14]

The Barbarian is creeping in. And here too as in Ephesus the temple made its international atmosphere: inferior in size and in the number of votive offerings, but far superior 'in the harmony and skill shown in the structure of the sacred enclosure, in size it surpasses all the sacred enclosures in Asia except two, that at Ephesus and that at Didyma'.[15]

To this deteriorating world the great uncouth ruins of the gymnasium where we rested belonged: but the older city, which was given to Themistocles in his exile for bread,[16] where he built his temple to Cybele Dindymene, and his daughter Mnesiptolema was priestess, has vanished with the banks of the Maeander on which it sat.

It is pleasant to think of Themistocles in Magnesia in his late middle age, enjoying the favours of the Persian king, looking over his fields of corn and his fig trees bellying out in their straight rows, their shadows under them as if they were galleons on an arable sea; and saying to his children, as he contemplated the well-furnished table: 'Children, we should have been undone, but for our undoing.'[17]

Plutarch loves him; and in life too he must have had the gift of being loved, for his friends served him and he constantly made new ones: his things were sent after him in exile; the captain and crew of his ship did not betray him; the wife of his enemy showed him how to ask for protection at the hearth; and the king of Persia, when at last he stood before him, presented him with the money which had been promised to whoever might capture and yield up Themistocles. His family life was happy: his little son, he said, was 'greater than any man in Greece; for the Athenians command the Greeks, I command the Athenians, his mother commands me, and he commands his mother'; and he refused a rich suitor for his daughter, for he 'had rather she should have a man without money than money without a man'.[18]

His mother was a foreigner in Athens, and possibly a Carian from Halicarnassus. However this may be, it is certain that his character had an Ionian cast, a maritime touch of the islands. He probably knew, even if he did not study under, Anaxagoras; and his enmity for Aristides, Plutarch reports, 'was nothing more than their regard for Stesilaus of Keos'. In the colonies and contacts in Athens of seafaring coastal Greeks of Asia that policy must have arisen which drew ' the attention of the Athenians to maritime affairs', and 'brought upon himself the aspersion of taking from his countrymen the spear and the shield, and sending them to the bench and the oar. Stesimbrotus writes that Themistocles effected this in spite of the opposition of Miltiades. Whether by this proceeding he corrupted the simplicity of the Athenian constitution, is a speculation not proper to be indulged in here; but that the Greeks owed their safety to those naval applications, and that those ships re-established the city of Athens after it had been destroyed . . . Xerxes himself is a sufficient witness'.

Everything goes to show that the sea-power of Athens was not a spontaneous event, but a novelty forced on her by a mind familiar with a less provincial and less conservative background. 'While others imagined the defeat of the Persians at Marathon had put an end to the war, he considered it as the beginning of greater conflicts, and, for the benefit of Greece, he was always preparing himself and the Athenians

against those conflicts, because he foresaw them at a distance.'
It was the activity of genius, but also perhaps the result of
knowledge and familiarity with the Asiatic world; and the
extremely personal note in his passion against the 'barbarian', the putting to death of the Persian envoy for presuming
to make use of the Greek language; the disgrace of the man
'who brought Persian gold into Greece'; the knowledgeable
diplomacy with which the Ionians in the Persian service were
treated; the sailorly postponing of the battle of Salamis 'till
that time of day when a brisk wind usually rises from the sea'
(the *imbatis* all Aegean sailors know so well), 'which occasions
a high surf in the channel'—all these things together build up
a reasonable picture of the young man of uncertain birth who
had his way to make and his foot in many societies; who induced the noble young Cimon 'with a gay air', to consecrate
his bridle to Athena and go 'down to the sea; by which means
he inspired numbers with courage to embark'; and who later
built and fortified Piraeus, 'which strengthened the people
against the nobility . . . as power came with wealth into the
hands of masters of ships, mariners, and pilots'. In this respect, Plutarch says, 'his politics were very different from
those of the ancient kings of Athens'.[19]

Against a background of familiarity with Asia, the later
history of Themistocles is humanly understandable, and one
may perhaps think better of all the diatribes that he has had to
undergo. It seems to me that the whole question of Persian
relations with the Greeks of Asia Minor is open to study, and
—I am treading where angels fear!—I cannot help thinking
that if the private memoirs of some Persian governor were
to be discovered, they would read very like an affronted,
disillusioned, ex-civil servant's present musings, in Africa or
Asia—full of references to the loyalty of the respectable,
the conservative, the inarticulate; full of the harms of the

'nationalists', misled and misinformed; and interspersed with frequent personal experiences of devotion.

Plutarch says that Aristides in exile 'was much regretted by the people, who were apprehensive that out of revenge he might join the Persians', nor did this (probably unfounded) suspicion detract from his consideration as 'the Just'. There are a great many records of such Pontecorvo flittings. Pausanias, the victor of Plataea, intrigued, and Demaratus, the deposed Spartan king, crossed over[20] and was 'received magnificently' by Darius, and enabled to give good advice to Xerxes about his private affairs when the moment came.[21] His descendants, and those of Pausanias' agent, still held Myrina and Gryneium and lands near Pergamum in later days.[22]

Darius 'remembered the benefit done by Histiaeus of Miletus and the admonition of Coes of Mytilene', who had saved him at the bridge of the Ister—and rewarded them. And when Histiaeus intrigued, not with Greeks but with Persians, in Sardis, he was killed, like Absalom, before the king's friendship could reach him.[23] The king also rewarded, 'with all manners of gifts', Mandrocles of Samos, who bridged the Bosphorus for him; and he made the brother of the ruler of Samos governor in Lemnos; and discovered Democedes of Croton the physician, who pleased him with a ready answer and became a table-companion of the king.[24] Scythes too, the ruler of Zancle in Sicily, 'arrived in Asia and went up to king Darius. And Darius held him to be the most righteous of all the men that ever came up to him from Greece, because he received the king's permission to go to Sicily, yet returned . . . to the king again, and so died of old age in Persia, blessed with great possessions.'[25]

This was the Lydian tradition, of kindness to political refugees. And prisoners too might be well treated. The captured son of Miltiades had fears because of his father's record, but the king 'did him no evil and much good; for he gave him a house and possessions and a Persian wife, by whom were born unto him children that are counted as Persians'.[26] And we hear of the 'men of Eretria', against whom the king 'cherished a terrible ire . . . but when he saw them brought before him and under his hand, he did them no more harm, but planted them in the country of Cissia',[27] near the oilfields today.

Later, during Xerxes' invasion, the number of Greek ships in the Persian ranks that wavered or deserted seems to have been very small: one only, before Salamis, 'Antidorus of Lemnos, alone of all the Greeks with the king, passed over to the Greek side'; and at Salamis 'a few . . . fought ill of purpose according as Themistocles had charged them, but the more part did not so. And I could rehearse the names of exceeding many captains of galleys who took Grecian ships'.[28]

When the Peloponnesian war transferred itself to Asia, the relationship became almost too intricate to follow. Who can ever keep pace with the motives of Alcibiades? But the three successive treaties that were made in 412 B.C. between the Spartans and the Persian general Tissaphernes, all admit the king's right to country and cities 'that belonged to his father or to his ancestors', and end by saying that 'the country of the king in Asia shall be the king's, and the king shall treat his own country as he pleases'. The only points of real difference in the treaties, which evidently preoccupied the armies, were those dealing with the mercenaries' pay:[29] even centuries later, fighting on the Granicus against Alexander, the main body of the Persian infantry was Greek.[30]

In the same year, 412, the same axiomatic concession of the land was made clear in dealings of the Persians and Alcibiades with the Athenians from Samos, who accepted 'without opposition' the cession of the whole of Ionia and of the islands adjacent to Persia, and only broke away when 'Alcibiades required them to allow the king to build ships and sail along his own coast wherever and with as many as he pleased', which was a threat to the Greek maritime supremacy.[31]

The failure of the Persians was probably one of time. When they invaded Greece, the Lydian heritage had been transferred to them for little over fifty years, while the Lydian conquest-alliance in Ionia had existed ostensibly for more than a century and, in fact, through many ages preceding. People of the coast were still living during the first Persian wars who remembered the days when their friends in Sardis were destroyed. With another century, and the Persians settled firmly in the old tradition, the Ionians might have heard the call from the Greek mainland with far less ready ears.

This was the Persian weakness. Their strength lay in the fact that they kept the old frame of things as nearly intact as they could. 'The Persians,' says Herodotus, 'receive foreign customs most readily of all men; and they honour the sons of kings, and though kings rebel against them, yet they restore the kingdom to their sons.'[32] They seem to have taken most institutions over ready-made—the payment of taxes, collecting of mercenaries, even the religion here and there. Artaxerxes Mnemon prostrated himself before the state of Hera,[33] and Cyrus consecrated a temple to the Persian Artemis.[34] In Magnesia, an inscription mentions Gadatas who had taxed Apollo's gardeners, and was rebuked by Darius, 'not knowing the mind of my ancestors towards the god'.[35]

The people in authority were, on the whole, decent civil servants, struggling with difficulties among a population more civilized and sharper than themselves. They seem generally to have been friendly and conscientious. 'Artaphernes, the governor of Sardis, summoned ambassadors from the cities and constrained the Ionians to make covenants among themselves, to oblige them to render justice and not to rob and spoil one another. And he not only constrained them to do this, but also measured their land . . . and imposed on each of them tributes which have continued without alteration . . . even unto my day. And Artaphernes imposed them nearly as they had been before.'[36] Herodotus, who was writing about his own country which he knew, is nearly always favourable, though he speaks his mind over 'unholy deeds' of resentful governors, such as the death of the magnificent Polycrates of Samos.[37] This too, incidentally, happened in Magnesia, where he was crucified: and a much later crucifixion is recorded, on the mountain above the city, of Daphitas the grammarian, who 'reviled the kings in a distich'.[38]

The Persian authorities seem also to have been extremely adaptable about women, though, 'jealous even to madness', they kept them hidden in the oriental way.[39] But they could accept independent females and this was proved not only by Artemisia, the rather unscrupulous queen, but by Mania too, the:—

'widow of Zenis the Dardanian, who fitted out a great retinue, took presents with her to give to Pharnabazus himself (the governor) . . . his concubines and the men who had the greatest influence . . . and set forth to visit him. And when she had gained an audience with him, she said:

"'Pharnabazus, my husband was not only a friend to you in all other ways, but he also paid over the tributes which were your due, so that you commended and honoured him. Now, therefore, if I serve you no less faithfully than he, why should you appoint another as satrap? And if I fail to please you in any point, surely it will be within your power to deprive me of my office and give it to another?"

'When Pharnabazus heard this, he decided that the woman should be satrap. And when she had become mistress of the province, she not only paid over the tributes no less faithfully than had her husband, but besides this, whenever she went to the court of Pharnabazus she always carried him gifts, and whenever he came down to her province she received him with far more magnificence and courtesy than any of his other governors; and she not only kept securely for Phamabazus the cities which she had received from her husband, but also gained possession of cities on the coast which had not been subject to him, Larisa, Hamaxitus, and Colonae—attacking their walls with a Greek mercenary force, while she herself looked on from a carriage. . . . She also accompanied Pharnabazus in the field, even when he invaded the land of the Mysians or the Pisidians because of their continually ravaging the king's territory. In return for these services Pharnabazus paid her magnificent honours, and sometimes asked her to aid him as a counsellor. Now when she was more than forty years old, Meidias, who was the husband of her daughter, was disturbed by certain people saying that it was a disgraceful thing for a woman to be the ruler while he was in private station, and since . . . she trusted him and gave him her affection, as a woman naturally would to a son-in-law, he made his way into her presence, as the story goes, and strangled her. He also killed her son, a youth of very great beauty about seventeen years old. When he had done these things, he seized the strong cities of Scepsis and Gergis, where Mania had kept most of her treasures. The other cities, however, would not admit him into their walls, but the garrisons that were in them kept them safe for Pharnabazus. Then Meidias sent gifts . . . and Pharnabazus in reply told him to take good care of his gifts until he came in person and took possession of them and of him too; for he said that he would not wish to live if he failed to avenge Mania.'[40]

Mainland Greeks, rather surprisingly, seem to have been more particular than the Persians in their disapproval of women in authority, and before the battle of Salamis they offered a prize of ten thousand drachmas to anyone who should capture the Queen of Halicarnassus alive, 'for they deemed it a matter of great shame that a woman should make war against Athens'.[41]

The story of Mania seems to give a likely picture of life under the Persians in Asia Minor, with its ups and downs. Intrigue was there, but so it always had been; and it would have been strange indeed if the success of the Greeks with their conquerors had aroused no envy. When Themistocles visited Sardis, he saw the statue of a water bearer 'which he himself, when surveyor of the aqueducts at Athens, had caused to be made and dedicated out of the fines of such as had stolen the water or diverted the stream'. He begged leave to send the statue back to Athens, but the Persian governor 'immediately took fire, and said he would certainly acquaint the king what sort of a request he had made him. Themistocles, alarmed . . . applied to the governor's women, and by money prevailed upon them to pacify him.'[42] The normal relations of oriental life were securely established.

Like Histiaeus of Miletus before him, he was treated with friendship and familiarity by the king, who 'took him with him a-hunting, conversed familiarly with him in his palace, and introduced him to the queen-mother'. He had obtained a year to learn Persian, so that his intercourse was easy; and charm and intelligence did the rest. Demaratus the Spartan, who was there at the same time, and not so gifted with tact, asked 'that he might be carried through Sardis in royal state, with a diadem upon his head. But . . . the king's cousin took him by the hand and said "Demaratus, this diadem does not carry brains with it to cover"' . . . and the king was displeased. Yet the climate in which such a demand could be made is not one of oppression.

More than against the Persians, the passions of Ionia were directed against their own 'tyrants', who—on the whole—supported the new conqueror. They were unpopular by the time that Herodotus wrote: they represented the foreigner, who found it easier to rule through a few individuals than to manage the unparliamentary Mediterranean form of democracy, just as the British found it easiest to govern through the princes in India or the pashas in Egypt. And when Darius was in Scythia, during the memorable discussion at the Ister, when the life of the king was in the hands of the Ionians to cut or keep the bridge, eleven out of the twelve there present proved themselves to be on the Persian side.[43]

The differences that counted in those centuries would now be called ideological. The city states of Italy repeated them and there are signs of their repetition today. They are super-national, and always bring a good deal of influence and intercourse to pass across the lines. Themistocles had no difficulty in finding access to King Xerxes before Salamis—a friendly Persian tutor was ready to his hand. Nor did Xerxes —a singularly unsubtle man—doubt the kindness of his intentions, then or later, when Salamis was over.[44] And as a final example in this illustration of the Ionian and Persian relation, we may cite Xenophon, a perfect gentleman, who found his ideal in the Persian prince; and Artontes, the son of Mardonius the Persian commander, who 'gave many gifts to Dionysophanes the Ephesian . . . and to others of the Ionians . . . who had spent some pains on the burial of his father' in the foreign land.[45]

I cannot think that Themistocles' conscience troubled him when he lived by the Maeander. There were no complications of inferiority complexes among the Greeks. It is always perhaps a happy chance when the governed feel themselves superior to those who govern them, and always advisable for the ruling power to avoid inspiring an inferiority complex if it can; the Athenians and the British, who were both careless about this, have suffered the relentless retribution. But Themistocles had no reason not to feel king of his world, whoever might be ruling: 'he who was born to command, and incapable of servitude, could never sell himself, and Greece along with him, to enemies and barbarians.' The Persians in Magnesia must have been very few; under Darius, the governor of Phrygia, Lydia and Ionia had one thousand Persian spear-bearers in Sardis[46]—not enough to trouble the daily life of the smaller towns. Themistocles was governor in his own district, and the people around him spoke his own language and lived the Ionian life on easier lines than Athens. It was an inland place, but the sea-fish came up the river and Miletus was almost in sight, with the island world beyond it. And by his death he was spared the hard choice of fighting his own country or failing the Persian king. Thucydides, the most reliable recorder, thinks that he died of disease. But I like to think that his death came as Plutarch tells it, with the king's messengers commanding him to perform his promises and exert himself against Greece, when:

'Regard for his own achievements, and the trophies he had gained, whose glory he was unwilling to tarnish, determined him to put such an end to his life as became his dignity. Having, therefore, sacrificed to the gods, assembled his friends, and taken his last leave, he drank bull's blood or, as some relate it, he took a quick poison, and ended his days at Magnesia, having lived sixty-five years, most of which he spent in civil or military employments.'[47]

And the Magnesians erected a very handsome monument to him, in the market-place, which was mentioned by Plutarch in his day.

Yürüks (Nomads) Descending to Winter Camps

Aydin: The Fountain of the Mosque

Aydin: The Mosque

Aphrodisias (Geyre): Byzantine Gate (East)

23

Aphrodisias

The Ease of Life

For whereas formerly they bore the names of heroes and
sea-captains and legislators, they now bear names such as
Lucullus and Fabricius and names of other blessed Lucanians.
For myself, I would rather be called Mimnermus.

PHILOSTRATUS. APOLLONIUS OF TYANA.[1]

The excitement of Ionia wanes as one follows the Maeander upstream, and something else takes its place—
the roughness and superhuman structure of Asia, formless,
less pure, but vaster, still modified by Greek humanity, and
welded by Rome. This mixture is the stamp of the Graeco-
Roman world. In a more violent, less subtle atmosphere
than that of Ionia the Seljuk mosque comes to its own. It
stood exquisite but subservient in Ephesus and Miletus; but
in Tralles (Aydin), it is at home even though—with the whole
Seljuk of the town around it—it stands derelict, tombs and

bazaar and fountain, burnt out and ruined in 1922.* Still it keeps, like a well-tailored suit, its nobility in destitution, and the modern town spreads prosperously beyond, 'as well peopled as any other city in Asia by people of means';[2] and the city described by Strabo is on its hill. It is still' trapezium-shaped, with a height fortified by nature, and the places all round are well defended'—by Turkish barracks now. The lower slopes, where later towns have grown, were eaten out even in antiquity by the wriggling Maeander, and the old sites are spaced along an upper shelf which remains jutting and still in process of erosion, overlooking the valley floor for many miles.

A magnificent fragment on the height of Tralles shows the best of the Roman invention, a gymnasium built with small solid bricks; a few truncated columns stand beside it, in the uncut grass. The olive groves come down like water, with sheep browsing and cows; the citadel walls, 'eight metres thick',[3] and the acropolis, gnawed down to ground level, are visible on the outer side from the town below.

Here Herodotus left me, for he mentions nothing on the middle reach of the Maeander, and I travelled in later company—with Alexander the Great, who sent his artillery to Tralles,[4] and the Seleucid kings who founded most of these Maeander towns,[5] and St. Anthemius who was one of the architects of St. Sophia, and chiefly with Strabo, who evidenly looked upon Tralles as his county town when he studied under Aristodemus in Nysa nearby. But the most important contribution of the place to history was the 'Tralles stone', the chief document we have for the Greek system of musical notation.[6]

---

* It is being repaired now, in 1954.

I had stepped into a train at Söke, and had changed into the Denizli express at Ortaklar. During the half-hour wait a very old porter had taken my bag and presently returned, brushing the crowd away on either hand, with a chair for me to sit on. He had shaken hands at parting, and word was passed along the train that an Englishwoman was inside it—for we were not above a little gossip as we loaded oranges and cotton on our way. It was a fine commodious train, with second-class carriages almost like the first, and the people, who climbed in and out loaded with baskets at little stations, had no idea of discriminating between them: the guard walked along every time, explained politely, and restored us to privacy till we reached Aydın, where the school children of the Medium School, going home up the line, were free to sit anywhere they pleased.

The great valley, still sodden with rainwash, grew drier, warm and golden under its last crops—the cotton plants crimson, the fig-tree leaves shrivelling brown at the edges, the pomegranates with red burnished fruit and green-gold bright, small leaves, falling in showers like Danae's rain. The road ran alongside, visible under ponds and ruts of water, and not to be negotiated by car. It was amusing to think that only in winter one can go up the Maeander by train, though here too, in a matter of months, the new road is planned.

Meanwhile I leaned out, and bought tangerines and gazeuse and circlets of bread sprinkled with sesame at stations; and looked up the side valleys, every one of which must have had a fortress—some still visible; and wished I could ride as Fellows did, thirty-two miles from Aydın to Nazilli in three days, finding 'scarcely a quarter of a mile in the whole distance without some wrought stone of a former age', and seeing the peasants dressed in 'light blue worked with sil-ver', and roses in their turbans, and the ' dazzling whiteness of the veils, and the splendid colours of the embroidered trousers, of the multitudes of women attending the market'; and sending a servant along, when one overtook the caval-cade of a governor, to ask for permission to pass:[7] and at Nysa, whose theatres and arcades are visible from the railway at Sultan Hisar, I might look down on fifty miles of the Mae-ander below, in country so rich that, in 88 B.C., Chaeremon could present 1,500 bushels of wheat to the Roman army.[8] I longed to get out, to visit the cave of Acharaca nearby, where in Strabo's day 'the young men of the gymnasium, nude and anointed with oil, take up a bull and with haste carry him up into the cave; and, when let loose, the bull goes forward a short distance, falls, and dies':[9] and the waters near are so greasy that persons who bathed needed no oil.[10] Here too one might find Homer's meadow of Asia, about three miles away from Nysa, on the way across Messogis (Kestane-Dagh) to Tmolus.[11]

Meanwhile the school children from Aydın pressed around, hemming me in. The entire French class of the Medium School was preparing to converse with me.

"We know French very well," they said, hunting for their syllables.

"You shouldn't say that," said I, exasperated. "You should say: 'We speak French hardly at all, but are anxious to learn.' And you should never crowd strangers as if they were animals in a zoo."

They made room at once with smiles, and politeness: and when we reached Nazilli, two of them took my bag from the porter and handed it and me, with many recommendations, to the owner of the Ankara Palas Otel. The smallest room was found, with three beds only, of which I paid for two; this is enough for a woman, as it is very unlikely that another female traveller will appear; and it seems to be the one advantage of being a woman in a Turkish provincial hotel. A man would have had to pay for about four beds to ensure privacy, and would then wash and shave in the middle of the corridor, at one of the two washstands provided. But I travel with two basins, and fill one and use the other to throw the water away, and keep myself clean in decent retirement—feeling that a woman has no reason to exist in a country which has not even a feminine termination for its pronouns. I asked the governor of Denizli what they contrive when their wives have to travel, and he told me that they send a servant ahead to prepare and furnish a room so that she may do so in seclusion. The hotel, outside the few chief towns, is looked upon as the caravanserai of a night, and not as a place where one can lodge a few belongings and stay for pleasure.

The owner of the Ankara Palas did all he could to make me happy. He sent little waisted glasses of tea at intervals, and offered supper in my bedroom; but I thought I would brave the *ristoran,* and found a room like any other anywhere else, laid out with table-cloths and hat-pegs and mirrors, in the High Street which is prosperous and modern, full of shops to cater for the wage-earners in the cotton-weaving factory, with money to spend. Here I ate chicken and lettuce, pilau and yaghourt and grapes, and the waiter arranged my napkin half-way under my plate and half on my lap, in a sensible way, and brought me three toothpicks with the bill. The business men coming in and out gave me a glance of curiosity and no more; for the idea of the foreign traveller is familiar, though the actual apparition is not. Soon, the proprietor told me when I got back to my hotel for the night, he was going to have a room with a bathroom, for tourists like myself.

The sun shone in the morning, drying the eroded foothills and the cotton expanses of the valley, that looks so permanent though one knows it to be travelling with unceasing disintegration down to sea. The Ankara Palas proprietor had found me a taxi to drive the forty miles to Aphrodisias; he had never seen the ruins himself, and was coming too. As we stepped in, a shrivelled little gnome tried to nestle in beside me and announced himself as the interpreter.

"Interpreter? Do you think I have travelled a thousand miles to learn Turkish, only to have an interpreter?" I asked.

The proprietor, who had produced him, was delighted to see him vanish, and we relaxed with a carefree Mediterranean holiday feeling for the day.

We crossed a fine new bridge of metal, and drove east between Maeander and his foothills, green from rain; till we came to the Morsynus valley, now the Vandalas Chay. Here, in Strabo's day, a bridge crossed at Antiocheia,[12] and this was the branching off, from the Southern Highway, of the road to eastern Caria. Hegesander, the sculptor of the Venus de Milo, was a native of this city. Two round hillocks show it across the Vandalas from Kurujak, a village deep in trees and with municipal pretensions, for a roller for the road was lying about there—the shaft of a marble column fitted with a metal handle. But the city was out of reach on its hills, a lichen of grey masonry shapeless and late; and there was no access for a car across the river, and we had no time to go on foot.

The valley, noble and open, without craggyness, with ample rounded hills, now began to lift itself as if with deep breaths like a Bach toccata, into higher air. Here and there, against pine hillsides, poplars made temple-colonnades of gold. The river wound silkily in the sun, far below. The ridges leaned like sleeping nymphs, so gently rounded, wooded or bare; smoke rose high up from the last nomad camps of summer. Behind us, lay the open spaces of Maeander; in front, in the south-east, mount Cadmus (Honaz Dagh), smooth too with female curves, but high and bold, and powdered with snow.

As we drove, we met the Yürüks descending from summer pastures above Karaja-Su. They were going to winter round Milas, a fortnight away by their pastoral travel. Their patchy camels of Anatolia, bigger than the Arab, came swaying along, browsing a wayside bramble, carrying loads of household furnishings among brighter rags of carpet woven in the tents: they gave the feeling which the nomad gives, of something so long repeated that it is as if the very earth had pulled its feet out of its own substance and were walking. They came down mile after mile, in groups and long caravans tied camel to camel, interspersed with flocks of sheep—sunk heads invisible and sunlight-catching fleeces—and with ponies trotting free and unsaddled here and there.

The women strode with thick knitted white stockings and shapeless boots, terrifically strong: their small pale eyes looked sharply out above weather-beaten cheek-bones; their bodies were wrapped in shawls and sashes over trousers, with tight-waisted jackets on top, and a kerchief like a veil tied with a circlet of another kerchief round the forehead. The halter of the leading camel was slung over an arm and they walked spinning, twisting the thread with the right hand and grasping the distaff in their left: the little lump of clay or stone that weighted their wool went back to neolithic times. So they passed, ageless, leading their clanking, untidy but solid caravans, with children and cooking-pots, and a few bright pieces of woven colour, spinning through the centuries—while the men moved here and there and shouted with their sticks in the air.

As we came into the thicker pinewoods, another sort of human being met us—the woodlanders or Tahtajis, who are not obliged by their flocks to move winter and summer, but stay shyly cutting the tree-trunks in their forests and bring them down to the road or the saw-mill, and never intermarry with the village life below. We came upon them by the roadside, in the shade of their trees round a pinewood fire, a company of all ages—the women with five rows or more of little coins under the kerchief, showing across their brows. When we left them, the road wound on in solitude, till it reached the fields of Karaja-Su and then descended, across the river, and up, eight miles or so, to the lifted sloping lands below Cadmus where the columns of Aphrodisias shine from far away, the temple of the 'rainbow-throned daughter of Zeus, immortal Aphrodite'.[13]

The history of the place, otherwise mostly non-existent, is written in its landscape: it has an open remoteness, a happiness of width and distance with tracks in all directions to cities out of sight; and Cadmus pours down his waters by unprecipitous gradations. The fierceness of Artemis in Heracleia is here forgotten: the solitude is kind and easy, under an open sky. *Ease* is the word that comes in Aphrodisias. Caesar made it inviolable, a sanctuary to Aphrodite,[14] and its events were municipal and pleasant in the later days when its Leleges were hellenized and forgotten.

The colonnaded square with a frieze of portraits (now in the museum of Smyrna) was dedicated to Tiberius, Livia, Augustus and the goddess of love.[15] The temple and baths are of the second century A.D. The gifts of gymnasium, aqueducts, the quadriennial festival of music;[16] the building of the stadium, still perfect; the later Byzantine life whose walls and three gates remain—all speak of comfort and prosperity. The town continued to exist, and became Stavrupolis, a bishopric in Caria, joined to Miletus, in A.D. 1369.[17] And even now, though the village huddles in a corner of the wall with barely 130 houses, and its mosque, pleasantly painted, is so poor that it cannot yet afford a minaret—there is an air of contentment. The district is famous for almonds—as innocuous a thing to be famous for as one can imagine, in a world unattended by gods.

Fourteen Ionic columns shine brighter than Cadmus, which shines with snow. One of them has fallen since Fellows saw and described 'a city built wholly of white marble'.[18] Chaotic stone, cornices and capitals in pieces, lie heaped under brambles and grass. And the easy atmosphere remains. I believe it to be due to something proper to be thought of in the precincts of Aphrodite—that absence of a feeling of inferiority which, we have noticed already, gives its lightness to these remnants of the Greek character tossed about in stone.

The inferiority complex is a modern disease. The antipodes of modesty, it is an inverted, hesitating, unavowed concern with Self and belongs to an age of doubt. No real humility produces it; and its hidden preoccupation makes it intolerable to others. It is, I believe, the chief disaster of western civilization today; for we cause it to spring up wherever we go, and our defeats need no other reason to explain them. We produce it, perhaps, by not being tender enough with traditions other than our own, by not accepting all good where we find it, weaving it in with our own good, remembering that the mixture makes the vintage and that the Absolute is out of reach. By discouraging the people who came to us in their own virtues, we have corrupted and weakened them, and have landed them half-way between, their own traditions and ours; and those only who are remote or strong enough to preserve their gods are saved—though with the loss of every advantage that we might have given them. In most we have inspired this desolate uncertainty—and having done so are now developing the same self-centred awareness of failure in

Temple of Aphrodite: With Mt. Cadmus Behind

The Baths in Aphrodisias (Geyre)

Aphrodisias (Geyre): Temple of Aphrodite

Aphrodisias (Geyre): The End of the Stadium

ourselves: and the only cure is a sense of Proportion, which is as near as we can get to the glory of God.

But the Greeks, in their later age, seem to have lived in Aphrodisias in undistinguished mediocrity and wealth, enjoying their world and untroubled by its opinions, except for a reasonable municipal pride in their city and its credit abroad. No doubt their attitude to the 'barbarian' promoted the inferiority complex in others and brought its nemesis in the course of time: but in themselves they had an inner security through all the centuries of their submissions, because of that genial interest in things for their own sake, which remained.

The great Ionian name declined into a synonym for trickery and fawning, and this became the picture of the Levant.

Yet the disease so common today seems to have been rare among them even in their degradation. They took their faults simply, as if they were somebody else's, even from the beginning:

> 'The shield I left because I must, poor blameless armament! beside a bush, gives joy now to some Thracian, but myself I have saved. What care I for that shield? It shall go with a curse. I'll get me another as good.'[19]

This was Archilochus, in the 7th century B.C., and, in that heroic age, the Private Angelo attitude was disapproved of. But Shakespeare echoed it centuries later, with Parolles:

> . . . if my heart were great,
> T'would burst at this: Captain I'll be no more;
> But I will eat and drink, and sleep as soft
> As captain shall, simply the thing I am
> Shall make me live . . . [20]

Surely one of the most charitable passages in all literature! Whatever the depths to which these voices sink, there is sanity about them—a saving sense of their unimportance in the scheme of things, which lets them still enjoy the pleasure and variety of life. The inferiority complex is absent.

When the Roman emperors came and the rapacity of the Republic was forgotten, the cities of Asia enjoyed their un-heroic architecture and florid riches, and showered their Roman rulers with titles and lands and inscriptions that beau-tified the market-places and pleased them and did no one any harm. Lavish heads on marble architraves, deeply cut traceries of acanthus, lie about beside the Roman brickwork of the baths of Aphrodisias, where the stadium stretches its long oval of grey stone intact. Small late columns, diagonally fluted, stand at the temple grounds. In the high air under the pale sky, where everything except the outline of Cad-mus has changed, the contentment of the bourgeoisie can be recaptured.

24

Hierapolis and Laodicea

The poor desireth small things as much as the rich desireth great; to have a plenty of everything is no pleasure to mortal men.

BACCHYLIDES, 5th cent. B.C. [1]

But as for you, most of you have abandoned even your names; nay, owing to this recent prosperity of yours, you have forfeited all tokens of your ancestors.

APOLLONIOUS OF TYANA. Epistle to the Ionians, Ist cent, A.D. [2]

Above all, remember that the door stands open,

EPICTETUS. Ist cent, A.D. [3]

When i returned to my hotel, in the November evening, I found Nazilli shining with electric lights, buzzing with new cars, and bursting everywhere into a general hum of radio, so distributed over the town, far and near, that it was pleasant, like a waterfall singing in Turkish.

The next morning, I boarded my train again, for Denizli.

The valley lifted itself from its eroded hills of reddish clay, its brown roofs, its pears and pomegranates, vineyards and olives and almonds, into barrenness and the rapturous feeling of the climb towards the bigness of Asia. We passed the gap of yesterday to Aphrodisias, wide as if with open arms to the sun: the plough had made patterns over the mounds of Antiocheia, in squares of varied colours. Our valley floor was cotton, and red skirts of women gathering it here and there; the main road kept along, rough as a cart track, and telegraph wires beside it; Maeander, cutting through low banks of red earth, ran loose in his bed, with poplars all about. His landslides were held up by oleanders, and—where the cultivation stopped—tamarisk, *agnus castus,* and liquorice spread thin-branched straggling arabesques. The air was grey and cold: mountains stood in the south—Cadmus, the side opposite to Aphrodisias, and a saw-edged ridge, and Honaz Dagh, a high dome—all white with the first light snows. The northern side of our valley, losing its jagged foothills, unrolled naked pale slopes; the gradient eased away, the sides sped into wavelike distances; across an imprisoned plain, Hierapolis showed like a discoloured scar on a shelf of the mountain, where the ancient road and the present railway swing out to Celaenae (Apameia, and now Dinar), and the armies of Xerxes marched down. I told the governor of Denizli next day that we were crossing the route of the most important of all Persian invasions, and he looked at me with a certain sharpness.

"Persians never came this way," said he. "I should have been told of it if they had."

It must always have been a windswept plateau, bare of trees and rich in harvests, even in the days of the legendary Lityerses who used to compel passing strangers, after feasting at his table, to reap with him, and when evening came would cut off their heads, and binding the trunk into a sheaf with the trusses of corn, would sing a song; but he was eventually slain by Heracles and thrown into the river Maeander—which is why in Phrygia to this day the reapers sing his praise as a champion reaper;[4] and it also shows that one never can be quite certain of what the Oriental will admire.

Swinging down from Sardis, Alexander marched here after the Granicus, and Cyrus before him.[5] The Persians built palaces round Celaenae, and Alexander made it the capital of Phrygia; and there Antigonus III gave up all he held north of the Taurus to the armies of Rome. Celaenae, which had become Apameia when the Seleucid kings developed all this region, was the chief market for Greek and Italian merchandise after Ephesus, when the Christian era began.[6]

Those great cities, Celaenae and Sardis, Ephesus and the southern places of Caria are all far away from the Hierapolis plain: but the four valleys that lead to them, each wide enough to enclose its own mists and look at its own horizon, curve away from here into their separate distances and produce the atmosphere of the cross-roads, which is as magical an atmosphere as that of life itself, since decisions must be made for journeys whose end is out of sight. I have sometimes wondered whether the suicide, who was obviously unable to make up his mind on his direction and gave it up in despair, was buried at the cross-roads for this reason? In the Hierapolis plain, the 'city of Cydrara on the borders of Phrygia and Lydia' must have stood—where Croesus set up a boundary stone, and 'one way leadeth to the left towards Caria and the other to the right unto Sardis. Here the army of Xerxes, marching into the shallow white northern spaces, came by 'Callatebus, where artificers make honey from tamarisk and wheat', and by the plane tree which Xerxes admired and—remembering perhaps his Persian *chinars*—adorned with gold, and gave in charge to one of his Immortals to keep.[7]

Here Herodotus appears again, describing the skin of Marsyas, flayed and hung up by Apollo and kept in the marketplace of Celaenae; and tells how Pythias the Lydian, the richest man in Asia, feasted the king.[8] But the army, and he and history with it, move away to the north; and centuries pass; and the perpetual earthquakes shake the anthills of men in all this region, and dig lakes and caverns and boiling springs, for 'nearly the whole of the country about the Maeander, as far as the inland parts, is subject to earthquakes, and is undermined by fire and water'; and the little village 'with inns for the reception of travellers'[9] mentioned by Strabo at Carura, is outshone by Hierapolis, near ancient Fliera (now Enjeli), where the kings of Pergamum built in the shadow of Rome.

Here the huge solidity of the Roman ruins spreads itself along a ledge, with hollow arches, and piers of cement, and ceilings cut into curves, and rafters entirely of stone. The baths meet one first, and later churches are away to the north and the theatre is held in the lap of the hill above: all look out across the plain to the lands of Maeander and with their blind eyes dominate the Ionian world. However impressive, one feels a deadness in the heart of this stone: the secret of life is not vivid inside it, as it is in the poorest remnant of an Hellenic wall. For the Romans, I have read somewhere, flattened their ground before they built on it—and incidentally that is how Augustus bull-dozed away the site of Priam's Troy when he constructed his temple. But the Greeks, out of poverty perhaps but perhaps also by choice, often fitted their fine blocks to the ups and downs of nature, and so—with this piety—acquired a share in her enduring and changing life: and though the Roman system has produced every later magnificence, using the world as if it were a clay tablet to write on it the vestiges of men, the very humanity of all our ruins makes them dead when their day is over.

There was this sadness under the vaults of Hierapolis, such as one cannot dream of on the hillsides of Teos. But the strange warm water spilled down the slope as it did in Strabo's day, green-white, light and gay, and full of bubbles, with a trail of steam in the cold air—building a swift incrustation of lime, delicate and dazzling as snowflakes, and solidifying rapidly. The peasants enclose their fields by guiding a little stream that grows and rises on a deposit of its own making, till a wall exists with the water running along the top. Down 300 feet of the steep hillside it has congealed in white cascades, huge heads of barbarian columns from below but flat above with shallow edges, like the growth of giant water-lily leaves out of a pond. Above, beyond the baths, is the Plutonium where the gods of the nether world were worshipped, nothing now but dry ditch filled with pedestals and fragments of old stone, but once 'an opening . . . large enough to admit a man . . . full of vapour and so misty and dense that one can scarcely see the ground.' Strabo threw sparrows in, and 'they immediately breathed their last and fell'; and a bull led into it would die, though it was apparently innocuous to eunuchs. The water here was 'remarkably adapted to the dyeing of wool', so that stuff dyed with the madder root rivalled that of the kermes berry or the marine purple; and then as now it poured down in such abundance that the city was full of natural baths.[10]

The *Vali* of Denizli was an active, intelligent man, full of schemes for his province, with two promising young sons and a friendly, hospitable wife; and we drove out from Denizli all together, with Mr. Hornstein, who was showing an exhibition of British photographs in the town. At Denizli itself, fifteen miles from Hierapolis, streams come down into a well-wooded southern bay, close to the ruins of Laodicea. Here are cobbled thoroughfares, and many new houses, snug and prosperous among the autumn trees, and snowy hills showing at the end of streets in a mountain air. It is a famous place, said the *Vali,* for wrestlers and horsemen, and huntsmen; and there are wild cats in the ravines. The schools were fine, as everywhere in Turkey; and I met delightful people, anxious to lead me out of my remoteness into their present world. This I would have liked if there had been more time; and I hope to return. Meanwhile my attention was torn between the fascist blocks of the Roman masonry, the photographing of the *Vali*'s wife in her neat pullover and trousers, and the *Vali*'s own planning of a tourist hotel, for which we found an agreeable site, in a corner with trees, where the view of the ruined city might not be interfered with. The *Vali* promised me warm water, running through every bathroom, as if it were Roman.

*   *   *

The day before, waiting at Gonjali station for a change of trains, I had noticed one of the two theatres of Laodicea tucked into the green hollow of a hill, with sheep browsing about it. My train had gone puffing up through the vanished city by a low valley where four piers of a Roman bridge remain. I drove out here, and found, still solidly in place, a water conduit from Denizli and the Lycus river, its mortar pipe laid through square joined blocks of chiselled stone. The gymnasium and a church or two hold bits of huge masonry together, Stone-henges against the sky; the sunken oval only of the stadium—the longest in Asia Minor—is clear; and of the two theatres one is shuffled away by earthquakes, but the western keeps the grass-grown rows of its seats intact. The rich indifferent city once spread for a great distance over a flattish range of pebbly hills welded with earth, a legacy of floods—and the buildings of Laodicea are now sunk almost as deeply as her rounded pebbles into their forgotten days. The plough turns them over, and a peasant was hacking with an axe at a squared Roman stone, sending a cloud of marble dust and a dull thud after it to roll lazily through the cold and heavy air with every stroke. Apart from this noise, there was no sound except, where the cattle browsed, the tearing of the short grass if one were near enough to hear it. Two shepherds leaned idly against the scattered pedestals; the ruins were everywhere and nowhere—in hillocks whence the corner-stones of foundations pushed through—in boulders that looked natural until one saw traces of chiselling, weathered grey—in fragments of alien marble, shapeless on the ground.

Many years ago, on the height where the palaces of Nimrud are now being excavated, I once watched the Beduin shepherd pasture his flocks where the stone wing of an Assyrian bull stood half out of the grass: and the same pastoral appeasement soothes the expanses of Laodicea. In the silence, among the browsing cattle, with the peasant in the distance cracking up the ruins as if he were Time incarnate, it was as if all the voices of these cross-roads were audible together: the voices of the Lydians, setting their boundary stones on the trade route; the Persian armies, vanishing with a flicker in the north; the voices of Laodicea, first known under Pergamene kings in 220 B.C.; the Roman city where, as in Ephesus, the tax-farmers had their bank and gladiatorial shows were first performed in Asia; Mithridates and the massacre of the Romans; the oppressions of the Republic; the enormous debt of Asia, unpayable, rising from 20,000 to 120,000 talents in thirteen years, until Lucullus reduced it and was never forgiven by

Ruins of Laodicea (Gonjali)
Stone Water Conduit at Laodicea (Gonjali)

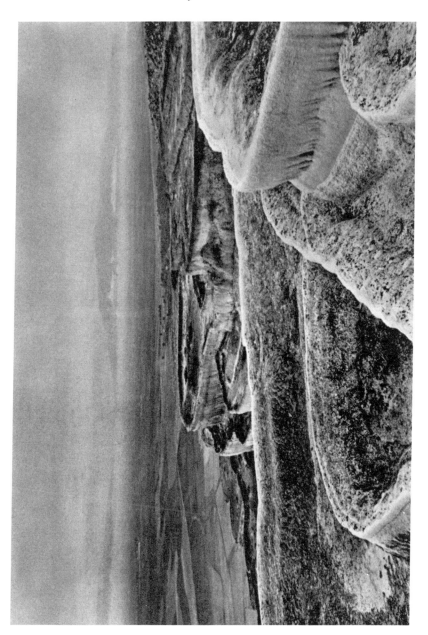

Hierapolis (Pamuk Kale): The Waterfalls

Hierapolis (Pamuk Kale): The Theatre

Laodicea

the business men in Rome; the billeting of troops on the householders, with sixteen drachmas a day and two sets of clothing for each soldier, and his friends to be entertained as well; the rifling of the treasures by Verres and the shocking trial of Philodamus in Laodicea, where justice showed herself a toy in the Roman hand; the city's resistance to the Parthians, with Zeno—a teacher of oratory—as captain in 40 B.C.; the fair-minded coming of Cicero; the gradual return of prosperity when the Empire cared for all;[11] the decadence and profusion.

The rich and coarsened material world had travelled far from that Ionia where ' to have a plenty of everything' was 'no pleasure to mortal man'—yet the morning light lingered. It grew darker and deeper, more conscious of itself, and weighted with intricate years. It played round St. Paul as he travelled, by Laodicea and Hierapolis to Ephesus down Maeander, through clouds that looked like sunset but were sunrise in the West. A few years later, born in Hierapolis, a slave in Rome under Nero's freedman, Epictetus speaks again with the voice that was heard in Miletus—not carefree now, but still happy and still brave.

'Why then are we afraid when we send a young man from the Schools into active life . . . ? Knows he not the god within him; knows he not with whom he is starting on his way?'[12]

'Thou art thyself a fragment torn from God: thou hast a portion of him within thyself. . . . In intercourse, in exercise, in discussion knowest thou not that it is a God whom thou feedest, a God whom thou exercisest, a God whom thou bearest about with thee, O miserable, and thou perceivest it not.[13]

'He hath entrusted me with myself: he hath made my will subject to myself alone and given me rules for the right use thereof!'[14]

'You think yourself but one among the many threads which make up the texture of the doublet. . . . But I desire to be the purple—that small and shining part which makes the rest seem fair and beautiful.'[15]

This is the voice that ever spake of immortality: that spake in Thucydides, when he wrote his work 'not as an essay which is to win the applause of the moment, but as a possession for all time'.[16] The ring of human dignity is in it, far from vanity, a notion of eternity under the breast. It began with the first philosophers when they discovered that the thing that has no beginning can have no end. With the passing of time, and the growth perhaps of riches as well as sorrows, the diffused eternity has come to reside more particularly in the souls of men: human bonds and human charities appear.

'Your own brother, that has God to his forefather, even as a son sprung from the same stock, and of the same high descent as yourself. . . . Remember who you are, and whom you rule, that they are by nature your kinsmen, your brothers, the offspring of God. . . .'[17]

'For what is a Man? A part of a City—first, of the City of Gods and Men; next, of that which ranks nearest to it, a miniature of the universal City. . . .'[18]

The voice of our day already lives in these syllables, and looks sadly, as we do, 'to the earth, to the pit, to those despicable laws of the dead. . . .'[19]; and has to speak what the earlier time knew clearly enough with no speaking, telling us to 'Keep death and exile daily before thine eyes, with all else that men deem terrible, but more especially Death. Then wilt thou never think a mean thought, nor covet anything beyond measure'.[20]

The world has become too full of many things, an over-furnished room. But, to make up for this loss, the immortality of the ancient poets has been lifted out of Time: it is made warm, like a garment, about us: it exists neither afterwards nor now, but always—the kingdom of Heaven, the Boundless of the old philosophers after six centuries of thinking, the house of many mansions, the eternity of the servants of God. Because of it, in spite of sorrow, happiness is the health of the spirit; nor is anything to be counted a disaster except the perversion of the soul.

This legacy must surely live within us; at these cross-roads of the ancient and the later time, far from my physical sight in time and space, but close in my heart, I leave the lands of Ionia—existent, like fairyland, like the kingdom of heaven, supremely beautiful, in and out of our everyday life ever available, yet not often nor easily found.

References

The works quoted are given once in full and then abbreviated or referred to by authors only. See bibliography for full titles and authors.

Preface

1 Simonides, *Lyra Graeca,* Loeb. II, 343.
2 Adapted from Alcman, 7th century B.C. *L.G.I,* 101.

Synopsis of History

1 Myres, *Who were the Greeks.*
2 Glotz, *La Civilisation Egéenne:* Hall, *The Civilisation of Greece in the Bronze Age:* Gurney, *The Hittites:* Hogarth, *Ionia and the East.*
3 Herodotus: Pausanias: Strabo. The term Asia Minor was not used till the 5th century A.D. so that it is here an anachronism. The name Anatolia was first used in the 10th century.
4 Strabo, XIV, 2, 28.
5 Herodotus, II, 97, 135, 178–9.
6 Radet, *La Lydie et le Monde Grec aux temps des Mermnades.*
7 *Lyra Graeca,* Loeb: *Elegy and Iambus,* Loeb.
8 Burnet, *Early Greek Philosophy:* Gomperz, *The Greek Thinkers.*
9 Grote, *A History of Greece.*
10 Plutarch, *Life of Cimon.*
11 Thucydides: Xenophon, *Hellenica.*
12 Magie, *Roman Rule in Asia Minor.*
13 Armstrong, *Grey Wolf.*

Chapter 1. Dawn in Ionia

1 Heraclitus, Loeb.
2 Burnet, 123: Xenophanes of Colophon.
3 Diogenes Laertius I, 25, Loeb.
4 Herodotus, VI, 9, 20.
5 Bacchylides, 5th century B.C.
6 Campbell's poems.
7 Semonides of Amorgos: *L.G.,* II, 339.
8 Stesichorus: *L.G.,* II, 67.

Chapter 2. Smyrna

Modern Izmir

1 *L.G.,* I, 255.
2 *L.G.,* I, 79.
3 Hall.
4 Herodotus, I, 16.
5 ,, I, 150.
6 Farrar. *Lives of the Fathers,* I, 77 ff; *Letters from St. Irenaeus.*
7 *L.G.,* II, 89 and 107.
8 Calder: *Studies in the history and art of the eastern provinces of the Roman Empire.*
9 Sir Charles Fellows, p. 4.
10 Declared sacred to Aphrodite by Seleucus II, Magie, 1, 98.
11 Calder: Strabo, XIV, 1, 37: Pausanias II, 24. (My copy has no paragraphs marked: I therefore only note the chapters, which are not long, and so entertaining that it is pleasant to be induced to browse about them.)
12 Sir Charles Fellows, 235.
13 Herodotus, III, 58.
14 Empedocles: 5th century B.C.: Burnet, 268 ff.

Chapter 3. Clazomenae

Modern Urla Iskelesi: 19 miles from Smyrna on Cheshme road

1 Herodotus, I, 6.
2 ,, I, 42.

3 ,, I, 148.
4 ,, II, 178. Amasis = Psammetichus I, 663–609 B.C.
5 Pausanias, VII, 3.
6 Burnet, 251 ff.
7 Herodotus, VII, 45.
8 Plato, Phaedrus, 270a; Plutarch's *Lives, Pericles,* 5.
9 Pausanias, VII, 3.
10 Archilochus, 7th cent. B.C. *E. and I,* II, 109.
11 *E and I,* II, 297.
12 5th cent. B.C., *L.G.,* III, 227.
13 ,, I, 73.
14 ,, I, 91.
15 ,, II, 85.
16 *E and I,* II, 101.
17 St. Cyr de Rayssac.

Chapter 4. Teos

Modern Sighajik: 38 miles from Smyrna, turning from Cheshme road through Seferihisar

1 Burnet, 112.
2 Herodotus, I, 76, 141.
3 ,, I, 94.
4 ,, I, 17.
5 *L.G., passim.*
6 ,, 17: Glotz, 344.
7 Pindar.
8 *L.G., passim.*
9 Pindar: Pythian I, 57.
10 Herodotus, I, 95.
11 ,, I, 94.
12 Burnet, 118.
13 *L.G.,* II, 147.
14 Herodotus, I, 168.
15 *L.G., passim.*
16 Ximenes, *Asia Minor in Ruins.*
17 Pliny, *Natural History,* V, 138.

18 Livy, XXXVII, 29 ff.
19 Magie, 45–9.
20 ,, 69, 80, 899.
21 Herodotus, I, 168.
22 *L.G.,* II, 159. Anacreon, 6th cent. B.C.
23 ,, 167.
24 ,, I, 69. Alcman, 7th cent. B.C.
25 Newton, *Travels and Discoveries in the Levant,* I, 90.
26 *E and I,* II, 487: Critias 5th cent. B.C.
27 *L.G.,* II, 269.
28 ,, I, 419, Alcaeus 6th cent. B.C.
29 ,, II, 155, 161.
30 ,, III, 331, Timotheus, 4th cent. B.C.
31 Strabo, XIII, 1, 54; Ximenes.
32 *L.G.,* III, 407.
33 Critias of Athens: 5th cent. B.C.: *E and I,* I, 491.

Chapter 5. Erythrae

Modern Ildir: 2 hours by motor-boat from Cheshme

 1 *E and I,* II, 103.
 2 Pausanias, VII, 5.
 3 *E and I,* I, 191, Xenophanes, 6th cent. B.C.
 4 Herodotus, I, 142–3.
 5 Pausanias, VII, 5.
 6 ,, VII, 3.
 7 Strabo, XIV, I, 31.
 8 Magie, 89.
 9 ,, 79.
10 ,, 615.
11 Herodotus, I, 18.
12 *L.G.,* I, 315.
13 Pausanias, VII, 5.
14 ,, X, 12.
15 *L.G.,* II, 187, Anacreon, 6th cent. B.C.
16 ,, II, 325.

Chapter 6. Chios

One hour by motor-boat from Cheshme

1 Attributed to Empedocles.
2 *E and I,* I, 161.
3 Herodotus, V, 98.
4 ,, VI, 1.
5 Radet, 98: Rostovtzeff: *Social & Economic History of the Hellenistic World,* 169, 462, 525, etc.
6 Herodotus, VIII, 132.
7 ,, IX, 106.
8 ,, I, 27.
9 Strabo, XIV, 1, 35.
10 Newton, I, 216.
11 Pausanias, X, 16; Herodotus, I, 25. The invention probably came from Asia Minor.

Chapter 7. Myrina

40 miles from Smyrna on Pergamum road beyond Aliagha.

1 *L.G.,* II, 403.
2 Strabo, XIII, 3, 2 and 4.
3 *L.G.,* II, 337, Simonides, 6th cent. B.C.
4 Herodotus, I, 161.
5 *See* Ch. 15.
6 Plutarch, *Life of Themistocles.*
7 Ramsay, *Asianic Elements in Greek Civilisation:* Strabo, XIII, 3, 6.
8 Herodotus, VI, 31.

Chapter 8. Gryneium

44 miles from Smyrna on the Pergamum road.

1 *L.G.,* I, 339, Alcaeus, 6th cent. B.C.
2 Herodotus, I, 142.
3 *L.G.,* III, 193, Bacchylides, 5th cent. B.C.
4 Newton, I, 80.

 5 Radet, 300.
 6 Strabo, XIII, 3, 5.
 7 Pausanias, I, 21: Strabo, XIII, 3, 5.
 8 Herodotus, III, 47.
 9 Burnet, 140.
10 *L.G.,* II, 337, Simonides, 6th cent. B.C.
11 Herodotus, VI, 21.
12 Pausanias, VI, 18.
13 Lucian trans. by H. W. L. Hince.
14 The population of Western Asia Minor alone was 25 million under Trajan.
15 Marcus Aurelius, trans. by G. Long.

Chapter 9. Pitane

Modern Chandarli: 58 miles from Smyrna

 1 Loeb trans. of Heraclitus, 6th cent. B.C.
 2 Diogenes Laertius, IV, 28.
 3 Gomperz, I, 492.
 4 Strabo, XIII, 1, 67.
 5 *L.G.,* I, 373.
 6 Magie, I, 227–8.
 7 Gomperz, IV, 377.
 8 Burnet, 223.
 9 Herodotus, I, 142.
10 Radet, 284: Herodotus, V, 49, etc.
11 Diogenes Laertius, I, 5.
12 Herodotus, II, 45.
13 *L.G.,* III, 133 : Bacchylides.
14 *E and I,* I, 93 : Mimnermus, 7th cent. B.C.
15 Burnet, 119, 121.

Chapter 10. Pergamum

Modern Bergama: 70 miles from Smyrna by road (and rail). There is a hotel.

 1 *L.G.,* II, 189, Anacreon, 6th cent. B.C.

2 Pausanias, VIII, 3–4.
3 Xenophon, *Anabasis,* VII, 8.
4 Magie, II, 725: Xenophon, *Hellenica,* III, 1,6.
5 Magie, I, 40, 41.
6 Radet, 190.
7 Herodotus, I, 160.
8 ,, VIII, 106.
9 Pausanias, I, 4.
10 ,, I, 4.
11 Herodotus, V, 58 ff.
12 Pausanias, V, 13.
13 Magie, I, 21 34
14 ,, *passim.*

Chapter 11. Cyme

Modern Nimrut Limani: 37 miles from Smyrna off the Pergamum road, track to Yeni Fochà, before Aliagha.

1 Diogenes Laertius, VI, I.
2 Freeman, *Ancilla to the Pre-Socratic philosophers,* (from Diehl).
3 Herodotus, VIII, 130: Strabo, XIII, 3, 6.
4 Statham, *A short critical history of Architecture,* 1, 54–6. Glotz, 517.
5 Choisy, *Historie de l'Architecture,* I, 337.
6 ,, ,, ,, I, 256.
7 Perrot and Chipiez, *History of Art in Lydia,* etc.
8 *Iliad,* III.
9 Myres, 492.
10 Ramsay, *J. of Hellenic Studies,* 1889, 14: Radet, 292.
11 Perrot and Chipiez.
12 Myres, 116; Hogarth, 66 ff.
13 Perrot and Chipiez, 220.
14 Pliny, *Natural History,* VIII, 74.
15 Radet, *passim.*
16 Pollux IX, 83 : Aristotle, fragm. 611, 37.
17 Herodotus, V, 49: I, 14: Radet, *passim*: and Hall.
18 *L.G.,* II, 157, Anacreon: Radet, 250.
19 Newton, I, 280.

20 Herodotus, VII, 73.
21 Perrot and Chipiez, 172.
22 *L.G.,* II, 5–7.
23 *L.G.,* I, 107.
24 Perrot and Chipiez, 29.
25 *Lycidas,* by John Milton.

Chapter 12. Phocaea

Modern Eski Focha: 45 miles from Smyrna, off the Pergamum road.

 1 Diogenes Laertius, IX, 28.
 2 *L.G.,* I, 249: Sappho.
 3 Strabo, XIII, 3, 6.
 4 Radet, 72, from *Nicholas of Damascus.*
 5 Herodotus, I, 137 ff.
 6 ,, I, I4I.
 7 ,, I, 152 ff.
 8 Strabo, XIV, 1, 2.
 9 Perrot and Chipiez, 65.
10 Quoted by Freeman from Diehl, Hecataeus of Abdera (4th cent.
    B.C.), fragm., 7.
11 Pausanias, VII, 3.
12 Herodotus, I, 169 ff.
13 ,, I, 164 ff.
14 Diogenes Laertius, VIII, 32.
15 Pausanias, VII, 5.
16 Herodotus, VI, 12 ff.
17 *L.G.,* I, 339, Alcaeus.

Chapter 13. Colophon

Modern Deghirmendere· 29 miles from Smyrna by track turning right, from the Ephesus road.

 1 Bowra, Early Greek Elegists, 32.
 2 Leake, *Journal of a tour in Asia Minor,* preface, V.
 3 Newton, I, 1, 137, 252. Ionians, i.e. from the W. Ionian islands, then under British jurisdiction.

4 Radet, 298.

5 Athenaeus XIII, 598.

6 Strabo, XIV, 1, 27.

7 Pausanias, VII, 5.

8 Strabo, XIV, 1, 29.

9 Pausanias, VII, 3.

10 Ramsay, *Asianic Elements in Greek Civilisation.*

11 *See* chapter 3.

12 Aristotle, *Politics,* IV, 1290b.

13 Herodotus, I, 14.

14 *E and I,* I, 195.

15 Strabo, XIV, 1, 28.

16 Radet, 198.

17 Pliny, *N. History,* VII, 196.

18 Athenaeus, XIII, 589.

19 ,, XIII, 600.

20 *L.G.,* III, 631; II, 167: Hall, 281.

21 Myres, 403.

22 *L.G.,* I, 197: Sappho.

23 Pausanias, IX, 35.

24 *E and I,* I, 299, Theognis, 6th cent. B.C.

25 Hall, 45: *Iliad II.*

26 Herodotus, I, 146.

27 Athenaeus, XIII, 572.

28 Herodotus, I, 93.

29 Athenaeus, XIII, 872.

Chapter 14. Clarus and Notium

Modern Ahmet Beyli: 38 miles from Smyrna.

1 Burnet, 119 ff.

2 Pausanias, III, 14.

3 ,, IX, 32: Xenophon *Hellenica,* I, 5, 12 ff.

4 Thucydides, III, 32.

5 ,, III, 34.

6 Pausanias, VII, 3.

7 Magie, I, 240, 498.

8 *E and I,* I, 361, Theognis, 6th cent. B.C.
9 Burnet, 114 ff.

Chapter 15. Sardis

Modern Sert: 73 miles from Smyrna: rail and road.

1 *L.G.,* I, 45. Alexander of Aetolia on Alcman.
2 ,, I, 209.
3 *E and I,* I, 99.
4 *Iliad,* II.
5 Strabo, XIV, 1, 45.
6 *Iliad,* II: Radet, 239.
7 Radet, 59.
8 Under Amenhotep III.
9 Hall, 85.
10 Radet, 265.
11 Radet, 288: Pausanias, VIII, 14.
12 *Iliad,* IV.
13 *See* Plato, *Republic* II, 3.
   Plato, *Republic* II, 359–360 gives the story.
14 Radet, 52, 269.
15 ,, 147, 16 ff; Strabo, XIII, 4, 17: *E and I,* I, 111.
16 ,, 75.
17 ,, 124 ff.
18 ,, 172.
19 Herodotus, I, 10.
20 Radet, 100.
21 ,, 173.
22 ,, 191–2.
23 ,, 55.
24 ,, 229, 230.
25 ,, 100, 101.
26 Herodotus, I, 15, 26.
27 *L.G.,* I, 363.
28 Diodorus Siculus, IX, 32: Radet, 215.
29 Radet, 180.
30 Strabo, I, 3, 21: Radet, 187.

31 Radet, 156 ff.
32 ,, 167.
33 Strabo, XIII, 4, 5.
34 Radet, 239: Herodotus, 1, 28 ff.
35 Aristophanes, *Wasps,* 1139.
36 Herodotus, I, 15.
37 Radet, 220.
38 ,, 276: Herodotus, I, 54.
39 Choisy, I, 259.
40 Gregorovius, *Kleine Schriften,* I, 1–47.
41 Perrot and Chipiez.
42 Vergil, *Georgics,* I, 56.
43 Radet, 40, 46.
44 Ramsay, *Asianic Elements in Greek Civilisation.*
45 Perrot and Chipiez.
46 Herodotus, VII, 74.
47 Radet, 58, from F.H.G. II, 186 (*Fragmenta hist. Graec.*).
48 Herodotus, I, 92.
49 Radet, 299, *passim.*
50 Herodotus, VII, 27–8: Plutarch, *Moralia,* I, 324: Radet, 225.
51 The Treaty of Antalcidas after Cimon's victory.
52 Spon, *Voyage d'Italie,* I, 206.
53 Herodotus, VI, 100.
54 ,, I, 84.
55 Xenophon, *Cyropaedia,* VII, 2.
56 Radet, 258.

Chapter l6. Ephesus

Modern Seljuk: 50 miles from Smyrna, rail or road.

1 Strabo, XIV, 1,4.
2 Philostratus, *Life of Apollonius of Tyana,* IV, 2.
3 Magie, I, 75, 705–6, 712: Alexander, 334 B.C. Goths 3rd
   cent. A.D.
4 Strabo, XIV, 1, 23.
5 Herodotus, I, 92.
6 Wood, *Discoveries at Ephesus.*

7 Seljuk: the coastal dynasties were not strictly Seljuk, but the term
   is useful for denoting the period of time, and I use it in this general
   sense.
8 Hogarth, 45.
9 Radet, 209: Herodotus, I, 26.
10 Magie, 89.
11 Pausanias, VII, 2.
12 Strabo, XIV, 1, 21: Magie, 826: Sartiaux, *Villes Mortes d' Asie
    Mineure.*
13 Sartiaux.
14 The chapel was restored 1951–2 by the Latin Archbishop.
15 *Byzantium,* ed. by Baynes and Moss, 161.
16 ,, 319.
17 Radet.
18 Burnet, 132 ff.
19 I have altered 'have one common world' 'to share one world'.
20 Radet, 196: Nicholas of Damascus, fragm. 65.
21 Ramsay, *A.E.G.C.*: Hipponax p. 23 in Loeb Herodes.
22 Magie, I, 142.
23 ,, I, 427–39.
24 ,, I, 75.
25 ,, I, 695.
26 *L.G.*, III, 301.

Chapter 17. The Panionium

Modern Güzel Chamli: 11 miles from Kushadasi as the crow flies.
Track from Kushadasi or from the top of the pass to Söke.

1 Diogenes Laertius, I, 41.
2 Heyd, *Histoire du Commerce du Levant,* I, 542 (from Ludolphi da
   Suchem *De itinere Sanctae Terrae liber,* 9).
3 Fellows, 205.
4 Herodotus, I, 148.
5 ,, I, 146.
6 Pausanias, VII, 24.
7 Plutarch, *Life of Aristides.*
8 Archilochus: *E and I,* II, 133.

9 *L.G.,* III, 657 ff.
10 ,, III, 493, *Daphnis and Chloe.*
11 Athenaeus, XIV, 619.
12 *L.G.,* II, 125.
13 *See* Ch. 12.
14 Herodotus, I, 170.
15 ,, VI, 7.
16 Magie, 66.
17 ,, 892.
18 Strabo, XIV, 1, 20.
19 'Here Sir William Gell found, in a church on the sea-shore, an inscription in which he distinguished the name of Panionium twice.' (From Leake's *Tour in Asia Minor,* 260.)

Chapter 18. Priene

Modern Gülbahche: 12 miles from Söke.

1 Freeman, 100.
2 ,, 40.
3 Magie, II, 893.
4 ,, I, 57.
5 Pausanias, VII, 5.
6 Magie, I, 91.
7 ,, I, 167.
8 Ximenes.
9 Magie, I, 168.
10 Choisy, I, 296.
11 Sartiaux, 141.
12 Herodotus, IX, 96 ff.
13 Magie, II, 822.
14 Herodotus, IX, 102 ff.

Chapter 19. Didyma

Modern Yeronda: (bus from Söke on Tuesdays): 15 miles from Maeander ferry.

1 Freeman, 141.

 2 Pausanias, V, 14.
 3 Newton, II, 149.
 4 Ximenes.
 5 Sartiaux.
 6 Pausanias, VII, 2.
 7 Magie, 74.
 8 Diogenes Laertius, VIII, 4.
 9 Herodotus, II, 158.
10 Sartiaux, 203.
11 Magie, *passim,* 1366–7.
12 Pausanias, VII, 2.
13 Strabo, XIV, 1, 5.
14 Herodotus, I, 19.
15 This story is quite unfounded according to W.W. Tarn—*See* below.
16 Quintus Curtius VII, 5, 28: Strabo XI, 11, 4 and XIV, 1, 5.

Chapter 20. Miletus

Modern Balat: distance from Söke (as the crow flies) 28 miles.

 1 *L.G.,* III, 325: Timotheus, 4th cent. B.C.
 2 *Iliad,* II 867, ff.
 3 Cretan Miletus: Strabo, XIV, 1, 6.
 4 Burnet, 2: Hogarth, 25.
 5 Hall, 160: Glotz, 499.
 6 Hogarth, 62.
 7 Glotz, 39.
 8 Hall, 229.
 9 Glotz, 43, 229: Hall, 21.
10 ,, ,,
11 ,, 120, 499.
12 ,, 38.
13 ,, 45, 501–2.
14 *Iliad,* XXIII, 700.
15 Glotz, 399.
16 Hall, 110: Glotz, 47, 124–5, 163. The word for brick is pre-Hellenic.

17 Glotz, 157, 216.

18 ,, 78, 83–97: Hall, 290.

19 Hall, 85–134.

20 Glotz, 128 ff, 478.

21 ,, 47, 53, 172, 502.

22 ,, 172, 183.

23 ,, 188.

24 ,, 60.

25 ,, 218 ff.

26 ,, 55: Burnet, 2.

27 Pausanias, VII, 4.

28 ,, VII, 3.

29 *See* Chap. 13.

30 Herodotus, I, 171 ff: Glotz, 252, 503.

31 Glotz, 61.

32 Egyptian hieroglyph quoted by Hall, 238.

33 Hall, 252.

34 Glotz, 63.

35 Hall, 246 ff.

36 Glotz, 67: Hall, 269.

37 ,, 69—hieroglyph of Ramses III.

38 *Iliad,* II 645 ff, III 232.

39 ,, XVIII 590 ff. The theatre at Phaestus has 10 seats, 25 metres in length, and an oblique stage of 20 cm.: date *c* . 1900–1750 B.C. There is another theatre at Knossos; Glotz, 333.

40 *Iliad,* VI, 235.

41 Herodotus, V, 65; I, 142: Strabo, XIV, 1, 3; 1, 6.

42 Pausanias, VII, 2.

43 Sartiaux, *Miletus—passim.*

44 Diodorus XIII, 104: Plutarch *Lysander,* 8 and 19.

45 Grote, 12, 38: Sartiaux, *Miletus.*

46 Magie, 92.

47 ,, 14.

48 Sartiaux, 173.

49 Ximenes, *passim.*

50 Magie, 706.

51 *Byzantium,* 167.

52 Wiegand, *Milet: Latmos,* III, I, 10 and 12.
53 Sartiaux, *Miletus.*
54 Herodotus, VI, 7; and *see* Chapter 12.
55 ,, VI, 18.
56 Ximenes, *Miletus.*
57 Pliny, *Nat. Hist.,* XXXV, 34, 8.
58 Diogenes Laertius, VIII, 1.
59 Athenaeus, XII, 30: from Asius.
60 Sartiaux, *Miletus.*
61 Glotz, 167.
62 Herodotus, V, 36: Burnet, 51.
63 Burnet, 40: Herodotus, III, 60; IV, 87.
64 Radet, 211: Herodotus, I, 170: Burnet, 41,46, and 47, Thales, *c* . 585 B.C.
65 Ovid, *Tristia,* IV, 3, 1–2.
66 Burnet, 1–79.
67 ,, 15.
68 Theophrastus, quoted in Burnet, 52.
69 Burnet, 66.
70 ,, 64.
71 ,, 67; Act II, 20,1.
72 ,, 73
73 *L.G.,* II, 189, from *Zenobius.*
74 *L.G.,* III, 539.

Chapter 21. Heracleia

Modern Kapa Keri: Söke by Serchin to lake Bafa—16 miles (as the crow flies).

1 Strabo, XIV, 1, 8.
2 ,, ,, 1, 9. 10.
3 ,, ,, 1, 10: Pausanias, VII, 2: Bean & Duyuran, road book at British Inst. of Archaeology, Ankara.
4 Magie, II, 883.
5 Wiegand, 178–9.
6 *Byzantium,* 143.

7 Wiegand, 179 ff.

8 ,, 182; taken from *Vita S. Paulus de Jediler* by H. Delahaye in *Analecta Bolland,* XI, S.1 ff. 1892.

9 Mentioned by Wiegand.

10 ,, ,, *See* above.

11 *Iliad,* II.

12 Wiegand, 2.

13 Pausanias, V, 1.

14 Sternbergia.

15 Pausanias, II, 5: II, 7.

Chapter 22. Magnesia on Maeander

Near Ortaklar: road and rail from Aydin, Smyrna or Söke

1 Plato, Protagoras 334d.

2 Thucydides, I, 138.

3 Diogenes Laertius, VIII, 12.

4 Strabo, XIII, 4, 15: Pliny, *Nat. Hist.,* XV, 19, 2.

5 Magie, I, 80, 167.

6 *E and I,* I, 361 and 43.

7 Radet, 131: Strabo, XIV, 1, 40.

8 Herodotus, I, 161.

9 Strabo, XIV, 1, 40: Magie, I, 78.

10 Magie, II, 884.

11 ,, I, 623.

12 Strabo, XIV, 2, 29.

13 ,, ,, 1, 38.

14 ,, ,, I, 41; quotes *Odyssey,* IX, 3.

15 ,, ,, I, 40.

16 Plutarch, *Themistocles.*

17 ,, ,,

18 ,, ,,

19 ,, ,,

20 Thucydides, I, 128.

21 Herodotus, VI, 67; VII, 3.

22 *See* Chapter 10.

23 Herodotus, V, 11: IV, 97: VI, 3, 29.
24 ,, VI, 88: V, 27: III, 129.
25 ,, VI, 24.
26 ,, ,, 41.
27 ,, ,, 118.
28 ,, ,, VIII, 12, 89.
29 Thucydides, VIII, 18, 36, 58 ff.
30 Grote, XII, 26.
31 Thucydides, VIII, 57.
32 Herodotus, I, 135: III, 15.
33 Radet, 257.
34 Tacitus, *Annales,* III, 62.
35 Radet, 257.
36 Herodotus, VI, 42.
37 ,, III, 120.
38 Strabo, XIV, 1, 39.
39 Plutarch, *Themistocles.*
40 Xenophon, *Hellenica,* III, I, 10.
41 Herodotus, VIII, 93.
42 Plutarch, *Themistocles.*
43 Herodotus, VI, 136: Plutarch, *Themistocles.*
44 Herodotus, VIII, 74, 110: Plutarch, *Themistocles.*
45 ,, IX, 83: ,, ,,
46 ,, III, 127: ,, ,,
47 Plutarch, *Themistocles.*

Chapter 23. Aphrodisias

Modern Geyre: 40 miles from Nazilli by Karaja-Su.

1 Philostratus, II, 471.
2 Strabo, XIV, 1, 42.
3 Ximenes, *passim.*
4 Grote, II, 45.
5 Magie, V,
6 Ximenes, *passim.*
7 Fellows, 244–5.

8 Magie, I, 213.
9 Strabo, XIV, 1, 44.
10 Athenaeus, II, 43.
11 Strabo, XIV, 1, 36: Iliad, *see* Chapter 15.
12 ,, XIII, 4, 15: Magie, I, 128.
13 Sappho, trans. by Sir Alexander Lawrence.
14 Magie, I, 418.
15 ,, I, 502.
16 ,, I, 586, 655.
17 Wiegand, *Milet,* III, 1; *see* Chapter 21.
18 Fellows, 252.
19 *E and I,* II, 101, Archilochus 7th cent. B.C.
20 *All's well that ends well,* Act, IV, Sc. 3.

Chapter 24. Hierapolis and Laodicea

Modern Pamukale: 11 miles from Denizli: modern Gonjali by Denizli[1];

1 *L.G.,* III, 133.
2 Philostratus, *Life of Apollonius of Tyana,* II, 471.
3 *The Golden Sayings of Epictetus,* 35.
4 Scholiast on Theocritus *L.G.,* III, 505.
5 Magie, I, 42.
6 Strabo, XII, 8, 15: Magie, I, 125–6.
7 Herodotus, VII, 31 ff.
8 ,, ,, 26.
9 Strabo, XII, 8, 17.
10 Magie, I, 127: Strabo, XIII, 4, 14. 'Mr. Cockerell found several small birds lying dead near the grotto; and though he tried its effects on a fowl for a whole day without any result, he was assured by the inhabitants that it was sometimes fatal to their sheep and oxen, but that it was not always equally dangerous.' (Leake, p. 342.)
11 Magie I, 127, 164, 127, 655, 217, 252, 237, 246, 430, 390, 257.
12 *The Golden Sayings of Epictetus,* 49.
13 ,, ,, ,, 48.

14 ,, ,, ,, 4.
15 ,, ,, ,, 7.
16 Thucydides, I, 1.
17 *The Golden Sayings of Epictetus,* 27.
18 ,, ,, ,, 45.
19 ,, ,, ,, 28.
20 ,, ,, ,, 138.

Bibliography

(Works in the order of their quotation)

Lyra Graeca. Loeb trans. 3 vols. (*L.G. in notes.*)

J. L. Myres. *Who Were the Greeks*. Sather Classical Lecture, Berkeley Calif, 1930.

G. Glotz. *La Civilisation Egéenne*. Paris, 1952.

H. R. Hall. *The Civilisation of Greece in the Bronze Age*. Methuen, 1928.

O. R. Gurney. *The Hittites*. 1952 (Penguin).

D. G. Hogarth. *Ionia and the East*. Clarendon Press, 1909.

Herodotus, trans. by Enoch Powell. Clarendon Press, 1949.

Pausanias. *Voyage historique de la Grèce,* trans. by l'Abbé Gedoyn, 1733.

Strabo. *The Geography*. Loeb, 1950.

G. Radet. *La Lydie et le monde Grec au Temps des Mermnades*. Paris, 1893.

Elegy and Iambus. Loeb. (*E. and I. in notes.*)

John Burnet. *Early Greek Philosophy*. Black, 1952.

Theodor Gomperz. *The Greek Thinkers*. Murray, 1949.

George Grote. *A History of Greece*. Everyman edition.

Plutarch, trans. by J. W. Langhorne. Cassell, 1858.

Thucydides. *Peloponnesian War* trans. by R. Crawley. Everyman edition.

Xenophon. *Hellenica*. Loeb.

David Magie. *Roman Rule in Asia Minor*. Princeton, U.S.A., 1950.

H. C. Armstrong. *Grey Wolf*. Arthur Barker, 1932.

Heraclitus. Loeb.

Diogenes Laertius. Loeb.

F. W. Farrar. *Lives of the Fathers.* A. and C. Black, 1889.

W. M. Calder. *Studies in the history and art of the eastern provinces of the Roman Empire.* 1906.

Sir Charles Fellows. *Travels and researches in Asia Minor.* Murray, 1852.

Plato. *Phaedrus* and *Protagoras.*

Pindar, trans. by Ernest Myers. Macmillan, 1888.

Ximenes. *Asia Minor in Ruins.* 1925.

Pliny. *Natural History.*

Livy. *History.*

C. T. Newton. *Travels and discoveries in the Levant.* 1865.

M. Rostovtzeff: *The Social and Economic History of the Hellenistic World,* Oxford, 1953.

W. Ramsay. *Asianic Elements in Greek Civilisation.* Methuen, 1928.

H. W. L. Hine. *Lucian the Syrian Satirist.* Longmans Green, 1900.

Marcus Aurelius, trans. by G. Long.

Xenophon. *Anabasis,* trans. by Rex Warner.

K. Freeman. *Ancilla to the pre-Socratic philosophers* (from Diehl).

Heathcote Statham. *A Short Critical History, of Architecture.* 1912.

Choisy. *Histoire de l'Architecture,* 1899.

Perrot and Chipiez. *History of Art in Phrygia, Lydia, Caria and Lycia.* Chapman & Hall, 1892 and Hachette, 1911.

Homer's *Iliad,* trans. by Andrew Lang, Leaf and Myers. Macmillan.

W. Ramsay. *Journal of Hellenic Studies.*

Athenaeus. *The Deipnosophists.* Loeb trans.

William M. Leake. *Journal of a Tour in Asia Minor.* Murray, 1824.

Aristotle. *Politics* trans. by W. Ellis. Everyman edition.

Diodorus Siculus. Loeb.

Aristophanes, *Wasps.*

Gregorovius, *Kleine Schriften.* Leipzig, 1887.

Vergil. *Georgics.*

C. M. Bowra. *Early Greek Elegists.* Oxford, 1938.

Plutarch. *Moralia,*

Spon. *Voyage d'Italie,* 1724.

Xenophon. *Cyropaedia,* Loeb.

Philostratus. *The Life of Apollonius of Tyana.* Loeb.

J. F. Wood. *Discoveries at Ephesus.* London, 1877.

F. Sartiaux. *Villes Mortes d'Asie Mineure,* 1892—Hachette 1911.

W. W. Tarn. *Alexander the Great,* Cambridge, 1948.

Byzantium. Edited by N. H. Baynes and H. St. L. B. Moss. Oxford, 1949.

W. Heyd. *Histoire du Commerce du Levant.* Leipzig, 1923.

Plutarch. *Aristides.*

Th. Wiegand. *Milet: Latmos III.* Berlin, 1925 ff.

Tacitus. *Annales.*

Plutarch. *Themistocles.*

Sappho. Ode trans. by Sir Alexander Lawrence.

The Golden Sayings of Epictetus, tr. by H. Crossley. Macmillan, 1925.

Index